JUST YOUR AVERAGE BALD, ONE-EYED BASKETBALL WACKO WHO

SIMON AND SCHUSTER

New York   London   Toronto   Sydney   Tokyo

VITALE

BEAT THE ZIGGY AND BECAME A PTP'ER

DICK VITALE
WITH CURRY KIRKPATRICK

SIMON AND SCHUSTER
Simon & Schuster Building
Rockefeller Center
1230 Avenue of the Americas
New York, New York 10020

Designed by Kathy Kikkert

Manufactured in the United States of America

10 9 8 7 6 5 4 3 2 1

Library of Congress Cataloging in Publication Data
Vitale, Dick.
  Vitale : just your average bald one-eyed basketball wacko who beat
  the ziggy and became a PTP'er / Dick Vitale with Curry Kirkpatrick.
  p.   cm.
  1. Vitale, Dick.   2. Sportscasters—United States—Biography.
3. Basketball—United States.   I. Kirkpatrick, Curry.   II. Title.
GV884.V58A3   1988
070.4'49796'0924—dc19
[B]   88-23053
ISBN 0-671-66040-3   CIP

ACKNOWLEDGMENTS

To acknowledge by name all the people who have helped me along the way would require another book twice this long, from my days as a teacher in elementary school through coaching in high school, college and the pros right on up to the grit and glitter of my career in television.

I owe so much to the people behind the scenes—the custodians who swept all the gyms so many years ago; the cheerleaders and the parents of all my players; the big-time administrators who took a chance hiring me, and their secretaries who were always so understanding; the basketball fans everywhere who have made my life so rewarding.

The play-by-play announcers and studio talent, both at ESPN and ABC, could not have been more helpful in guiding me along in TV, but they have been no more important to the productions and to me than the technicians, the producers, directors, graphic people, the office staff, the camera crews, all the people behind the scenes whose reviews count more to me than anything anybody could ever put in the newspapers.

But there are some special names I do want to mention; without any single one of them I'd probably still be in some nine-to-five job itching to get out.

From Garfield, New Jersey, I'd like to pay tribute to Carl Pecoraro, my first superintendent of schools; Roger Sullivan, my first principal at the Mark Twain Elementary School; Ciro Barcellona, the high school principal; Robert Nork, the athletic director; and coach Frank Dawson and Vince Rigolosi.

At East Rutherford, my thanks to administrators Clayton Hitchner and Warren Meniketti, the superintendent of schools; Hugh O'Neal, my principal at the Franklin school; Vincent Ziccardi, my principal at East Rutherford High; coaches Robert Stolarz, Lou Ravettine, Al D'Amato, Bill Jones, Tony Trause, John Subda, Fred Paul and Ken Sinofsky; athletic director Bill Eigenrauch; and my friends Peter and Daryl Murray, Charles and Connie Nylander.

At Rutgers University, coaches Dick Lloyd and John McFadden and alumni boosters Herb Carmen, Abe Suydan and George Mackaronis were terrific to be around from start to finish.

I was lucky enough to make lasting relationships at the University of Detroit with Fr. Malcolm Carron, S.J., the president of U of D; athletic director Bob Calihan; sports information directors Dave Seifert and Bill Kreifeldt; trainer Jack Moores; and secretary Madeline Hazy Ward. I had a great time working with my staff: David Gaines, Jim Boyce, Brendan Suhr, Tim Domke, Rick Bloom, Michael Brunker, Joe Berkowski, Pete Roddy, Jerry Opalinski, Dale Tucker, Frank Marino, Dominick Volpe and Sal Malek. We all benefitted from having terrific friends and boosters like Dennis Flynn, Bob Cicci, Stan Bartnicki, Ken Elliott, Juan Diaz, Steve Wall, Phil Di'Mambro, Bill Ebben, Rocky Ross, Sam Washington, Charles Nichols, Arnie Mistura, Dick Letscher and John Tomey.

I may not have lasted long with the Pistons, but I will always be grateful to owners Bill Davidson, Oscar Feldman and Herb Tyner for giving me a shot at the big time; and to my staff, Wil Robinson, Al Menendez, Richie Adubato, Harry Hutt and trainer Mike Abdenour for keeping me going.

And then it was on to televisionland. If I had a hat I'd tip it many times over to Bill Grimes, the president of ESPN, and all the rest of the gang who have made me feel so at home at that sports fan's paradise: Roger Werner, Scotty Connal, Bill Fitts, Steve Bornstein, Loren Matthews, Tom Odjakian, Chris LaPlaca, Rosa Gatti, Steve Anderson, Mo Davenport, Fred Gaudelli, John Wildhack, Chip Dean, Ralph Mole, Jay Mullin, David Miller, Marc Payton, Terry Lingner, and Julia Barfield. And at my second TV home, ABC, nobody could ask for a better boss than Dennis Swanson or more capable colleagues than Dennis Lewin, Bob Apter, Geoff Mason, Ken Wolfe, Bob Iger, Jack O'Hare and Craig Janoff.

My career in television has opened a lot of doors for me; without it I wouldn't have had the chance to work with and get to know Shelby Whitfield and Fred Manfra at ABC Radio; Greg Gumbel and Peter Goldberg at WFAN in New York; Bill Conerly and Tom Barton from the Anheuser-Busch college basketball show; through the Indiana Pacers network, Mel and Herb Simon (owners of the Pacers), Donnie Walsh (their GM), Roger Blaemire, David Alcorta; in Chicago, Chet Coppock and Cheryl Raye; at Nike, Sonny Vacaro and Ed Janka; at Preview Publishing Company, publishers of the *Dick Vitale College Basketball Yearbook*, Shane O'Neill, Doug Weese, and Kyle Heinrich; from the Washington Speakers Bureau, Georgene Savickas, Harry Rhoads and Bernie Swain; at Fisher Nuts, Janice Manemitsu, and at the Edelman Public Relations Company, administrators of the Fisher Nuts Sports Nut of the Year contest, John Eckle, Jeff Sernick, and George

Drucker; Larry Donald at *Basketball Times*; my buddies at International Management Group, Barry Frank, Michael Glantz, Chuck Bennett and Sandy Montag; and my editor at Simon and Schuster, Jeff Neuman.

Finally, I want to thank my wife and daughters, who suffered still more lost time away from me while I suffered through my induction into still another brave new world, the world of literature.

It's been a winding road from the Ziggy, but what a wild ride along the way!

For my mother and father, Mae and John Vitale, who in adversity always provided inspiration, motivation, and love, and who taught me everything I know about the most important commodity on earth: people.

CONTENTS

THE SOUND IS FAMILIAR

Hold me back! Calm me down! Don't let me get too excited here or I'll make my own All-Hallucination team! But are we talkin' about a PTB here? A prime-time *book?* Are you kiddin' me? A book about basketball, my one favorite thing in all the world? Where I get to talk about hoops and say whatever I want for as long as I want? And I don't have to break for a commercial or even get interrupted by a game? Oh, baby. This is a true M&M'er if I ever saw one—and I've seen a lot for a guy with only one good eye. Dick Vitale on basketball! Little Richie, the bald, one-eyed Italian from back in Jersey who couldn't run or jump or play more than a lick,

now gets all the minutes! (Notice I didn't say couldn't shoot, because—mark this down, store it away—Richie could always shoot the rock.)

Okay, okay. Right away I'll admit it, I'm a kid in a candy store, a junkie, an out-and-out addict when it comes to basketball. I live and breathe the game. Always have. Always will. Don't ask me to explain it, at least not in so many words. You know what that might mean. There would be many—so many we'd have to give hernia warnings with each copy of the book.

I'm such a wacko about basketball I speak a different language about it: lots of initials and words and phrases and hoopalogue which you may not be able to follow without checking the glossary up ahead in Chapter 12. But you've heard this kind of stuff before. Probably committed similar shortcuts with words in the privacy of your own home. M&M'er—that's a Mismatch. Or it's an NC—which means No Contest. PT is Prime-Time when used with another P, as in Prime-Time Performer. By itself, PT might be Playing Time. You never know. You just have to pay attention. A Dow Joneser—that's a player who's inconsistent, unreliable, up and down and all around the town. Got it now? These are just a few examples. But hey, don't sweat it. This is no contrived, made-up deal. This is the way I've always talked about basketball. Or about living, which is one and the same to me.

I still have a love for the game that, other than my love for my family—my wife, Lorraine, and my teenage daughters, Terri and Sherri—transcends just about anything I've come in contact with in my life. It's a childlike wonder, a passion, an absolute obsession. My soul has always been in basketball. I will probably die someway, somehow, somewhere in the game.

As if I have to say this, let's agree right here that basketball is the finest of all sports. I won't even begin to get into the athleticism the game demands—the brand of athlete in hoops compared to our other fun and games. You can't be a specialist like in football, where Bernie Kosar just throws the sidearm

flutterball into the flat or Refrigerator Perry throws his balloon cheeks over the goal line. We're not discussing baseball's under-aerobic-achievers: Juan Berenguer pitching the Minnesota Twins to the World Series (or was it the clubhouse buffet?) with his gut hanging out is not my idea of a tremendous ath-lete. No, my hardwood guys are absolutely, positively the finest athletes in the world. To paraphrase the great former football coach at Florida A&M, Jake Gaither, they're a-gile, mo-bile, not too fra-gile and, when needed, a little bit hos-tile as well.

Basketball, especially at the college level, is just a happier event than any other sport: more vibrant, more colorful, more exciting. Without a doubt, pro and college basketball are bet-ter—if not more skillfully or more efficiently—played, better coached and, yes, better officiated than other sports. They're more enthusiastically followed by their fans and more artfully covered by television; certainly they're esthetically superior, technically more correct, measurably more meaningful. And, to me, vastly more inspirational. Hoops remains spontaneous, adventuresome, imaginative, consistently different and, above all, great fun. Doesn't something like that simply deserve a language all its own?

Give me the razzmatazz of the game on campus—and I include Madison Square Garden, the New Orleans Super-dome, Rupp Arena, and little Sullivan Arena up in Anchor-age, Alaska, as on campus; let's face it, baby, the *world* is my campus—give me the noise and spirit and enthusiasm and passion and all the rest and I'm in hoop heaven. I love this game with my mind, my heart, and my soul, and every night I get to put that feeling across to millions of wackos just like me from coast to coast. That's why my single, number-one, absolutely favorite thing ever written about me was when Steve Rudman of the *Seattle Post-Intelligencer* wrote that Dick Vitale *sounds* like college basketball. Baby, that one lit up my day, my week, my season! Make my career, Stevie baby!

I know just what he means, because I know that sound. Essentially, I've patterned the chords of my entire life up there on the basketball scale. Growing up in New Jersey, I was halfway between the meccas of the game: the Garden in New York and the Palestra, that magical, mystical bandbox on the campus of the University of Pennsylvania in Philadelphia. Oh, what a pair of juke joints to hear a symphony in!

I remember Joe Lapchick coaching at St. John's. Louie Carnesecca was his assistant back then. Lapchick, the Chief: tall, distinguished, in control, bigger than life. I remember Frank McGuire bringing in his clubs from North Carolina and later South Carolina. Dapper, handsome Frank flashing his cuffs as much as he did his smile. You think, watching guys like this, I didn't envision myself as a coach one day? To love the game like I did and to think of myself as part of it in these places—what a fantasy for a kid!

And not just a kid. I wasn't a kid anymore when Bill Bradley played for Princeton in the early sixties. The Palestra was sold-out one night when a bunch of my buddies and I wheeled and dealed with the ticket taker at the old barn off Chestnut Street so we could somehow sneak in to watch Bradley, the great All-American, do his thing in one of those doubleheaders the Palestra practically invented. Back in the old days I just bounced from gym to gym, filling up my days with basketball, whatever the level. All throughout my playing in junior high and high school and in CYO ball, throughout my years in college at Seton Hall University, throughout my early career as a coach in high school, I was a total freak for the game.

I'm still surprised at how many people come up to me and say they didn't know I was a coach. I guess they think I just emerged one day as this wacko hoop nut out of some TV test tube gone berserk or something—that I burst full-grown into your living room wailing, "Yowooo, a Slam Jam Bam, Dipsy-Doo Dunkeroooo!" without any formal training in the game. Not that I was any threat to John Wooden, the Wizard of Westwood, of course, but I coached at every level of the game and put together a pretty good track record before reaching the pros. In 1971 I was a sixth-grade teacher in East Rutherford, New Jersey, picking up some change coaching the local high school team, and seven years later I was coaching the Detroit Pistons in the National Basketball Association.

In my seven years coaching the varsity at East Rutherford High we won four sectional championships and two straight state championships. As an assistant coach at Rutgers University, I recruited the key players for the Scarlet Knights team that went to the Final Four in 1976. By then I had taken the head coaching job at the University of Detroit, where in four years we won 78 games, including 21 in a row in 1976–77. (You might recall that was the year Marquette won the national championship with somebody named McGuire coaching. But when Marquette played Detroit that season, *Vitale whipped McGuire.*) And then I went on to the Pistons, a long, sad story we'll get to all too soon, where for the first time in my life I experienced what every coach fears most in his career: The Ziggy. The big Z. Pack the bags. The end. That's all she wrote. Go home. It's over. You're fired. The Ziggy. And then, it was ESPN, here I come.

I still do a lot of coaching clinics and camps and I can x and o with the best. One of my strengths as a coach was my ability to teach, to show how to break down offenses and defenses—to adjust to moves, attack the seams in a zone, or alter formations to get odd-even matchups. If a team has a 1-3-1 front, attack it with two men on top, split the point, establish triangles inside. Stuff like that. But I don't want to make this sound complicated, like football or something. It's not. Coaching backetball is easy. Simplifying it is the trick. The key is to communicate. How does a Bobby Knight or a Dean Smith or a John Thompson go to practice and get his people to execute while Joe Zilch who knows all the terms and strategy can't get his people to do squat? It all comes back to communication. That was always my strength, and now it's my business.

For me, it all goes back to the late nights—I should say early mornings—that my coaching compadres and I spent sitting around the Ross Diner up on Route 46 in New Jersey.

We had it all figured out back then. We were all geniuses headed for the ACC or the Big Ten or UCLA. The plays worked perfectly with the salt and pepper shakers. Sometimes they worked even better outside the diner where we would set up game situations with garbage cans. One night we got stopped by the police for making such a racket. We called it a new pick 'n' roll; they called it disturbing the peace.

One March night in 1967, we were reading the next day's early edition of the New York *Daily News* about the NCAA Final Four in Louisville, Kentucky, when my best buddy, Tom Ramsden, another basketball sicko, looked at me with a zoned-out expression. I looked back, in the same zone. We knew exactly what we were thinking and what we were going to do: We were going to Louisville. We didn't have hotel rooms or game tickets or directions and hadn't made any of the other normal preparations. We just suddenly knew we *had* to go. We each ran home, threw some clothes in a suitcase, and then headed down the interstate for Kentucky. It was the middle of the night but that hardly mattered. We were going to our first NCAA finals.

The 1967 Final Four was the first for one Mr. Lew Alcindor (who later would become Kareem Abdul-Jabbar, of course), the one in which his UCLA team destroyed Houston and Dayton. Afterwards Houston's Elvin Hayes ran off his mouth about how Alcindor wasn't that good and how the Big E would dominate him the next time they met. That turned out to be the following year in a game in the Houston Astrodome, a game created by a little TV impresario named Eddie Einhorn, a game that merged television with college basketball forever and ultimately enabled yours truly to get and keep a job.

But I want to tell you, being around the NCAAs was everything I expected. I don't even remember now how we got a place to sleep; I think we stayed up all night a few times. We went over to where the UCLA team was headquartered—for a look at the Bruin song girls, of course—and hung around while bands played all over the hotel for most of the night. I don't know how the UCLA players ever got any rest. Then we managed to get a couple of tickets over at another hotel where all the coaches were staying. The national coaches are always in convention at the Final Four, which makes for as great a circus as the games themselves and, for a coaching groupie like me, an even more amazing show. Because of my basketball camp and clinics back in Jersey, I knew a lot of the younger assistants in those days, so hitting them up for tickets wasn't that difficult.

The Final Four atmosphere was utterly fantastic to me. Just being there, even having had to drive a car all night and never being sure where the next night's bed would be, was ecstasy, an unbelievable high. I couldn't wait to get back and tell everybody how I had hobnobbed with the John Woodens and the Adolph Rupps and the Guy Lewises.

The contrast between my first Final Four—I wonder if Mr. Abdul-Jabbar realizes we share that in common as well as goggles and bald heads—and my second one will never cease to amaze me. Until I came to ESPN, in all those intervening years I was so wrapped up in my coaching career that I couldn't get back to the coaches' convention and the national tournament. I always felt I had to use that postseason time to get a head start on recruiting. I would be out getting players while the others guys were conventioneering; I was struggling in the valleys in order to get to that mountaintop.

Then in 1983 ESPN wanted me to go to the finals in Albuquerque, both to send reports back to the studio and to meet and mingle with the network's advertisers and other clients at the tournament parties.

This was the year the Houston Cougars with Akeem (The Dream) Olajuwon (and you can look this one up: Akeem became "the Dream" nationally after none other than Dicky V gave him that nickname on ESPN at a Christmas tournament in Houston during his freshman year) were the dominant team in the nation and at the top of the wire service polls for much of the season.

I had gotten a lot of ink after I said that I didn't think Houston could win it all. (You may remember the Coogs were upset by Jimmy Valvano's North Carolina State Wolfpack in the championship game.)

Sixteen years earlier I had gone to the Final Four a nobody, driving all night in a beat-up sedan. And now I was back, but this time it was by jet plane, with a hotel suite, catered parties and all the rest. But my fondest memory of that weekend is when our group from the network arrived at the Pit, the arena at the University of New Mexico, for the semifinal double-header that Saturday afternoon. As I walked into the Pit, I heard this chant . . .

"DICK VI-TALE! DICK VI-TALE! DICK VI-TALE!" The Houston fans yelled it quite a few times that day as the Phi Slamma Jammas blew away a fine Louisville team in as spectacular a dipsy-doo-dunkaroo contest as you can imagine. Even before that, as I walked through the corridors and aisles, I could hear people saying, "That's Dick Vitale," and "There goes the ESPN guy," and calling to me: "Hey, Dick, we're going to win today," and "Over here, Dicky, take a picture with us." The Houston fans put a big cowboy hat on me and grabbed me and posed me around and I was loving every minute of it. The hot dog in me came out immediately. We were sitting right next to the Houston section during the semis and I just couldn't believe the reception I got. I think this was the first time I realized the reach of ESPN. I knew we were growing in numbers—from one million homes when we started in 1979 to roughly 50 percent of the homes in the United States, about fifty million, by 1988. But I didn't think about the terrific capacity for influence an announcer had in this format.

If I wasn't convinced of it then, what happened three years later at the ACC tournament in Greensboro sold me for good. You've got to understand what a hero Oscar Robertson was to me. Oscar! The Big O! Just standing next to Oscar Robertson was one of the great thrills of my life. Back in college I wasn't good enough to make the Seton Hall varsity, remember, and one night in 1958 the Pirates were playing Cincinnati in the Garden. I was sitting in the stands. The Big O was on the court. If I tell you that that night the Hall got 54 and Oscar got 56—alone, by himself, solo—would that be saying enough? I think Cincy won 118–54 or something. The point is Oscar may have been the greatest player ever, period, done, over-and-out, back to you in the studio. They talk about Magic Johnson's triple-doubles? In the 1961–62 season the Big O *averaged* triple-doubles for the Cincinnati Royals in the NBA. And while he was in college, Robertson's performance against my school was one of his finest moments.

Fast-forward ahead now to 1986, the ACC tournament in Greensboro. There I was, standing courtside with the Big O himself when a group of kids gathered around asking for autographs. But they weren't asking Oscar Robertson for his. No, they wanted the signature of the player with no name, no game, and no reputation besides, the nobody talking to Robertson, the one-eyed bald guy, Vitale!

"Who're you, Willis Reed?" some kid asked Robertson.

"Uh-oh," Oscar said to me. "I bet I hear about this at a future banquet."

"Only every time I speak at one," I told him.

But talk about humbling, or rather unhumbling! Was it really possible that I had finally made it in the big time of the game I adore as much as life? If a man is known by the friends he keeps, or in my case the telephone conversations he wallows in, I guess so. Eddie Sutton, the coach at Kentucky, accepts calls from Dick Vitale. Dave Gavitt, the commissioner of the Big East, does. So does Denny Crum at Lousville, and Ed Steitz, the head of the NCAA rules committee. Eddie and I have an ongoing contest to see who can make more of Eddie's beloved invention, the three-point basket. I still say: Move the line *back,* Mr. Steitz. Even my daughters can shoot 50 percent from 19-9!

Hey, Dick Vitale can even ring up the General at Indiana, Bob Knight.

"You got thirty seconds, starting now," Knight snarls.

"Listen, Knight, I can't say hello in thirty seconds," I answer.

"You media guys blow these kids' heads out of all proportion," Knight said to me early in the '88 season. "Keith Smart has a perpetual case of Final Fouritis; he's gonna have to sit next to me on the bench." This is Knight's typical way with the media. Intimidation City.

"Hey, General, ease off," I said. "Smart may be sitting next to you now, but when you're up in Ann Arbor down five to the Wolverines with four minutes left, he's not gonna be sitting next to you."

I'm a member of the media now and I've really adapted to that role. When I was a coach I always liked rapping with writers, and now that I'm on their side of the lines I still enjoy it. If there's one thing I've learned in this business, it's that the media's favorite people to talk to are other media people. We know more than everybody about everything anyway, right? So at times I seem to take on a dual role and it's schizo city. Like at a press day for the Big East in New York one time. All the coaches were mingling with the print and electronic boys when Big John Thompson of Georgetown got the floor for his turn. But I guess I was doing my schtick, too, answering some questions over the microphones for some local TV and radio guys. Just then one of our ESPN producers, Mo Davenport, came over and said Thompson was getting all over my case. Big John is like E. F. Hutton—when he talks, you listen. What he had said was, "Look at Vitale over there. He's supposed to be doing the interviewing. Except he's always the interviewee. And he's got more cameras around him than the rest of us put together."

My friend Dale Brown down at LSU, the Preacher Man, must think I have some influence as well. One time he called me to get me to use it. This was when he was still trying to recruit Arvadis Sabonis, the big center from the Soviet Union, to come to Baton Rouge. Never happened. Never would happen. It was all over before it began. But Dale is one of these guys who doesn't know it's over even *after* it's over. "You have to tell the true story about Sabonis," Dale fairly shouted over the phone, as he sometimes does. Hmmm, does that remind you of anyone? "You have to get this out; Sabonis doesn't have Achilles tendon problems. There's nothing wrong with the guy. The Russkies are just afraid to let him come to America because he loves it here and might defect. Get this truth out!"

Hey, Dale, do you want me to start World War III? Do you think they get ESPN in the Kremlin? Think I'm a PTP'er to the KGB?

Sure, I love being seen as part of the rah-rah spirit of college ball. I won't ever deny that I'm a promoter of the game, an advocate, a spokesman for the positives of basketball. A house man? That's all right, I'm proud to be a guy who speaks for the good things in the game. Not that I duck the issues. Not that I'm not critical when I see something wrong. But I'd much rather be known as a cheerleader, an ambassador for roundball, the rah-rah guy. And the fans have been great to me while I've played that role.

For example, when our crew from ESPN walks into the Duke Indoor Stadium down in Durham before a game—this started a few years ago—they have a standard chant. Half the crowd yells "Bald," the other half yells "Head." And then, alternately, "Bald!" "Head!" "Bald!" "Head!" And they're pointing at me and stomping and everything. Of course I play it up. I go get a towel from the manager and start shining my dome, and the crowd goes absolutely bananas. My paisan Valvano over at N.C. State was amazed. He came into Durham when I was doing a Duke–State game once, the crowd started chanting "Bald! Head! Bald! Head!" and he just shook his own nonbald head. "I can't believe you, Dick," he told me. "You're building your own personal hot dog stand in my back yard!"

We were doing some taping before the teams came out on the floor for the pregame warmups. I was rapping with the students—"Hey, how you doin'?" stuff like that; they love those Southern expressions—and those maniacs proceeded to go nuts. They started writing DUKE across my head and group-groping me and lifting me and throwing me around.

Finally they passed me up through the stands to the top of the arena and passed me back down. "Bald! Head! Bald! Head!" Being the ham that I am, I was acting about as nutsy as they were.

And then I started teasing these kids over TV. Here they were with their faces painted blue and they had no shirts on and they were jumping around and screaming at the top of their lungs. "Would you believe," I intoned to the viewing audience after I finally got my sea legs, "that these are our future secretaries of state, our great attorneys, our doctors, our leaders of the Western world? Fourteen hundred on the college boards, we're looking at here, ladies and gentlemen. These are wackos!"

And I love every creative, wacko one of them.

I cherish my relationship with all the young people connected with the college game: fans, players, wackos all. I've built up some strong relationships with certain teams, to the point where I can rag the guys over the air and they rag me right back. Especially when I'm wrong. Like in the 1987 NCAA tournament when I made a doozer of a pick—me and everybody else: North Carolina to easily beat Syracuse in the East Regional final. That was the game where Rony Seikaly and Derrick Coleman had their way with J. R. Reid, and where Jim Boeheim finally confirmed that he could win the big game and reach the promised land of the Final Four. Hey, I didn't mind the egg on my face; Jimmy B is the all-time whiner and crier, but he's also a great guy who deserved a win like that after so many years with the Syracuse fans on his back.

Anyway, a week later in New Orleans I was walking along in the French Quarter with my wife and daughters, just relaxing before the Final Four, when, sure enough, we ran into all kinds of Syracuse rooters who really let me have it. Then all of a sudden this pack of giants came sprinting up from behind us and Sherri was momentarily terrified.

You've got to picture this now: a bunch of guys, 6-8, 6-9, 6-10, roaring down the street right at us. It looked like a gang rumble or something. No wonder Sherri grabbed me and squeezed me like heck. Well, it turned out to be the Syracuse Orangemen themselves! Seikaly and Coleman and a bunch of the other guys were out on the prowl on Bourbon Street. "Where's J.R.? Where's J.R.?" they chanted. They got all over me because I had said Reid would get the Syracuse big men in foul trouble and take them apart. "Where's your baby, Dick?" Seikaly said. "You going to cry now that your baby, J.R., isn't playing anymore?"

They were really on my case and in my face. But I loved it and had a ball with them. A crowd gathered and we sort of strolled along, talking about the tournament with the boys from Syracuse and anybody else who wandered by. That same weekend I hosted a Final Four pep rally with my buddy Al McGuire, along with the cheerleaders from the participating schools, and we had a blast. I think even Al was surprised by the reception ol' Dicky got down in New Orleans. "I can't believe this, Dick," Al said. "You've really connected. You've become the Pied Piper of college hoops."

How can anybody not be turned on by college hoops? The variety, the changeability, the unpredictability. The dancing girls at Memphis State. The Dome Ranger and the Dome Orange—or whatever that furry little orange hairball is—at Syracuse. The Buckeye band playing at Ohio State—they play the "Here's Johnny" theme from the Carson show, only they change it to "Here's Dicky" for me. The great chant at Kansas, maybe my very favorite cheer in all of sports: "Rock . . . Chalk . . . Jay . . . Hawk!"

The atmosphere around the college game is something that can't be matched anywhere. People often ask me what my favorite environments in the nation are for basketball and it's awfully difficult to narrow it down. But let's start right there in Lawrence, Kansas. Such tradition and history! James Naismith himself, who invented basketball, was a teacher and a coach at Kansas. Phog Allen was the mentor there for so many years. Clyde Lovellette. Those NCAA championships. Wilt Chamberlain. Dean Smith played at Kansas. The framed pictures of all the greats decorating the halls around Allen

Field House. That amazing run to the 1988 NCAA title. Whenever I think of Kansas, I remember listening on the radio to the great NCAA final game between Kansas and North Carolina in 1957 when Lennie Rosenbluth, Tommy Kearns and the Tar Heels beat Wilt and Kansas in triple overtime. Now you go into Lawrence where Larry Brown and Danny Manning revived all the echoes. High rankings, full houses, the kids sitting outside in all-night lines waiting to buy tickets.

Another terrific area is the triangle down there in North Carolina. They call it the Research Triangle: Raleigh, Durham and Chapel Hill. But for my purpose it's the Basketball Triangle, with Carolina, North Carolina State and Duke. I've already mentioned the maniacs at Duke. But then down the road there's the Dean Dome, more than twenty thousand seats strong, a gorgeous place named for the master in Chapel Hill. The arena is just a great facility, absolutely state of the art. Everything in Chapel Hill is first cabin, first class. There's something about Carolina that I get a special excitement about. It's like the Dallas Cowboys or something. The uniforms, the cheerleaders, the people. The whole situation there reeks and reeks of Class with a capital C. Don't get mad at me, Jimmy V, for saying this, but in college hoops, North Carolina is America's team.

Valvano goes nuts at the way I go on and on about the Tar Heels. He thinks I'm in love with Dean and company, calling him the Michelangelo of coaching. "Hey," he says to me, "a few years ago in the Carolina–State game there's four minutes left and you're talking about Michelangelo and how brilliant he is down at the end of the game and meanwhile *we're kicking Carolina's ass*." But I tell Vee, "Hey, we're all Italians in this. I even gave Deano an Italian name. What do you think Michelangelo is, Dutch?" But Valvano is a spectacular part of the triangle himself. He's always a special show. Going out with him to dinner. Attending practice. Then his histrionics in the game. Postgame interview. Manicott' and wine afterward, served up with Vee's one-liners. Like when he com-

plains about getting the blame when his players drop out or
flunk out of school. "Hey, Dick, at worst I'm even; if they
can give me the heat for my players not graduating at N.C.
State, they've got to credit me with all the doctors I developed
when I coached at Johns Hopkins." It's all showtime. With
Vee, you're watching one of the great entertainers in sport.
You're watching Francis Albert Sinatra. Or in the business
world: Lee Iacocca. That's his stature, his personality and
pizzazz.

Bloomington, Indiana, has to be on the list of the top environments in the game. Bloomington means the red sweater,
the volcano, the explosion. It might mean flying chairs or a
game called on account of darkness: a darkness of mood. It
means the General, Robert Montgomery Knight. Indiana on
the basketball court is like John McEnroe on the tennis court:
when's the thing gonna blow? Going to an Indiana practice,
baby . . . you talk about motivators. If I wanted one guy
alongside those 50-by-94-foot lines for one special game, I'd
want the General. His practice is like a clinic, and when he
starts attacking, when he jumps on his best players all the
time, eats them up alive, lets out all his profanities and hos-
tility but above all gets them ready to win, well, he's just a
sight to see.

Then there's Syracuse. Got to have the Carrier Dome near
the top of my list. Just mingling with the fans down on that
humongous floor is a treat. A lot of the SU students always
strain our ESPN ropes there at courtside and give me the
business about the Pearl: Dwayne (Pearl) Washington, one
of the most enigmatic college players I've ever known. Does
enigmatic mean strange, weird, inexplicable? That was Pearl.
One night, the greatest. Another night, he's absolutely AWOL.
His presence made Carrier Dome games something special.
And they haven't lost any enchantment without him.

Remember, Syracuse draws over thirty thou to the Dome
for most of its Big East conference games and marquee intersectional battles. There might be a blizzard outside—in
fact, there probably is a blizzard—but still those thirty thou

show up to root for the Orange and criticize Boeheim. And then most of them try and cram into Freddy Grimaldi's place afterward for some of the best Italian food this side of Capri.

Syracuse may be cold and snowy but Orange basketball is so hot it's unbelievable. As Steve Thompson, one of those kids Boeheim got to leave the Los Angeles area to enroll at his Rustbelt paradise, said, "It may be minus degrees outside the Carrier Dome, baby, but it's always seventy inside. And when the fans start rolling in, it's like ninety-five."

If there's one place that rivals the Carrier Dome in fan intensity, it has to be the lobby of the Hyatt Regency in Lexington, the final entry on my list of top hoop environments. Kentucky matches Kansas in tradition—Rupp, Hagan, Rupp, Ramsay, Rupp, Beard. Kentucky matches Carolina and Syracuse in its awesome facility, the twenty-thousand-seat-plus Rupp Arena. Kentucky matches Indiana in interest; basketball is still king in the state long after the Baron of the Bluegrass, Adolph Rupp, has gone. And forget about breathing, much less moving, on a Kentucky game night in the lobby or even up on the floors of that Hyatt that sits adjacent to the basketball palace in downtown Lexington.

They love their Wildcats in Kentucky. I've never seen so many basketball periodicals published about one team—from the *Cat's Pause* put out by Oscar Coombs to *Cawood on the Cats,* another magazine done by the Kentucky radio legend, Cawood Ledford. And oh, baby, the pressure to win! As the present Wildcat coach, Eddie Sutton, told me: "Kentucky fans don't expect much; they just want us to win more games than we play." And the biggest fan of all still might be Kentucky's former governor and commissioner of baseball, the ninety-year-old A. B. (Happy) Chandler, who each season at the final home game sings "My Old Kentucky Home" until there's not a dry eye left in the house. Three quarters of the way through Sutton's first season at Kentucky, after the 'Cats had upset all predictions, won 20 games and were on their way to an appearance in the NCAA Final Eight, the coach finally got a vote of confidence. It arrived in a note to Sutton from

Chandler. The note read, simply, *Eddie: Unpack. Happy.*

If college hoops hadn't captured the imagination of the general public before the 1980s, it sure has now. In six of the last seven NCAA Final Fours the national championship has gone down to the last basket. That kind of excitement and spectacle is one important factor. But another is the total unpredictability of the animal. Who could possibly forecast a Cleveland State in 1986 or an Austin Peay in 1987? And what about the biggest upsets—the ballplayers who develop from ugly ducklings to beautiful swans right in front of our eyes? Remember Houston's Olajuwon as a freshman in the 1982 Final Four? He wasn't a pretty sight. And Navy's David Robinson was a complete NC as a frosh in 1983–84—and I don't mean a Non-Com. Who could have predicted they'd become so great? Nobody on this planet.

For these reasons everybody seems to be a fan, and we in the television business helped create this boom by turning college youngsters into media superstars almost before they know how to shave. You think I'm on television a lot? How about the North Carolina Tar Heels or the Syracuse Orangemen? Rony Seikaly and J. R. Reid get more air time each season than Bill Cosby, and they don't get to use reruns.

Even athletes in other sports follow college basketball. I went to speak at a banquet in Midland, Texas, that also featured Brian Bosworth of Oklahoma and the Seattle Seahawks. The Boz, big and bad, punk haircut and shades, wanted to talk hoops. I met Tommy Lasorda, the manager of the Los Angeles Dodgers, during a layover in O'Hare Airport in Chicago, and we talked basketball so long we both missed our flights. I see Sparky Anderson of the Tigers; he wants to know if Michigan is better than Illinois. I see Darryl Strawberry of the Mets; he starts imitating baby jump shots. I talk to Tony Peña of the Cardinals, he *does* Dick Vitale to me!

I met the richest man in America. *He* wanted to talk basketball. Get this: There I was, speaking at the National Retailers' Convention at the Fontainebleau in Miami, with the chairmen of the boards of all the leading stores in America, and I was supposed to talk to them about motivation! Well, I had done my homework, baby. I did a whole shtick on Sam Walton of Wal-Mart, how he went from a five-and-ten-cent store to the megabucks of the universe. And afterwards Sam the Man himself sought me out. He wanted to play tennis the next morning, he invited me to his home down in Arkansas, but most of all, he wanted to rap about the Hogs! I loved Sam's comment when he lost about two billion in the stock market dive in '87: "It's only paper." Hey, it's only a game. It's only paper. Same thing.

Then there was this reception at the Fiesta Bowl in Phoenix in '87—I was out there with my daughters, who were playing in a tennis tournament. I was hobnobbing with some football players from Miami—Vinny Testaverde, Alonzo Highsmith, Mike Irvin, they all kept coming over to say hi and to rap about basketball. "Who are the PTPs this season?" they asked; they all knew the phrases. Then the band stopped playing. Everybody stopped talking. Even I stopped. The guest of honor, Bob Hope, was making his appearance. I was thrilled.

When Hope came over my way, I puffed up just like one of the big shots. "Bob Hope," somebody said, "meet Dick Vitale." I gave him a firm handshake. Bob Hope looked at me like I had just landed the weirdmobile from Mars. He didn't say, "Who the hell is this guy?" But he might as well have.

I knew immediately there was at least one guy college basketball hadn't reached yet. I still have work to do.

OPINIONS ARE LIKE BUTTS—
ONLY I HAVE MORE THAN ONE

One thing you can say for me as a broadcaster: I've never held back with my opinions. I've never steered clear of controversy. I say what I think, and I don't care about the consequences; I'll face those when they come. And they come—do they ever come!

Frankly, I think this whole thing about me as a guy who tries to stir up controversy is overrated. I don't try to create controversy; I try to create conversation. If something I say gets people talking about college basketball, that's not promoting myself, that's promoting the sport. Back in Jersey I used to scream that I loved Willie Mays when my buddies

liked Mickey Mantle and somebody else might have liked Duke Snider. It's not a right-or-wrong thing, it's just my opinion. I try to get the same kind of arguments going about hoops, only now I've got a lot more people listening.

One year I tried to challenge people when I said that my choice as the best player in the Big Ten was Steve Alford of Indiana. Immediately I had people going bananas in Columbus, Ohio, saying, "Wait a minute. What about Dennis Hopson here at Ohio State?"

When I went to do the Purdue–Illinois game that season, Terry Boers from the *Chicago Sun-Times* was at the game being interviewed. It was right before the opening tip-off and they had me jump in when the topic of Alford came up.

Right there at courtside we got into a big imbroglio when Boers told me he wouldn't pick Alford on the all-league team in the Big Ten. That was it. I said, fine, I was out. "If you want Hobson I can listen to that," I said, "but don't tell me I'm irrational if I pick Alford and then you don't even have him on your first five! I can't even argue with you anymore on that basis." Now I knew how easy it could be to drive people wacko!

But this is just the kind of healthy debate I try to create. I did it with Patrick Ewing vs. Akeem Olajuwon and with Ralph Sampson vs. Michael Jordan. Any time you do that stuff, you really can create some noise.

I believe the first time I got involved in any kind of controversy on the air was during a DePaul–Old Dominion game, when ODU broke a long Blue Demon winning streak in Chicago.

This was one of my earliest games with Jim Simpson for ESPN. I told the producer and director that I wanted to do an interview with Mark Aguirre of DePaul before the game; I had been all over the newspapers that week about how I wouldn't pick Aguirre on my All-America first team because he didn't come to play every night. I explained I was going with Kelly Tripucka of Notre Dame in the small forward slot

because when you blew the whistle, Tripucka always came to play.

This became a big deal in the Midwest, especially in Chicago among the DePaul lovers who wrote to ESPN accusing me of racism and downgrading an inner-city black kid in favor of the white Fighting Irish guy. This had nothing to do with it, of course; my choice was purely based on the fact that in my heart Tripucka was an everyday player and I didn't feel Aguirre was.

So Simpson and the ESPN guys thought it was very gutsy to want to face Aguirre after that. But I've never been afraid to speak my opinion to a guy's face.

On camera I simply told Aguirre what my beef was. "Mark, let's be frank," I said. "I say sometimes you don't come to play. You can be as great as you want to be, but to me you're just a Dow Joneser, an up-and-downer." (Funny thing, that's probably the first time I used "Dow Joneser" on the air).

Mark was real nice about it. He said everybody's entitled to their opinion. He didn't get nasty or defensive or anything. And today we're great friends—but I still get on him about his play.

The game that night proved everything I'd said. Aguirre had been loafing in practice the day before and I got all over his case about it. I told him I didn't think it was fair to Ray Meyer, his teammates or his school. Then in the game I got on him again about his lack of effort.

For a long time I'd been tired of seeing players treated like prima donnas just because they wanted to be billed as All-Americas. You've got to come to practice every day, pay attention, cooperate and bust your gut. That's how you get better in this game. DePaul got beat in the last minute at home by Old Dominion, and if Aguirre had been ready to play for a full forty, it never would have happened.

Simpson always had the knack of being a catalyst for me, bringing out the candid comment that might stir interest and . . . okay . . . okay, controversy.

He'd sit there during the dead of the game and say, "OK, Dick Vitale, here's one for you. You've never been a guy to dodge the question. I'm going to put you on the spot. I want an All-America center. You can only pick one. Will it be Ewing or Olajuwon?"

That would be the cue for me to go into my whole shtick and I wouldn't duck at all. "Right, Jim," I'd say. "I've got to go with the big guy at Georgetown, the intimidator, Mr. Defense, Patrick Ewing. Because they're going to win it all, Jim. They're going to win big, the national championship, and Ewing's the reason." Georgetown did wind up beating Akeem the Dream and Houston in the national championship game in Seattle that year.

Patrick and I go back a long way. On ESPN, as a matter of fact. Back in 1981 I was doing the Dapper Dan high school all-star game in Pittsburgh when Ewing got into a fight and punched a kid. And it really took away from his performance. He was a vicious player, vicious in a positive way. But he always seemed to be angry, too, on and off the court.

Patrick didn't seem like a happy kid at all. When we interviewed him following the game, Patrick was just fierce. He had the gold trophy and the adulation and all, yet he was still saying he didn't care if players got rough with him or if the press questioned his tactics, he wasn't about to take any "nonsense." Only he didn't say "nonsense."

Patrick was not easy to talk to back then. On camera he seemed surly and spoiled. I was glad they never ran the interview. Here was a seventeen-year-old kid mouthing off, and airing those comments would only have given a bad impression of the kind of player who was coming out of high school. The game would not have been represented well at all.

During his college career I touted Ewing enough so that I felt comfortable being a bit critical of him as well. I was mostly unimpressed with his posting up and his drop-step moves. "Patrick," I said on the air, "you've got to work a little more on those pump fakes inside."

The next time I did a Georgetown game, sure enough, Hoya

coach John Thompson grabbed me and practically pulled me into the locker room. Thompson, who is 6-foot-10, about three-hundred pounds, carries a milk carton around for his ulcers and speaks in a booming thunderclap of a voice. "I want you to get in here," he roared. "And tell Patrick about his post moves. Explain some things to him."

I guess the word had gotten out that I was being a little critical. I didn't want a bad confrontation. I had been one of the prime salesmen for Patrick Ewing and the Georgetown program for years. I thought he was the most intimidating, dominating center to come down the road since Jabbar and Walton. I thought he was great! Now he was going to eat me alive while Thompson watched, drinking from his milk carton.

But I wasn't about to back down. I felt strongly that everybody has some areas they should work on. I looked up . . . up . . . up at Patrick. " I still think you should work on those drop moves," I said.

Ewing stared down . . . down . . . down at me. Then he got the biggest grin on his face. "I do, too," he said. Then he laughed and laughed. So did Thompson. After a while, so did I.

At Georgetown, I heard, Ewing was sometimes withdrawn, bitter, sullen, surly. Now with the New York Knicks in the NBA his personality has come out a lot more. Maturity does so much for a person it's unbelievable. This guy has made a 180-degree turnaround. Recently I spoke at an event sponsored by Nike, and Patrick was there with his little son, smiling and laughing and fooling around. He came over and put his arms around me. All I could think was how fast these kids really do grow up.

When I picked Ewing over Olajuwon in '84 it really stirred up a Cougars' nest in Houston. Immediately the letters and phone calls came rampaging in. The *Houston Post* even came up with a big voodoo doll with a Vitale face and pins stuck through it. I became a marked man in Houston, talking about their guy, their basketball hero, being only a second banana.

But hey, my point was not to downgrade Akeem. I *wasn't*

knocking him. I loved the way Olajuwon played. If you say a guy is number two in the nation . . . wouldn't you like to be number two at what you do?

The mentality that exists in our country, though, whether it's in sports or anything else, dictates that to be anything less than number one is to be a failure. It's amazing. If I picked Ewing, that meant I was anti-Akeem. Wrong! But if I was this, I was that. The Big East had Vitale in its pocket. I was locked up with Thompson and Dave Gavitt, the Big East commissioner. You should have heard the complaints.

Nothing was negative in the choice between these two great players. I mean this was a pick for an All-World team! So I chose Ewing one and Olajuwon two—where's the negative? And yet that's how the Houston fans reacted. But then, I should have known.

They undoubtedly remembered the previous season, when Houston kept winning while I kept insisting on ESPN that the team couldn't win the national championship because of a lack of experience at the point.

The Cougar point guard was Alvin Franklin, a freshman that season. Down the stretch, for shot selection, decision making, giving the ball up at the right time, I just think a team needs a veteran at that position in order to go all the way in the tournament. And Franklin wasn't a pure point guard, anyway; he was a scoring guard.

Bear in mind that Houston was always a suspect team on the free throw line, too. And what's a freshman usually do on the line at the end of big games? *Kannnng.* But Houston had a great season in 1982–83 after making the Final Four the previous March in New Orleans when Akeem was just a rookie. And the next year they got to be number one during a season in which they showed up constantly on our ESPN basketball review show.

Naturally, Bob Ley, my partner in the studio, and I talked about Houston a great deal. But as I made my position clear and stuck to my guns, we had writers and radio and TV people calling me from Houston all the time, and I took some heavy criticism.

That was the first year ESPN decided to cover the Final Four live. We set up interviews and talk shows and carried on business from the site of the games. Let's set the stage. Houston had just destroyed Louisville in their famous dunk-athon semifinal game. One of the more amazing games in the history of the Final Four for sheer athleticism and spectacular moves. Akeem. Clyde (the Glide) Drexler. Larry Michaux. Benny Anders. Even Alvin Franklin. They did their stuff. And stuffs.

So now I went into the locker room to face the music. Remember, I had said all year they'd never get there because of Franklin at the point. And they had just absolutely run out a terrific Louisville team where the point guard had as much bearing on the game as my dog.

Well, the Houston Cougars were really ready for me. They had my name up on the chalkboard in the locker room, for one thing. This wasn't the first time I'd been immortalized on a locker room wall—after all the stuff I've said through the years I'm a walking locker room wall. It was just the first time I'd come face-to-face with such a thing.

I didn't have to venture into the Cougars' lair to congratulate them, mind you. But I did. And they went wild. They all started teasing me. "No point guard, huh?" "Can't make the Final Four, huh?" "Opinions are like butts, Dick Vitale," Reid Gettys said to me, repeating a line I'd read from him earlier in the season. "Everybody's got one." Only he didn't say "butts."

What could I say? Now I had changed my mind. I thought Houston would be a lock in the championship game against Valvano and North Carolina State. But I teased them back. "It's not over yet. You didn't win the gold yet," I said.

Then they ended up losing the final game in that unbelievable upset. I didn't visit the Houston locker room after that one. I went to the press conferences and sat with Valvano's dad. I learned that Vee's mother's maiden name is Vitale. But she said it was pronounced in three syllables, long E, Vi-Tal-E.

She probably didn't want to be recognized by Alvin Franklin.

Speaking of unbelievable, there aren't a lot of impossible upsets in the NCAA tournament and I've sure as heck made it known what I think of the M&M'ers that crop up every year. But, boy, is it embarrassing to miss them when they do happen. How about Austin Peay in 1987? Remember the Governors in the first round that year against Illinois?

There we were, Bob Ley and I, sitting in the studio doing the all-day tournament roundups, the cut-ins, evaluations, analysis, and really having some fun. And I really went after the Illinois–Austin Peay first rounder in Birmingham. "A mismatch, a total M&M'er, I don't believe this game," I said on the air. "We're looking at Rolls-Royce versus Volkswagen. Bo Derek versus Dr. Ruth. There's no way." My evaluations, as you may remember, are calm, well-reasoned, and calculated not to offend. Right.

At the end of that regular season I had worked Illinois against Indiana on ABC with Keith Jackson, and the Illini beat the Hoosiers. Right after that Illinois blew out Michigan. They had the Wolverines down 30 points at Ann Arbor. They beat Ohio State late in the season by 20. I couldn't believe the scores, they were on such a roll. So I picked them to reach the Final Four. I thought it was a lock.

So I really stuck my neck out, or my mouth. That day in the studio, I said I would stand on my head if Austin Peay beat Illinois.

Well, don't you know the Governors just played their hearts out. They were quicker, faster, and they wanted it more. They had the crowd. They had a big, huge forward throwing in one-hand *push* shots for three-pointers. Illinois looked dead. Still, there was no way Austin Peay was going to win. Was there? Yeah, there was.

I was sitting there watching when Illinois had the last shot for the win. Everybody knew the ball would go to Ken Norman. I used to get a lot of heat from the Illinois fans when I jumped all over Norman for being lackadaisical. I always teased the Illinois coach, Lou Henson, about his hairstyle. But now, believe me, I wanted them to pull this baby out.

So Norman got the ball and threw up a brick and Austin Peay won and here they came back to me in the studio. Will he? Won't he? Is he going to stand on his head?

Hey, NC. No contest. Of course I was going to honor my pledge. I put my head down and tried to prop myself up a little behind the table on the set. The crew was laughing hysterically. Actually, this was before the cameras came back live, so they were taping it. I tried my best, but it wasn't a great headstand, believe me.

During the break the production people came out and said they didn't have that good a shot on tape so they were going to get two guys to hold me up. I was worried about getting hurt, but they did it anyway and it came out fabulous. They got it all on the tape. But then Steve Anderson, our producer, nixed the idea. It was his decision, his call. And he thought the gimmick was just too hokey. I disagreed, but they ended up running only my original effort on ESPN.

I wasn't embarrassed about the headstand at all. People were calling in like crazy asking if I was going to do it, but Steve felt it didn't look right.

Following Austin Peay's victory, the Governors' coach, Lake Kelly, came into the press room in Birmingham and the first thing he said was, "Now I want to see Dick Vitale stand on his head." One of the Governor players called home immediately after the game and talked to his family. "Mom, did Dick really stand on his head?" Kelly must not have been that mad because he also said, "Maybe now that Dick stands on his head, his brains will rotate to the right place and he'll get some sight back in that bad eye." And later that month he invited me to speak at the Austin Peay banquet.

You should have seen me in Clarksville, Tennessee. I loved

it. First they had a press conference, and two Austin Peay players were there with a sweatshirt for me that had the school name written upside down. Of course when they held me standing on my head for the cameras, *Austin Peay* was right side up.

Then at the banquet a couple more players came up to the dais before it started and stood me on my head again. The crowd went nuts. I got a standing ovation before I even opened my mouth. And the emcee led them in the fans' favorite chant: "Let's go, Peay. Let's go, Peay. On Vitale." It was a riot.

The year before the Austin Peay upset, the prime story early in the tournament was little Mississippi Valley State. They played the favorite, the number one team going in, Duke, and scared the living bejesus out of the Blue Devils. Nobody knew about them. Nobody figured they had a shot. But who would? Not Dicky Vitale, at least.

Mississippi Valley State led most of the game, and as the updated score kept circulating on the wire to the different tournament sites, people were amazed. It was almost as if the Valley guys didn't even have to win the game; they had already won the respect of the tournament. It was like an upset just for them to be hanging so close. They played on guts, quickness, great athletic ability, and they challenged Duke all the way down the stretch, never letting Johnny Dawkins and the Dookies go off on one of their patented 12–0 runs.

As it was, Duke did end up surviving. But the thing everybody remembered about the game was the effort of Mississippi Valley, that and the fabulous threads that the team's coach, Lafayette Stribling, wore on the sideline. Right away Lafayette was an automatic for my All–GQ team.

I had said from the beginning that the Valley had no chance, no shot. But it was an incredible performance, and a few days later they called me to speak at their banquet. The president of Mississippi Valley State University called me, that's who. It was the first time I ever had a president call me.

After I flew into Memphis, the Valley people picked me

up at the airport and drove me to Itta Bena, Mississippi. And they really rolled out the red carpet. I walked around the corner in Itta Bena, saw the post office and the grocery store, and that was the town. That was it. But the people were so friendly and beautiful to me down there.

In my speech I said everybody should have known something about Mississippi Valley State because of the great wide receiver Jerry Rice, who played there before going to the San Francisco 49ers. I teased Stribling about his clothes, of course. "Lafayette spends more money on those duds than he does on recruiting, that's for sure," I said. "The question is, do his suits cost more than the athletic budget?"

I went on and on about the Duke team and what a great player Johnny Dawkins was. But later I thought about it, and realized I'd made a mistake. The Delta Devil kids were the kind of players who couldn't care less about an opponent's reputation or ability. They just went out and played their socks off against him. That's what got them into such a great position against Duke in the first place. They were the perfect definition of "try."

Mississippi Valley State was a valuable lesson to us all.

Probably none of my remarks stirred up more fan interest or anger than when I said Michael Jordan of North Carolina should be player of the year over Ralph Sampson of Virginia in 1982–83.

I became a Jordan fan very early in his sophomore year; I was amazed at his athletic grace and his intelligence on the floor. I kept selling Jordan over the air, Jordan and the North Carolina program.

I had the honor of doing one of the greatest games I've ever seen, a true Tar Heel–Cavalier classic, featuring an unreal show by Jordan in January 1983. The Tar Heels were behind 16 points in the second half but came back to win when Jordan made an offensive tip, stole the ball and went in and dunked, then tipped a defensive rebound away from Sampson on the last Virginia shot to save the game. It was the most unbelievable sequence of plays by one individual I've ever seen in a big game. Carmichael Auditorium was delirious. They still play this sequence on tape in the Tar Heel Hall of Fame wing of the Dean Dome, along with highlights from the Carolina NCAA championship victories of 1957 and 1982. That's how incredible it was.

Well, I was doing the game with Jim Thacker from Charlotte, Mr. ACC-TV basketball, and he was just about as excited as I was. And yours truly was just raving on and on. "Forget about Mr. Sampson," I wailed. "Forget about everybody. The player of the year is Michael Jordan. The award has got to go to this young guy from North Carolina. America's premier player. He's the best."

That was the end of me in the commonwealth of Virginia. A surge of feeling against Dick Vitale like you wouldn't believe. I had to go down to Virginia a couple of weeks later for an ACC game and feelings were so high that Dick Schultz, now the executive director of the NCAA but then the athletic director at Virginia, called up ESPN. Schultz wanted Scotty Connal to know of the emotions swirling around that game and to complain that Sampson might have been hurt professionally by my comments.

I talked to Schultz personally and told him I felt Ralph was first-team All-America, that it wasn't a knock against him that Jordan was the best player in the land. But I really believed Michael deserved the award, not Sampson. And in no way was I out to hurt Ralph's reputation.

The local reporters in Charlottesville soon got into the act. One of them called the night before this game and asked if I had changed my evaluation of Sampson. "No," I said, "and I'll go one step further. I don't even know if Ralph is number two. I would go Jordan and Dale Ellis at Tennessee, then Sampson."

The next day the headline read: *Vitale Says Jordan Number 1 and Sampson Number 3*. No sooner did I arrive in the parking lot at University Hall in Charlottesville than the fans got on my case something fierce. I went into the arena and everybody blasted me. During the warm-ups I tried to make small talk with Sampson. Not much pleasantness there, either. Afterwards he nailed me too: "What does Vitale know? Who's Vitale anyway?" Ralph said.

During the telecast I stuck to my opinion about why Jordan was the best in the nation. But I also praised Ralph. At the press conference afterward, Sampson continued to let me have it. And Terry Holland, the Virginia coach, also verbally attacked me. Ralph had the unkindest cut of all, though. "Who cares about Dick Vitale?" he said. "Al McGuire says I'm the best."

Al McGui-ah?

The upshot came later when Ralph and I made up. During his rookie year in the NBA I did Sampson's debut game with the Houston Rockets. Ralph against Moses Malone. We met several times in the hotel lobby and we teased each other. "Here comes Michael Jordan's agent," Ralph would call out when he saw me. "You got that right, big fella," I said. "But if I'm an agent I want a piece of your pie, too."

I think Ralph understands now. It wasn't taking anything from his soul or manhood—and certainly nothing off his professional worth—to have said somebody else was a better player. I consider Sampson a friend now. No problems. And looking back, it's hard to believe that people were outraged at the idea that Michael Jordan was the best player in the country.

All my opinions about what player or team was the best— a guy says give him a reaction, I give it. That doesn't mean I'm right or that whoever I don't pick as the best is a hound. Sometimes I'm very disappointed that people get so upset and can't respect an opinion without getting personal and attacking the commentator.

There are attacks and then there are attacks, of course. When I'm being critical I try and spice the criticism with humor. Doing pro games I think an analyst should have more latitude. These guys are getting paid the big bucks and they should be held accountable. Darryl Dawkins called himself "Chocolate Thunder." But once I had a game in which the big Dawk played so badly, I called him "Vanilla Pudding."

But I've been involved in some controversies that I consider much more serious. Take the case of Scott Skiles a few years ago at Michigan State. Scott was a great college player, a scoring guard who could shoot, drive, penetrate, dish, defend and, most important, lead his team. He was a gutsy, hard-nosed, inspirational player whose Spartan team was beaten in the Midwest Regional of the NCAA tournament in 1986 by Kansas only after a ridiculous incident in Kansas City when the timekeeper didn't start the clock, giving Kansas the extra time they needed for a come-from-behind win.

I had only one problem with Skiles. I felt he should never have been allowed to play that season.

I'm a traditionalist, a purist. Always have been, always will be. I believe our college athletes are role models for kids and should be forced to meet high standards. Certainly they should be treated no more lightly than anybody else when they've broken the law.

Skiles had been involved in a number of altercations involving liquor and possible drug possession prior to his senior year. He was found guilty of drunk driving. He was on probation. Michigan State allowed him to play his senior year when I felt the proper move would have been to redshirt him and make him sit out a full season as a penalty. I thought it was very hypocritical of the University and of Jud Heathcote, the Michigan State coach, to allow Skiles to play.

I had been pursuing this tack all season when the NCAA tournament came roaring into March. Here we were, monitoring the games in the studio and hearing messages all tournament long from the NCAA about drug abuse. Then we flashed to the screen to watch Scott Skiles tearing it up for Michigan State. The hypocrisy of it all just crashed down on me. Finally, we came back from one of these dissertations and I said, "Isn't it ironic that here we have Mark Price [of Georgia Tech] speaking against drugs on the tape and now we're going to watch Scott Skiles? I'll say it again. I think it's wrong, wrong, wrong."

The Michigan State people were furious and Heathcote was especially upset. But that's the way I felt. I'm glad I got the chance to elaborate on my views later in front of all the coaches' board of directors at their national meeting at the Final Four in Dallas.

John Thompson of Georgetown, the president of the group at the time, called me and invited me to speak to the coaches about some of the issues of the day. When I got there and John introduced me, we went right into it. "Dick," he said, "several of our coaches have been upset about some of your comments, mainly Mr. Heathcote here."

And I said, "Fine, let's go, Jud. I know you want to go for my throat. So I'm going to tell you up front why Skiles shouldn't have played this year." And I did.

The one thing I've always respected about Jud is that he never leaves you hanging about how he feels. He'll come out and tell you face to face. The one mistake I might have made, and he agrees, is I probably should have called him directly and found out more about the situation with Skiles before I went on the air with it.

Nevertheless, the facts were there. I wasn't making the decision about whether Skiles was involved or not. He was. I believe in giving people who've made a mistake another chance. My feeling was that the chance should have come *after* Skiles had been made to sit out a year.

Since then I see Scott from time to time in my capacity as part-time TV commentator for the Indiana Pacers' games. There are no hard feelings. He's another guy who understands everybody is entitled to an opinion.

Speaking of which, while my mouth has often expanded to a size approaching the Union Gap, even I've rarely been confronted with so public a word-munching and opinion-swallowing as I faced during the Larry Brown Will-He-or-Won't-He-Leave-Kansas Sweepstakes last March. And unless you were living under a rock during the NCAA tournament, you know what I mean by *sweep*stakes.

My part in the scenario started back in February 1988 when I was in Norman, Oklahoma, to do the Kansas–Oklahoma game. All the rumors were in full cry then: Larry to the new Charlotte franchise in the NBA. Larry back to UCLA. Larry to the Houston Rockets. Larry to Arizona State. Larry to the moon. Larry to anywhere but back to Kansas. At lunch the day of the game against the Sooners, I was ragging Larry about the whole thing. "You'll never survive those 12–70 seasons at Charlotte," I told him. "C'mon, 'fess up, Larry. You'd love to get back to the sunshine in Westwood."

Brown kept insisting he wasn't going anywhere, that finally after Danny Manning left Kansas and everybody saw that Brown was staying, all the rumors would stop and he could get on with a normal recruiting and coaching cycle at Lawrence.

I didn't believe a word of it and I kept on him. I was so sure he wouldn't be back. John Feinstein of the *Washington Post* suggested that I promise on the air that night that if Brown did stay at Kansas and coach there in 1988–89, I would do an entire telecast *without saying a word!*

Of course, that would be ridiculous—wouldn't it?—not to mention impossible. So that night I amended that to promise that if Brown came back I would show up in Lawrence at midnight on October 15, the first day of practice, at Kansas's big 'do they call "Late Night with Larry" and I would get down on my hands and knees and scrub the floor of Allen Field House. Actually, what I said was that I would scrub the floor with a toothbrush, but I hoped people weren't going to remember that. No such luck.

As the Jayhawks went on their late-season tear, recovering from all those injuries and the adversity and that 12–8 record to sweep through the early rounds of the NCAA tournament, whip Vanderbilt and Kansas State in the Midwest Regional and advance to the Final Four—as Larry Brown's cult-hero

status in the plains just mushroomed, that vow became more
and more prominent.

On the Thursday afternoon prior to the NCAA semifinals
in Kansas City, I drove down to Lawrence with a couple of
friends to have lunch with Larry at one of his favorite spots,
the Wagon Wheel. By this time our little bet was a cause
célèbre in the midst of all the NCAA goings-on. Kids on the
Kansas campus wouldn't let up when they saw me. "Hey,
Dick, get your soap and water ready for next year," they
shouted. Larry had his TV producer show me a tape of Kansas's game with Oklahoma State where the announcers brought
out a pail with my name on it. And the razzing didn't stop
there.

That night Larry brought the Kansas team into Municipal
Auditorium in downtown KC to watch the second half of the
coaches' all-star game. Mike Patrick and I were minding our
own business telecasting the game for ESPN when Larry came
over to our courtside table for an interview. Little did I know
he would present me with a mop right there on national TV.
"I'm staying, Dick," he said, "and here's a little something
for you to bring down to Lawrence next October."

Well, it wasn't TV's ratings "sweeps" period, but Dickie
V's never one to miss a trick, so I got right up during the
telecast and started mopping the floor in front of our broadcast
location. Brown wasn't about to let the subject rest, either.
After the Jayhawks upset Duke in the semis, we had him on
again, this time on "Sportscenter" on Sunday night from our
set in the lobby of the Westin Crown Center Hotel. This time
Larry gave me a scrub brush inscribed with my name and the
October 15 date. Again, I got down on my knees during the
show and started practicing my cleaning technique. But I still
never believed I'd have to use it.

You know the rest. Jim Valvano backs off the UCLA job.
Kansas wins the championship. UCLA opts for Brown. Larry
goes out to UCLA, assures them he's coming. Then, after he
gets back to Lawrence, he changes his mind again and an-

nounces he's staying. And then he goes and takes the NBA job in San Antonio. Sometimes I think he went through all that drama just to keep my travel agent guessing.

Well, I'd have to say that I've never taken more grief for a prediction that turned out to be right. I know that, as disappointed as people were that Brown was leaving, they were even more upset that they didn't get to see me down on my knees with all of their brushes. And I was disappointed too—I was all set to get a sponsor for this gig. I thought "Late Nite with Larry, Dick and Mop 'N' Glo" had a kind of a nice ring to it. But the guy who ended up doing the sweeping was Mr. Brown—sweeping out of town, and sweeping up those big pro bucks that he'll need a couple of buckets to carry to the bank.

MY WEEK AND WELCOME TO IT

I don't usually keep a diary—as you'll notice, I barely have time to brush my teeth during the basketball season—but I decided to jot down some notes about my travels over a few days: where I went, who I saw, what I talked about, and talked about, and talked about . . . I don't think I'll do it again. I thought I was tired after this particular trip. [ ] got finished reviewing my notes, I realized I was *exh*

DURHAM AND CHAPEL HILL
WEDNESDAY, JANUARY 20

This was a special week for me because it was the only time this season that my wife and daughters would be able to join me on the road. Normally I arrange for them to be at the Final Four, and the girls get excited about that. They had a ball in the French Quarter in New Orleans in 1987. But this would be a real treat because they were coming to North Carolina for the Duke–Carolina game in Chapel Hill, a place they've heard me talk so much about over the years.

The other reason for the trip was that Terri, 16, and Sherri, 14, are starting to get interested in colleges. Both of them attend St. Stephen's Academy in Bradenton and the Nick Bollettieri Tennis Academy which is practically next door. Terri, a sophomore, has already been getting letters from colleges because of her tennis, and while we were out in California the previous summer she was shown around the campuses at UCLA, USC and Stanford. I wanted the girls to get a look at Duke and Carolina, to see the environment, the excitement during a basketball season, the whole package. Lorraine had never been in the area for a basketball game either, and she wanted to see the Research Triangle in the Raleigh–Durham–Chapel Hill area.

The game is Thursday night, so I came a day ahead to do some advance work. At the airport I asked a skycap where I could get a cab. "Dickie," he said. "We're so disappointed. When McGuire comes to town, the stretch limo is waiting. Here you are, getting a cab?"

"Yeah," I said. "Al puts his megabucks into transportation. I'm one of you people. I save all my money for *tips*." That got 'em hopping.

At the Europa Hotel in Chapel Hill—a little piece of the old country right there in College Town USA—I returned phone calls and answered messages for a while. Art Chansky, a freelance writer and old friend who used to ghost Jimmy the Greek's columns, called to invite me to lunch the next day. I don't know about football, but basketball was always all Greek to the Greek, so anytime you read Jimmy on hoops, the expertise came from Chansky. Art also used to be the main contributor to the *Poop Sheet*, a terrific little periodical of news, views and information on all the ACC schools. Now Chanksy edits *Carolina Court*, a slick magazine about Tar Heel basketball.

Art is the kind of knowledgeable inside guy I've tried to cultivate over the years so I can keep up with what's going on in the different regions. Believe me, if it's happening in Tobacco Road, Art knows about it.

I also made contact with a couple of other newspaper guys in the area—Frankie Dascenzo of the *Durham Sun* and Rick Bonnel of the *Charlotte Observer*—who wanted to hang around with me and write stories about Dickie V.

I had arranged to meet with Carolina coach Dean Smith that afternoon in his office at the Dean Dome. I don't know what I expected, but nothing I had heard about this place compares with actually being there. Talk about state of the art! This was the Taj Mahal of basketball offices. I was in awe. All high-tech dials and buttons and totally plush. Push one button and a screen comes down on the back wall. Push another and video highlights of Michael Jordan's career start rolling on the screen. Press something else and here come James Worthy and Sam Perkins, Walter Davis and Phil Ford, on and on. Even Dean doesn't know what all the buttons do yet. Dean has all the gadgets he could ask for, except maybe a cigarette machine. (Dean's trying to cut down on his one real vice, all those cigarettes he puffs underneath the stands.) Even the closet door is computerized; Dean said it took him a while before he could figure out how to hang up his jacket!

"I heard you the other day on the Duke–Maryland game," Dean told me. "You were talking about the outstanding academic institutions like Duke and Stanford and Northwestern. Hey, don't forget about North Carolina." The man was right on top of it, working me like a referee. He whipped out a chart and showed me a *US News & World Report* study that ranked the top ten schools in America; North Carolina was one of them. Dean's eyes lit up. "We're right with them," he said.

Dean invited me to watch practice later in the day, but first Duke was coming over from Durham, about seven miles away, for a shootaround. The Duke coach, Mike Krzyzewski, had never done this before, but he put it to a vote among his players and the team elected to drive over so they could get more familiar with the court at the Dean Dome. Mike said he was relying more and more on the old John Wooden theory of game preparation. "I'm not going to worry about J.R. [Reid] and Carolina," he said. "I'm concerned with *us*, our game plan and execution, our health and frame of mind. I'm only concerned with that."

I kidded Mike about his association with Bob Knight, the General, whom he played for at Army and later assisted at Indiana. "I got you ranked as a Colonel now, but you're moving up, K," I told him. "I had you as a Captain and now you're a Colonel." So he started to give me a breakdown of the ranks in the military. "Someday you'll get there and be a General," I told him. "You just have to do it for twenty more years."

Duke only stayed a little while and then Carolina came on the floor. The 'Heels, Blue Heaven. Michelangelo himself. Before they got down to serious business I went over to J. R. Reid. "What's this I hear about you leaving school?" I asked. (There had been a rumor that Reid was planning to go pro after his sophomore year.)

"I'm not going anywhere. I'm staying here," he said. I used that in the telecast the next night. Then I got to teasing Dean. The Tar Heels are always one of the top teams in the country in field goal percentage and free throw percentage. Great discipline and concentration, and much of that is attributed to their coaching. Ricky Fox, a freshman, was standing nearby.

"Gee, Dean," I said. "Look at Ricky's percentage. He's about forty percent from the line." I didn't mention it again, but at the end of practice Dean said to Fox, "Ricky, prove to Coach Vitale you're a clutch free-throw shooter. Go to the line right now. Twenty thousand are in the stands. The game is tied. Let's see you make the one and one."

Fox drilled both.

Dascenzo, the writer from Durham, was watching practice with me. This was a rare treat for him, because the local guys don't usually get to sit down so close to the court during the workouts. "Usually we're given a card and we have to stay up in the second tier behind the walkway," Frank whispered. The atmosphere seemed to call for whispers. I felt like we were in a boardroom overhearing the master plan, or in a winery witnessing the final touches before that champagne was bottled.

I keep hearing that the master wants to coach only a few more years, but sitting there it was impossible to think of a North Carolina team without Dean Smith. Who would his successor be? Eddie Fogler, Dean's assistant for many years, did a fine job as head coach at Wichita State and is said to be the favorite now, but my pick is still another Carolina guy. Even though he's going back to the NBA, and despite the many bridges he's burned behind him (stealing Greensboro's Danny Manning out from under Dean's watchful eye, among them) I still think Larry Brown will eventually be the man at Chapel Hill.

That night in the hotel lounge I had a long talk with another guy who's moved in recent years: Don Nelson, the former coach of the Milwaukee Bucks who left the sidelines to become vice president and general manager of the Golden State Warriors. (He added the job of coach, too, later in the season.) Nellie was in town scouting—actually he was sniffing out the rumor about Reid—and he was in rare form. The man can tell stories and put away the beer with the biggies in the business.

A part-owner now, Nelson gave me a hard time about how the Bucks tricked me and the Pistons into switching draft positions so they could get Sidney Moncrief. While Sidney's eventually going to the Hall of Fame, I wound up in the Hall of Shame. I thanked Nellie for ultimately being responsible for my going to television.

When Nelson told me about his travails with Chris Washburn (the former N.C. State star who had gone hardship to the Warriors, experienced drug problems, and finally got traded to Atlanta) it was easy to imagine the characteristics that made Nellie such a great competitor as a player and coach. Simply, Nelson was a tremendous overachiever. He wasn't a blue chipper, but he worked his guts out to be a player in the pros. And what really drove Nelson nuts about Washburn was his lack of work. The kid flat-out didn't want it. Nelson said he was lazy, prideless, a prima donna who didn't care.

Nellie saw all this talent in Washburn going to waste, and it drove him nuts. He called Washburn into the office one day, Nelson said, "and I flat wanted to fight him. 'Let's fight,' " Nellie said to Washburn. " 'C'mon, right here, we're getting it on. You hit me and I'll hit you. Because I can't stand a guy who doesn't want to work and you don't want to work.' "

Nelson had gotten rid of Washburn long before our talk. He got rid of Joe Barry Carroll for the same reason in that big trade for Ralph Sampson. And those aren't the only non-workers in the pros, either. Oh no. I had seen the Clippers' center Benoit Benjamin just a week before play a game in which he might as well have announced to the crowd and his coach and teammates: "I don't care. I couldn't care less if we win or lose. I am sitting this one out. I'm getting my check, what else matters?"

It was an ugly scene, one I despised so much that in the locker room later I told Benjamin exactly how I felt. I went right up to him and told him he should add another 0 to that 00 number on his uniform—no points, no rebounds, no heart. I told him he disgraced the game that night. His own teammates were nailing him. It was sad; I can't understand players like that. There are so many guys who would kill just to put on a pro uniform, and then there are guys like Benjamin and Washburn pulling down a million a year playing like they don't give a damn. It just drives me nuts.

Meanwhile, though, listening to Nelson at the Europa, I remembered how great it was to be out of that pro rat race. And one other irony occurred to me.

Here in one day I had been with two of the outstanding coaches in the game; Smith on the college level, Nelson in the pros. Here I was, the nonsmoking, nondrinking Dick Vitale. And I was talking baskets with two hoop geniuses, one of the great smokers of our time and one of the major, heavy-duty suds hitters in any tavern. It made me think that maybe if I had taken up the weed and put away some more brews, I could have collected a lot more W's.

THURSDAY, JANUARY 21

This was a big game for me not only because my family was here, but because the ESPN brass was flying in from Connecticut to host a postgame party for the Duke and North Carolina people, as well as for Dave Cawood and Tom Jernstedt of the NCAA. The network wants to get involved in some more contracts with NCAA basketball, so ESPN president Bill Grimes, executive VP Steve Bornstein, and VP of programming Loren Matthews came down to Chapel Hill. We all were really up for the game: Mike Patrick, my announcing partner; producer Mo Davenport; director Chip Dean. We were ready to roll.

I was ecstatic when Lorraine and the girls arrived at the hotel late in the afternoon. We had a light dinner, then went over to the Dean Dome. I think it's still a shock for Terri and Sherri to see everybody make such a big deal over their dad. Or maybe to see me make such a big deal over a basketball game. But as soon as I walk into the arena, it's showtime, baby. First I kissed some of the Duke cheerleaders and the Carolina crowd booed. Then I went up into the crowd and helped judge a zaniest costume contest. I teased the kids about their subdued manner. "You're not wild and crazy like they are at Duke," I said.

"You mean we're not maniacs," some kid yelled back.

"This crowd's like Pavarotti in concert," I said. "The Duke crowd is Springsteen in concert." Because of the theater seating in that twenty-thousand-seat arena in Chapel Hill, because of the chair-back seats, the modernness, the fact that the students don't get the best seats down by the court, you don't get that spontaneous madness you get from the Duke kids who stand in the bleachers over at Cameron Indoor Stadium and do things like throw packets of uncooked macaroni when Craig (Noodles) Neal of Georgia Tech is introduced—to take one unusually mild example.

Before the Duke–Carolina game Terri wanted to put on the earphones to hear some of the things being said from the production truck. We were testing some graphics when something went wrong and Davenport blew up. "Dick, you can start in as soon as we fix this f—— graphic," he shouted into the earphones.

"Mo . . . uh . . . my daughter is . . . uh . . . listening," I said. My ears turned red, but not Terri's.

The game itself was a typical Duke–Carolina barn burner. I could not believe the intensity of the Duke D for forty minutes from the entire team. Coach K has ten guys he can play without a dropoff and they stick it to you with just about the best team defense of any club I've seen in years. The Blue Devils' co-captain Billy King may be the best individual defender in the nation; this guy can guard anybody—from big forwards to small guards. [At the end of the season he would receive the Hank Iba Defensive Player of the Year Award— over Gary Grant and Tim Perry.] No way would Mr. Oscar Schmidt of Brazil score thirty on King; no way would the U.S. lose the Pan American Games gold if King had made our team and played for Denny Crum in Indianapolis the previous summer.

A few weeks later King would turn in what I thought was the defensive gem of the year when he absolutely buried David Rivers of Notre Dame, holding him to 3-of-17 shooting in a Duke victory at Durham. In a four-game series that week

King had to guard Jerry Pryor of Clemson, Tommy Hammonds and Duane Ferrell of Georgia Tech, Vinnie Del Negro of N.C. State and then Rivers. Show me anybody else who can do that. Tonight King was nothing short of magnificent as he shut down Carolina's deadly shooting guard, Jeff Lebo. King fought off screens and picks all game to stay in Lebo's face, made him miss 12 of 14 shots, and turned him into a non-factor, if you can believe that.

As a result everything was churned in to J. R. Reid inside. And man, did J.R. want it. Duke stayed in control most of the night until Reid started simply grabbing the ball, turning and putting it in the basket as if he was Moses Malone or Akeem Olajuwon or somebody. It was Man-against-Boys stuff. I think Reid scored on something like seven straight Carolina possessions, baskets or foul shots.

It looked like Carolina would win after all, with Reid dominating so handily, but then that strangling Duke defense came to the fore again. The game turned in the last minute when the Blue Devils prevented Carolina from getting the ball to Reid in its last three possessions. Lebo had one of the final shots, baseline, about 15 feet. A gimme for him, right? Wrong. Out of nowhere came Robert Brickey, switching off from J.R. A leap. A piece of the ball. And Lebo's shot fluttered harmlessly away like a wounded duck; Duke won, 70–69.

"Hey, Swofford," I called out jokingly to John Swofford, the North Carolina athletic director, at the party after the game. "You've got no guts. If you had any guts, you'd get rid of a coach who's so dumb he can't figure out how to get the ball to J.R. down the stretch."

CHAPEL HILL AND DURHAM
FRIDAY, JANUARY 22

The Vitale women and I ate lunch today in the Four Corners, a neat little spot right by the post office on Franklin Street in downtown Chapel Hill, which used to be co-owned by, wouldn't you know it, Art Chansky and Eddie Fogler. It's a small world.

In between ordering the salads and sandwiches, which are all named after former Carolina basketball heroes, I noticed the waitress was severely depressed.

"Why do you look so down?" I asked.

"Don't you know what happened last night? We lost to Duke," she said.

"Did you go to the game?" I asked.

"No, I watched it on TV, right on this giant screen over here," she said.

"Well, who were the announcers? I'm curious," I said.

"Oh, Vitale was one. I couldn't stand him. At the end of the game I wanted to turn him off. All he kept talking about was Duke this and Duke that and how much he loved Duke."

"Oh, really," I said. "Well, I want to introduce myself. My name is Dick Vitale."

Aaggggaaaggg.

Well, her face absolutely dropped to the floor and she went sprinting into the kitchen. The manager had to force her to come back out. I ended up giving her a big tip and, I hope, making a fan. But it's the old story. If I'd gone over to a restaurant in Durham the next day, they'd think I had been rooting for Carolina. North Carolina State fans would have nailed me for rooting for both North Carolina and Duke. People hear what they want to hear.

We split the day between the North Carolina and Duke campuses. The tennis coaches at the schools talked to Terri and Sherri and showed them around. It's almost like one big happy family down there. For instance, Jane Preyer, who played on the team at Carolina and later spent some time on the Virginia Slims tour, is now the tennis coach at Duke.

Over at Durham in the afternoon we saw the Blue Devil center, Danny Ferry, who took my daughters to the tennis courts and told them about the bonfire that three-hundred Duke kids set after the game last night. He pointed out the students' cars that had the 70–69 score painted on the windows. Back in Chapel Hill that night, we had dinner at Slug's, where the new UNC football coach, Mack Brown, and his assistants were eating. They asked my daughters about their tennis. Then the Tar Heels' guard Ranzino Smith came in. I chided him about being a better football running back than a basketball player. He was a star running back in junior high.

"How did you know that?" Zino asked me.

"I just know," I said. (Art Chansky told me.)

You can imagine how my daughters felt after their head-spinning visits. When we were leaving the Chapel Hill campus they got in the car and said, "We love Carolina. This is where we want to go to school." When we finished at Duke they said, "We love Duke. We've decided we want to go here."

All I know is when I got home a couple of weeks later one girl had on a Carolina shirt and the other wore one from Duke.

LAS VEGAS
SATURDAY, JANUARY 23

Preparation Day again. If there's one thing I've learned in television it's to be prepared. I don't want to be surprised by anything that happens, so I try to arrive at every telecast equipped to know about the coaches, the players, the numbers, strategy, everything. Different people have different methods, but what I do before a game is make a list of every player on both teams and jot down not only their biographical information and key stats, but also anecdotal tidbits that might be of interest to viewers.

On the plane out to Vegas for the Temple–UNLV game, for instance, I ran down the Owls: Mark Macon, the terrific freshman guard from Michigan whom I would be seeing for the first time; I knew already that this was one smart, serene, thoughtful kid who turned into Mr. Gangbusters Confident when he hit the floor. Ramon Rivas, the Temple center, played for the Puerto Rican national team. Tim Perry, one of the best rebounders in college, is from Freehold, New Jersey, and went to the same high school as Bruce Springsteen. Perry himself was a musician. He played drums in a local band and also played the instrument in the school marching band before he realized his basketball talent late in high school and ended up selling his drums to a buddy. Next year when he gets his pro contract Tim can buy the drum company.

Oh, yeah, and Mike Vreeswyk, Temple's three-point wing man; I wanted Mike to hit some treys against Vegas so I could call his baskets "threeswyks." I had it all planned. "A three by Vreeswyk, folks," I was going to scream, "Call it a three-swyk."

I had my Vreeswyk story all ready. One day last year I got a phone call out of the blue from a guy I went to college with at Seton Hall–Patterson, a big scorer named Eddie Vreeswyk.

"Eddie! A voice from the past," I said.

"Dick, you know that kid you've been crowing about from Temple, Mike Vreeswyk?" Eddie said. "He was the leading scorer in high school in Pennsylvania. He's my son."

Well, I hadn't put the names together then, and I hadn't seen Mike Vreeswyk since. But when I got to Vegas and went to the Temple practice, I saw he was a chip off the old block. "Just like your old man," I told Mike. "Your next assist will be your first. Eddie Vreeswyk hasn't passed the rock yet."

Watching John Chaney's team practice, you can tell by the way they protect the ball and the way they make every pass that there's no room for carelessness. The Owls work so much on catching and passing the ball, the simple fundamentals, concentrating on preventing turnovers. You can also tell that Chaney lets Macon get away with a little more than the rest, a little more individuality in his dribbling and penetrating. John doesn't want to hold him back or break him; Macon is like a young colt and Chaney's the trainer, meticulously teaching him how to race.

There was a big difference between the Temple and Vegas practice, but not in the way you might think. It's the difference between offensive ball control and defensive ball control. While the Owls stress discipline and shot selection on the offensive end, Jerry Tarkanian's team tries to overcome that with the emotion and intensity of their abnormally quick pressing defenses.

Stacy Augmon is Tark's newest budding star. The prototype Vegas athlete, he can run and jump. Long arms. Defends out on the point. Augmon's shooting leaves a lot to be desired, but I told him he reminded me of Paul Pressey of the Milwaukee Bucks, a great defender and one of the most underrated players in the NBA, the man who invented the position of point forward. I don't think Augmon knew who Pressey was.

Then there are my other favorite Rebels: Gerald (Furniture) Paddio, the great long-range bombardier who I had on my All-Improvement team. This year he can at least dribble, pass, and defend; when Vegas went to the Final Four last season, he didn't have to and couldn't have if he had to. Then there is Jarvis Basnight, the Squire. That's his real middle name. I told the kid he should go by both names, but the Squire is a bit embarrassed by the highfalutin sound of all those monikers. There's also Richard Robinson, a player who tends to disappear for weeks at a time, usually getting his game together in time for a TV appearance. "Boy am I glad to see you," Tark told me. "Robinson hasn't played at all since you did our game with the Soviets in the preseason."

Vegas has such a misleading image. Everybody thinks the Runnin' Rebels are run and gun and that's all, but the team gets almost all of their offense in transition off the steals and rebounds and tipaways and loose balls forced by their defense.

Another difference I noticed today was that when Temple was on the floor, John Chaney and his assistant, Jim Maloney, did all the teaching: two guys, drills, spare and simple like the old CYO days. When Vegas got out there Tark operated the Shark Tank almost like it was General Motors and he was in charge of a huge board of directors; there were assistants everywhere.

"Tark, doesn't it get too wild?" I asked him.

"Dick, I love it all," he said. "I have one guy who does nothing but specifically get into the faces of my defensive unit while I'm coaching the offense. That's Ralph Readout. He's my Intensity coach."

Speaking of fired-up, while I was watching Vegas practice with Keith Jackson of ABC, who should come walking in but T. C. Ciricione himself. Now we're talking characters.

I mentioned preparedness? Luckily, Maloney had prepared me for T.C. because Jimmy had just received the Ciricione treatment the day before when the Temple bus arrived at the team's hotel. Almost before Maloney could check in, T.C. had nailed him for a pair of tickets to the game. If you don't know T.C. (commonly referred to as Tootie), you haven't been around college hoops very long. Everybody knows Tootie Ciricione.

I first met Tootie during a high school all-star game years ago. "Vi-TAL," Tootie squealed today in that high-pitched voice, reminding me. "Vi-TAL. It was Pittsburgh. The Dapper Dan Roundball Classic. 1970. The Chatham Center, Vi-TAL. You had Les Cason [my star high school player]. I drove you everywhere, Vi-TAL. Don't you ever forget it, Vi-TAL."

Keith was going bananas over my guy Tootie. I could translate the look on his face. It said, "Who is this piece of work?" I've got to describe Tootie. He's about 5-foot-6, short and wiry, glasses, high forehead, not much hair left. He's about fifty, give or take a decade. You'd never think he'd be a basketball guy, but then again I'm not the suavest-looking Tom Selleck around, either. As a matter of fact, Tootie probably identified with me long ago and that's where we made a connection. That and the fact that unlike a lot of guys, I give Tootie the time of day.

Tootie is a basketball junkie, the all-time junkie. Forget anybody you ever met who devoted his life to one thing. They all pale in comparison to Tootie. He's always trying to get a legitimate coaching job somewhere but always falls short. He carries around recommendations in his pocket wherever he goes. He had them with him today: letters from Tark, George

Raveling, Dale Brown, and his main man from the University of Hawaii, Riley Wallace. And me?

"I got all the biggies but not you anymore, Vi-TAL," Tootie said. "You're not a coach anymore. You're with the TV boys, Vi-TAL. Your letters don't mean nothin' anymore."

Tootie has been living in Vegas for a while. He still works some basketball camps in the summer; he was at Thompson's camp and Michael Jordan's camp. He still wants that legit assistant coaching job, or a scouting position. Hey, the guy knows the game.

Both times I got head coaching positions, Tootie was on the telephone to me practically before the press conferences were over. "Vi-TAL," he screamed through the phone the day I was named coach of the University of Detroit. "Congratulations, Vi-TAL. What time you meeting me at the airport? I got all the recruits listed. Here's what we need. Send the ticket prepaid, Vi-TAL." He had the flight numbers and times, the works. I told Tarkanian about this later—he's known Tootie for years—and he said it reminded him of the time a legendary Eastern recruiter named Spook showed up at Tark's office at Long Beach State in California and asked Tark if he wanted André McCarter to come play for the 49ers.

"Sure I want McCarter," said Tark.

"I can get you McCarter," said Spook. "Of course, I'll need a little cab-fare to Philadelphia."

Tootie once heard my "A Boy, a Ball, a Dream" motivational speech. Now every time he sees me he practically begs me to do a little riff from it. "Give it to me, Vi-TAL," he squealed today at the Vegas practice. "Vi-TAL, c'mon. A boy . . . a ball . . . a dream. When I hear that, I get a basketball orgasm."

One season when Tootie was coaching junior high ball, they say, he dressed up like an Indian and ran through a hoop as a pregame gimmick. His team was 0–17 at the time. The team actually beat up Tootie and put him in a hospital for two days. But I have another favorite story about Tootie. A true story—it's in the court documents.

Once Tootie was subpoened to testify as a character witness for a man accused of murder. "Mr. Ciricione," the judge intoned, "what can you tell us about the defendant?"

"He gives it up, your honor," said Tootie.

"What?" said the judge.

"He gives it up."

"What do you mean? Gives what up?" said the judge.

"He gives up the rock," said Tootie. "You ever watch basketball, your honor? Everybody wants to shoot it these days. Everybody wants to score. This is a good man, judge. This is a man who *gives it up.*"

Tootie has nothing on Tark for basketball single-mindedness. Two nights ago the UNLV coach was watching the closed-circuit telecast of the Mike Tyson–Larry Holmes M&M'er at the Hilton Hotel and a fan walked up. "It's been a bad night for old guys [the fan had bet on Holmes] but a great night for autographs," the guy said to Tarkanian. "First, I got Mikhail Baryshnikov. Now you."

Jerry murmured something about "great, great." But I knew he had no idea who Baryshnikov was. The only Mikhail he knows plays for the Celtics. Later Tark was at dinner with some friends when Colonel Tom Parker, Elvis Presley's old manager, walked up to say hello to Tark's dinner companions, whom Parker knew. Again, the Shark had no idea who the Colonel was. Friends say when Watergate was going on, Tark had no clue about that, either. They told him the President was about to be impeached. "That's a shame," Tark said. "What for?"

Tark invited me and Sonny Vacarro to join some friends for a Mexican feast at Cafe Santa Fe, which is next to the Thunderbird Hotel, just off the Vegas strip. Sonny is Nike's main basketball man, the guy whom every coach in America should get down on their knees and thank for raising the stakes of the coaches' promotional sneaker contracts. Sonny and Tark are really tight; they spend a lot of time together, because Sonny does color for Chick Hearn on UNLV telecasts, and nobody rides Tark like he can. Vacarro is always giving Tark grief about his team, his players, the schedule, the weather, whatever.

Right away another guy named Bob Duncan joined our party. He turned out to be one of the original members of the Diamonds, the singing group who made "Little Darlin'" so popular way back in the fifties. Wow, was I impressed. Duncan, who sang the high falsetto on the song, was still going strong with the group. They were appearing that very week on the Strip. We talked about an old neighbor from Garfield, New Jersey, Joey Dee, who made "The Peppermint Twist" famous with his group, the Starliters. Naturally, I broke into my own version of both songs. *Uh . . . uh . . . little darlin', oh little darlin'*. Bob told me to stick to basketball.

Anyway, you think Tarkanian knew what in the world we were talking about? No way. Sonny ragged Tark about Brian Williams, Maryland's fine freshman center, whose dad, Gene, was a member of the Platters for eighteen years. *Oh-oh-oh yes, I'm the Great Pretender*. Williams had played at Bishop Gorman High School in Vegas as a junior, the same school Tark's son Danny attended, right under Tark's nose. "My biggest mistake in coaching," he said. Williams was rapidly becoming the best freshman big man in the country. Sonny ragged Tark about all the great redshirts he had sitting out this year. "Redshirts always look great when they're ineligible," Tark said. Sonny ragged Tark about everything. For all his legal battles with the NCAA and his outlaw reputation, Tark is at the point now where he just laughs off the slings and arrows.

Vacarro mentioned the famous episode a couple of summers ago when a kid showed up at the Nike development camp with a shaved haircut spelling out the word *Adidas*. The kid didn't go to class, wouldn't obey rules and finally got kicked out of the camp. "Sounds like my kind of player," Tark said. [Sure enough, Tark ended up getting the kid, Antoine Dauson, who will enroll at UNLV in the fall of '88.]

After dinner Tarkanian took us over to his new club, Sharks, an enormous multi-level disco. Limos, bright lights, long lines. I thought I was a celeb until we hit this place and Tark was the man of the hour. After a while you couldn't budge anywhere near the bars without making a very close acquaintance with the person next to you, who usually happened to be a breathtaking debutante of one kind or another.

Tark left me in Danny Tarkanian's hands and went home to look at some more film of Temple. Danny, the former Runnin' Rebel point guard, was on a weekend break from law school in San Diego. Sure enough, Danny let me have it. "How could you say last year UNLV would finish fourth in the Big Ten?" he asked me over the throbbing music. I think my answer was drowned out by some rap group. At least I hope it was. Another stranger insisted I come see his son play tomorrow. The son had scored 21 points in his last game. The son was six years old. When somebody yelled out, "Dickie Baby, this is Intimidation City," I knew it was time for beddie-bye.

SUNDAY, JANUARY 24

Before the game today it seemed like Old Home Week for Dickie Baby. First, I saw Billy Kesgen, a kid who played for me on one of my first teams at East Rutherford High School. Billy's now the recreation coordinator for the town of Henderson, Nevada. Then I saw Tootie again. Bob Lanier was broadcasting the game for the Mutual Radio network; the Dobber played for me when I was with the Pistons. And Al Menendez was scouting the game for the Nets; Al was a scout for me at Detroit. And then here came Charley Theokas, the athletic director at Temple; he was the GM for the Nets when I was in the league. We made a great trade once: Eric Money for Kevin Porter. It killed both clubs. Finally, a guy named Chuck Vitale came up to say hello. I didn't know anything about him. Turns out Chuck is a pit boss at the Desert Inn, and from Jersey besides. "I'm getting hassled at the office,"

Chuck said. "Either go easy on the Rebels or announce to everybody that we're not related." We aren't. Okay, Chuck?

Tark's teams always bring out the celebrities in Vegas and today was no different. Steve Wynn, Frank Sinatra's guy who owns the Golden Nugget, sat courtside. Steve's good friend Whoopi Goldberg sat next to him. Alongside them was Irwin Molasky, and his family. Irwin is a partner in Lorimar Productions and was one of the main guys in the conglomerate that used to own the La Costa Resort near San Diego. Now he owns most of the part of Las Vegas that Wayne Newton— or Tark—doesn't own. Boy, are they fans, especially Susan Molasky, Irwin's wife. She gives hell to the refs. She gives hell to the opposing team. She even gives hell to the opposing team's cheerleaders.

Don't ever put the Vegas loonies in the same hemisphere as those laid-back Californians who impersonate basketball fans. We're talking rabid. On our ABC telecast today I gave the player-of-the-game award to the fans, who rocked and rolled when Vegas was behind and ultimately pulled the Rebels through to a one-point victory over a Temple team that had not lost all year [and would not lose again in the regular season].

I couldn't believe the Temple freshman, Macon. I loved his control, his style, his confidence! It was amazing the way he kept the game in the palm of his hand even though he had a terrible shooting afternoon. He was only 9 for 22 from the field, but shooters have to shoot and leaders have to lead and Macon did a whole lot of both. Here was an eighteen-year-old in his first game against a Top Twenty team, with nineteen thousand of those Gucci-rooter boosters in the Thomas and Mack Center cackling all over him, and he was as calm and serene as if he was back in his hometown of Saginaw, Michigan, playing in the backyard.

[I went absolutely bananas over the kid: he was the closest thing to Oscar Robertson I'd seen in nine years of broadcasting. I hyped him so much that the next week the Philly papers burned me for praising Macon so much. Then a couple of weeks after that when he scored 31 points against Villanova and destroyed Massimino's club—Rollie said he'd never seen anything like Macon—the same papers wrote him up as if he was the new Messiah of basketball.

Even the president of ABC Sports, Dennis Swanson, who was at the Vegas game—he's a graduate of Illinois and a basketball fanatic, a super-supporter of the Fighting Illini—asked me if I hadn't gone overboard on Macon given his miserable shooting day. But I tell you, the kid did everything on that court. He dominated the game.]

Today was also the day ABC let me use the Telestrator for the first time. That's the machine that lets me draw x's and o's and lines and scribbles to show how plays develop. Keith said it was like a crayon coloring book—he's not a big fan of the Telestrator—but I had found a new toy. I scrunched down in my seat to play with the thing because it was practically under our courtside table and I went nuts diagramming stuff, especially once when Macon went into his shakin', bakin', fakin' routine.

John Chaney is such a master of tempo that Temple was able to stay ahead nearly the whole game. The Owls average under nine turnovers a game; it's no wonder because when one of them gives up the ball, John screams at him as if he'd just broken a Ming vase. Talk about discipline. Chaney won't even let the Temple kids talk on the team bus, and they tell the story of the time the Owls were riding along in their bus when a fire broke out in the back and nobody dared say a word!

Temple led by 12 points in the middle of the second half. But in the face of the visitors' composure and this great new player introducing himself to the nation right on their own dance floor, the Rebels' crowd stayed uproarious and wouldn't let their team fold.

Vegas rallied to within 47–49 before Macon stripped Paddio clean for a fast-break layup with about eight minutes to play. Then the kid followed that with two more buckets after some creative juke moves. But the Rebs kept on coming. The James brothers—not Jesse and Frank, but Keith and Boobie—both hit three pointers from downtown to cut the Temple margin to 57–58 in the closing minutes, so Macon simply set up for one last attempt at the game-clinching basket.

He would have got it, too. Except for one thing. He threw the ball to the wrong man. When Macon drew a defensive double-team to him, he delivered a sharp entry pass to Temple's sub freshman center, Duane Causwell, with seventeen seconds left. But all was not well that ended with Causwell. Immediately about three Rebels attacked Causwell, fouling him. No way were they letting him shoot the layup, baby!

When Causwell missed the front end of the one-and-one, Vegas had possession. I saw Tark whirling his arms on the sideline for a timeout, but then he waved off his own signal— lucky none of his players were looking at their coach, as is sometimes customary—and the Rebs started up the floor. At the time I questioned his decision, but I can see in retrospect that Jerry knew if he called time, it would allow Temple to set up in another of its shifting, confusing zone defenses that had been stopping the Rebels' half-court offense all afternoon. Vegas is an open-court animal, and Tark let his guys run free in their element.

Sure enough, as the home team roared along amid the bedlam, with four guys who had been ineligible last year and a fifth who'd been in junior college, the ball went to Anthony Todd, a transfer from Lamar. Todd rose over Temple's Perry from about 12 feet away and stuck the jumper that gave Vegas its first lead since the opening basket as well as an enormous victory, 59–58.

After doing the game I went to a banquet with Sonny Vacarro, a "football fantasy" deal celebrating the end of the grid season. Met a lot of nice people, including Paul Gleason, the actor who played the teacher in the movie *The Breakfast Club.* Paul's playing a football coach in a new flick, *Johnny Be Good.*

He's also a baseball nut and we decided to get together next spring when he comes down to Florida for spring training.

Sonny asked me to say a few words to the audience, which wasn't so difficult, if you know what I mean. Monte Clark, the former coach of the Detroit Lions, was the emcee, and I told everybody how Monte and I had one thing in common: we both got the Ziggy in Motown.

Nobody puts a gun to my head to do this sort of thing, so I can't complain; but sometimes I wish I could say no once in a while. Because I had another speaking engagement and another game to do—Iowa at Wisconsin—several hours later and a couple of time zones away and I probably should have tried to catch some z's. To make matters worse, while I was waiting in the hotel lobby to go to the airport I got greedy with Mr. One-Armed Bandit whom I had relieved of about a hundred silver dollars the day before. Mr. Bandit got me back twice over. Viva Las Vegas.

MADISON
MONDAY, JANUARY 25

I slept a little on the red-eye flight to Chicago where at dawn I was greeted with snow and a temperature of 11 degrees. Of course my commuter to Madison was cancelled and I had to wait out the sleet and snow for a flight out on one of those tiny planes that do so much for Dramamine sales. Ah, Big Ten basketball.

Madison had a nice blizzard going as we got a ride into town past ice fishermen on Lake Mendoza. I told the driver this was exactly what had forced me to move out of the Midwest. I picked up this morning's Wisconsin State Journal: *Underdog UW Eagerly Awaits the Vitale Effect.* Now I was making headlines. But what the story said was all too true; whenever I showed up, upsets seemed to happen. I was two for three in Big Ten upsets on ESPN's Big Monday telecasts. Two weeks ago Northwestern stunned Indiana at Evanston and last week Ohio State surprised Michigan at Columbus. Would Wisconsin nail Iowa tonight?

I had promised another old high school player of mine, Bobby Ferraro, that I would speak to the Badger Boosters at their luncheon today. Bobby had gone off to the University of Wisconsin from Jersey and had never come back. He was in the insurance business now in Madison, but what was aggravating was that he also spent a lot of time being a *referee*. I had to bust his chops for that.

I thought I had the lunch audience rolling when I did my shtick on teams playing "cupcake" schedules until Ferraro piped up from the head table, "Hey, Coach, isn't that what we played in high school?" Can you believe him? I fly all night to do this gig as a favor to my guy and now he's stealing my laughs. I had to bust him for that, also.

Truthfully, though, I love getting out and talking to the people about hoops. Doing my gig. Spreading my lingo. It makes it worthwhile when I realize sometimes I make an impact. Cute story: a Badger booster named Jim Scheidler told the audience that his seventh-grade son was asked to describe in class the other day what kind of president Abraham Lincoln was. "A Rolls-Roycer," he said.

When I had met with the Badger Boosters the year before, I closed my speech on a crescendo: a play-by-play of the final seconds of the game that night, in which I had Wisconsin upsetting Indiana. You might recall that in the actual contest the undermanned Badgers took the future national champs to three overtimes in one of the great Big Ten games of the decade. Today I repeated the forecast: "Five seconds left. Iowa up by one. WISCONSIN STEALS. DANNY JONES IN FOR THE SLAM-BAM-JAM. BADGERS WIN!"

Hey, always leave 'em smiling.

Unfortunately tonight's contest turned out to be one of the real stinko games of the decade. Wisconsin never had a chance. Jones scored only 10 points and Vitale didn't have the greatest of nights, either.

First of all, I was totally wiped out from lack of sleep. On the ride over to the gym the snow was so heavy it didn't look like there'd even be a game. Freddy Gaudelli, a great kid who used to be a driver and hot dog–fetcher for ESPN, was now our producer. Freddy's gone big time: "We'll do the 'Vitale Speaks Out' segment at six-thirty, guys," he said.

"What are we doing at seven-thirty?" Mike Patrick said. First Ferraro, now Patrick. My partner is always busting my chops. We bet on how many takes I'll need to get a perfect "Vitale Speaks Out." I think I do pretty well for an ex-jock right out of the locker room, but Mike claims I owe him about $87,000 from last year alone. Hey, I don't rehearse it or anything, it's straight off the top of my dome. I always think I'll get it the first couple of times, and I'm always wrong. I think it took me five takes tonight.

Jerome Lane of Pittsburgh had taken down a glass backboard against Providence in the first game on ESPN, and the delay meant the network was coming to our game late. On our telecast a screwed-up graphic on Iowa point guard B. J. Armstrong appeared on my monitor and I announced to America that B.J. "had to penetrate for Wisconsin." Plus the earphone static was so thick I couldn't hear Patrick. Plus I think I pronounced Des Moines "Dez Moinz." Plus the game was awful. Plus exhaustion was setting in. Oh, it was a long night in Madison. We get those once in a while in a season and all you can do is hang loose and roll with the turnovers.

"Stay tuned everybody, we're going to make this interesting," I said at one point. "Gimme some topics, Mike, get me rolling. We're going to the blowout material." Soon the score was 60–30. "Rudy Martzke, the guy who bangs the typewriter and reviews television sports for *USA Today*," I said. "Rudy used to be a ballboy here at Wisconsin. Used to sweep up the floors, just like these kids here." Man, you knew I was searching for material. There was no Vitale Effect this time. The final was 104–89, and the game wasn't nearly that close.

NEW YORK
TUESDAY, JANUARY 26

"Did I really screw up Des Moines last night?" I asked Patrick
as our car crawled through another snowstorm to the Madison
airport.

"The glamour never wears off," Mike grumbled through
the smoke of his approximately eighth cigarette that morning.
If Dean Smith ever wants a doubles partner in a smoke-off,
Patrick's the guy.

On the commuter flight back to Chicago I talked to some
of the Rapid City (South Dakota) Thrillers, a CBA team that
had lost the night before in LaCrosse, Wisconsin. They were
7–18. And I thought I had it rough. I spotted Duane Washington, who played at Middle Tennessee State last year when
I worked his team's upset victory over Michigan. "You've
seen the tape, Duane. I know you've seen it. 'It's not the
Pearl, but his name is Duane,' I said. Bet you've watched that
replay thirty times, Duane. Does it still come out the same?"

In the Chicago airport I hooked up with John Eckle, a great
PR guy who is handling the Nuttiest Sports Nut of the Year
contest for Fisher Nuts. I'm a spokesman for Fisher and I'm
judging the contest again this year to find a successor to defending champion nut Pop Shortell, a sixty-four-year-old father
of eleven kids from Connecticut who has officiated more than
thirty thousand basketball and baseball games and has watched
or listened to every New York Yankees game for the last
thirty years. And Fisher thought I was a nut.

Fisher's interest is in the fan. I got involved with the company because, bottom line, a fan is what I've always been as
well and, let's face it, the fan has never gotten enough credit.
Naturally, too, I could always use the mucho smackers these
nutty people were willing to pay me for promoting something
I believed in anyway. Eckle and I toured ten cities last year.
Today in New York I did a couple of TV and radio spots for
Fisher, talked to writers from Dallas and Hattiesburg, Mississippi, on the telephone, worked on my diary, made my

thrice-weekly live call to WFAN in the Big Apple, taped a few more interviews, and then collapsed in my hotel bathtub with the daily papers.

One thing about New York, New York. You can always relax.

Also, you can get papers from everywhere. I'm a newspaper addict. Couldn't live without them. When I'm in the city I dive into about twelve a day from all over the country.

Refreshed, with an off-day from basketball telecasts, what better way to spend an evening than to catch a Knicks game at the Garden?

I was still stewing about "Dez Moinz," though. I knew I blew it because Lorraine told me so on the phone. And my buddy, Garf, let me know it, too. Garf is Howard Garfinkel, the guru of all basketball gurus, a New York guy who is the pioneer of high school player ratings and all-star summer camps. And another two-fisted smoker. In a round robin between Deano, Patrick, and Garfinkel, I might go with Garf.

Garfinkel claims he "discovered" most of the members of that Jersey coaching clan, the Hubie Browns and Mike Fratellos and Rick Pitinos. And he probably did. I know he was the person most responsible for my getting my first college job as an assistant coach at Rutgers; he'll be a friend for life. I talk to Garf on the phone probably four or five times a week, usually after every TV game I do, sometimes at halftime to get a critique. Garf is hardly sparing in his critiques. If I had called him from Madison at the half last night, I could have corrected "Dez Moinz" right on the telecast.

"There's a big problem with watching the Knicks versus the Nets," Garf said as we sat in a flat, morguelike Garden. "Neither team has any player who can make the other team."

During the warm-ups the Nets' Pearl Washington came over, the real Dwayne Washington. "You still burying me?" Pearl said.

"You guarding anybody?" I said.

"No way," said Nets assistant coach Bob Wenzel, standing nearby.

"But they can't guard me, either," said Pearl.

Wenzel is the former Jacksonville University coach who had recovered from a serious brain aneurism and was considered a future star in the coaching ranks before he left for the chaotic situation in New Jersey. A Rutgers grad, he asked me what I knew about the head coaching job there. I told him he would be a natural for it. [Wenzel got the job at the end of the college season.]

Meanwhile, the Nets were dead as a doornail. They were embarrassing themselves. Interim Coach Bob MacKinnon called a timeout once and just stared at the players. What a disaster! They've got to do something to restore life to that franchise. The Knicks–Nets rivalry should be like the Dodgers–Giants was in the old days. Now the games are just a giant bore. [The Nets later hired Willis Reed as coach and drafted Chris Morris out of Auburn—two big steps in the right direction.]

Later—the Knicks won but who cared?—Garf and I repaired to a favorite postgame hangout, the Carnegie Deli on Seventh Avenue, for some more hoop talk. Fred Klein, another basketball fanatic and friend of all the coaches, owns the place and he always holds a table for us. After I stuffed myself on the most awesome ham and cheese sandwich—this baby was as big as my mouth—we talked to a couple of other fans who had been at the game: James MacArthur, the actor, son of Helen Hayes, co-star on Hawaii Five-O—remember "Book 'em, Dano"—and Dr. Fletcher Johnson, a leading cardiovascular surgeon in New York who used to play on the great Duquesne University teams with Sihugo Green.

I couldn't resist doing some play-by-play right there in the deli. "Johnson along the base . . . He passes to Green . . . Sihugo with the jumper . . . It's two for the Dukes!" I told Dr. Johnson it's too bad he wasn't playing now, I'd make him a star. Book *me*, Fletcher.

The doctor started massaging my heart. "You've got a lot of years left in you," he said.

Not if I don't get some sleep.

ALL OVER NEW JERSEY
WEDNESDAY, JANUARY 27

First things first. I cleared my conscience of "Dez Moinz" by going right to the horse's mouth. I telephoned WHO and KLYF radio stations in Des Moines to apologize personally. They didn't believe it was me at first and challenged me to do a little Dickie V to prove it. They put me live on the air and this time I not only pronounced the city's name right but I described a little B. J. Armstrong shake and bake and I even had him on the right team.

Actually, this was a day I'd been looking forward to for a long time. ESPN was doing Syracuse–Seton Hall from the Meadowlands tonight, and when Fisher Nuts sprang for a limo, I asked Eckle to come along for a nostalgic visit back to my roots. After leaving Manhattan, right out of the box the limo driver got lost in Passaic. But that's okay. Hey, I knew all about Passaic. Dick Tarrant, one of my candidates for coach of the year at the University of Richmond, architect of their run past Indiana and Georgia Tech to the NCAA's Sweet Sixteen, is from Passaic. Craig (Ironhead) Heyward, the monster fullback at Pittsburgh who just announced this week he was leaving Pitt for the pros, is from Passaic. I rolled down the window and yelled out, "Ironhead: Stay In School!" Oh yeah, in Passaic we also passed just a couple of blocks away from St. Mary's Hospital, where Dickie V himself was born.

I hadn't been back to my father John's house in Elmwood Park for a couple of years, and he was waiting for us with my cousin, John Scarpa, and my uncle, Mike Scarpa. My mother passed away five years ago. He didn't show it, but I know my dad was impressed when we took him for a ride in that fancy stretch limo. He thinks I'm Vince Lombardi and Walter Cronkite rolled into one anyway; boy does he do some bragging on me! And I bet after we left he went straight to the phone and called all his buddies to tell them about the limo ride and the big-time PR guy hanging around his son Richie.

That's what everyone still calls me back home. "Rich, where's your suit and tie?" demanded my dad, resplendent as usual in all the accoutrements: tie tack, pocket square, the works. (I was wearing a warm-up outfit.) "A man in your position should always wear a suit and tie." Here I was, 48 years old, and my dad was still telling me what to wear.

We drove around town past the lovers lane, past the church where I was married the first time, past the ballfields I played on. We had lunch at the Elmwood Park Diner just like old times. Uncle Mike recalled the time he coached the Elmwood Park Bombers, the glamour grade-school football team in the area, and I took my team from nearby Garfield, the Garfield Boilermakers, and beat the Bombers 46–6. The league wouldn't let my big kid, Ken Bohannon, play halfback, so we just stuck him at end, told him to step back from the line on the snaps and threw the ball out to him. He ran over Uncle Mike's team like they were lilies of the field. Yeah, I'd trick all my relatives to get a W.

Tricks? My cousin John and I reminisced about how we used to sneak into Yankee Stadium early, try to get some batting practice balls or even a bat, then trade them to kids for better seats. Once we told a kid we had a ball that had just been hit by Mickey Mantle. The kid forked over box seats for that one. Now John plays cards at the New Jersey Country Club in Wayne with Yogi Berra himself.

"Next time, don't embarrass me. Wear something," my dad said when we dropped him off back at the house.

My trip back in time was just getting started. During the next few hours we drove through the town of Garfield, past the grey clapboard house where I grew up—372 Madeline Avenue—and over to East Rutherford and the Franklin School, where I got my first job as a teacher. The sign on the playground said *No Ball Playing*. I think I was responsible for that: One day I drove one over the fence and broke a window in the house next door.

Boy, were Augie Novello and Louie Ravettine shocked to see me! Augie is still the maintenance guy at Franklin just as he was at East Rutherford High when I coached there. Me and Augie had a lot of deep, dark secrets about what I put my players through that Augie promised me would never leave the locker room at East Rutherford. "Little Vince!" he called out today when he saw me. Augie always said I was a mini-version of Lombardi. He snuck me down the hall so we could surprise Ravettine. Louie was my boyhood pal, a guy who could really play some hoops. He was a wild sonofagun too, and—hard to believe—now he had grown up to be principal of the East Rutherford grade school system. Man, it was great to see these guys! Some of the same teachers I had worked with were still at Franklin, too. I used to make so many calls from the teachers' room they took the phone out and put it in the nurse's office. They told me today the phone's never been put back in.

Ravettine hopped into the limo and we drove around some more. We went over to East Rutherford High to see the gym where I coached. We went by the Cornerstone Inn, a restaurant where one of my former assistant coaches, Albie D'Amato, who made some dough in real estate, now works the salad bar for a hobby. We went by the municipal building to see my former sister-in-law, Daryl Murray, who is a deputy court clerk. Lorraine and I were married in this building. Upstairs, I couldn't believe how another old classmate of mine, Pat DeVasto, had changed. He's the tax collector now.

"Pat, my man, you're getting so fat," I said with my customary diplomacy. "You used to be so skinny."

"No I wasn't, Richie," Pat said. "You only saw me with one eye."

I got so caught up in the past, I totally blew the present—an ESPN production meeting at our Meadowlands hotel. First miss in nine years. But since the limo driver couldn't find a way to get to the hotel for a half hour after he saw it from the highway, I'm not counting it as an official miss.

It was easy to get up for the game that night inasmuch as I knew a whole bunch of my former players would show up. Sure enough, there were Duffy Alberta and Charlie Grillo and Joey Gladis from my first teams, and Dwight Hall, who made the winning shot to win our first state championship. There was Bobby Stolarz, my right arm as an assistant coach at East Rutherford. He was Hank Raymonds to my Al McGuire: the worker, the brains. There was even Lennie Loran, one of the referees in that state title game. Lennie now works the scorer's table at the Meadowlands.

As if there wasn't enough nostalgia floating around the place, one of the officials tonight was Pete Pavia, who made the gutsiest call I've ever seen one night in Olean, New York, when I was coaching Detroit against St. Bonaventure.

"You remember that, Pete?' I said. "We were up one point and the Bonnies hit a seventy-five-footer at the buzzer. When you came running down to the table waving off the basket, I ran out of there with my team so fast they couldn't have gotten us back with a fleet of patrol cars."

"Remember it?" said Pavia. "How could I forget? You jumped on my back and kissed me before you ran off. I've never worked a game at St. Bonaventure since."

Smaller gyms like the one in Olean seem to me to be the right places for the college game. The problem with Seton Hall playing in the Meadowlands is it's such a pro atmosphere. There's no spirit, no enthusiasm, the fans are in a coma. I think the Big East would be better off without some of these huge arenas in the regular season. Mike Patrick said the place sounded like a Class C high school game, but as my contingent from Elmwood Park and Garfield and East Rutherford knew, our high school crowds were much better than this.

I don't know which was more dead, though, the arena or the Syracuse team. I mean, c'mon! This was the returning national finalist team. This was Rony Seikaly and Derrick Coleman and Sherman Douglas. This was the team that *Sports Illustrated* ranked number one in the preseason. I think the Orange was ranked number one by more polls than any other team. And yet Jim Boeheim's club had struggled much of the season, losing four close games in which the team averaged barely 50 percent from the free-throw line. Boeheim had even called in a high school teacher from New Jersey to teach the team foul shooting. How much did it help? Well, Coleman was "up" to 62 percent, but he had made eighteen in a row at one point, so what about consistency? Seikaly only missed two tonight, so maybe . . .

Look, I just think Syracuse underachieved all year. We're talking three big-time pro players, first-round draft choices, but Seikaly has had his eye on the NBA lottery all season and Coleman, a sophomore, was rumored to be going hardship himself. I asked Derrick before the game and he said if he could be a top-five pick he would go, but the youngster is dreaming. Top five? Come on. He can't shoot, for one thing. He has a severe attitude problem, moping and sulking when things don't go his way. The problem with Syracuse is, some nights the team just doesn't play with intensity. The Orange-men don't play that hard. They think they can do it on physical talent alone. They hate all the zones that people throw at them because that negates their great one-on-one ability, but they've got to learn to beat them anyway.

Douglas, too, occasionally plays out of control. Put Sherman's great games up against, say, B. J. Armstrong's, and Douglas comes out ahead, probably on his defense. He also is the master of the lob pass. But I don't think Sherman can nail that stationary J like Armstrong can, and he doesn't have the consistency B.J. has. That's not to take anything away from Douglas—he's one of the top five point guards in the nation.

Syracuse stayed in touch just long enough to win tonight, 87–76, in front of an announced 10,911—but it sounded like just ten. Douglas had 18 points, but it was Stevie Thompson, Syracuse's slashing 6-3 forward—the Orangeman who plays the hardest no matter the opponent—who was the star of the game. He had 26 points and 9 rebounds. And Boeheim really controlled the game when it counted in the last four minutes, using his timeouts and setting the tempo down the stretch.

The disappointing crowd sat on its hands—after the public address announcer welcomed me home, of course—enabling

Syracuse to get away with standing around before finding enough energy to beat the Hall. I plugged the Seton Hall coach, P. J. Carlesimo, over the air—he doesn't have the facilities to recruit with the marquee names in the Big East; there's just no way—because I'd heard he was in danger of getting the Ziggy. P. J.'s biggest mistake, ironically, was beating Georgetown twice the year before. Expectations rose to the point where the Hall's alumni thought he should at least battle for a first-division spot in the league. Tonight didn't help P. J.'s cause any. [Two big wins over Pitt and the Hall's first-ever NCAA bid got him a new five-year deal before the season was over.]

When my father and brother, John, came down before the game, I got our ESPN crew to tape everybody for a shot to use later during a lull in the action. There were plenty of those. After the picture of all my guys appeared on the screen, Mike Patrick put the cap on my all-day trip into Nostalgia City with another zinger: "I've got a few photos of my wife in my wallet I could break out anytime," he said.

BRADENTON
THURSDAY, JANUARY 28

From my old home to my current one is a direct flight: Newark to Bradenton/Sarasota. Usually I'm so zombied out by the time I get back to Florida that the only way I can tell I'm really home is the sight of Ron LeFlore handling the bags at the airport. That name ring a bell? Yeah, it's the same Ron LeFlore who played for the Detroit Tigers and the Chicago White Sox, who was discovered in prison by Billy Martin and came all the way back to make it in the big leagues. Ronnie got into some drug problems in his last days with the Sox, but now he's straightened out. He's vowed to get back to the majors—as an umpire.

Ronnie wasn't working today, and when I asked the baggage guys why, they told me that, true to his word, LeFlore had enrolled at an umpires' school. [I heard later that at the end of school he wasn't offered a job in the minors because, at age thirty-nine, he was too old.]

Home. Wife. Daughters. Rest.

Rest?

Messages.

Larry Donald, the editor of *Basketball Times*. Larry was a great friend after I took the Ziggy from the Pistons. He called to give me a boost after some critical remarks appeared this week in *Sports Illustrated*.

Harry Rhoads, the president of the Washington Speakers Bureau. Harry told me he was at the Maryland–North Carolina State game in College Park the other night when some kids across from the State bench unfurled a huge banner: *Dick Vitale Says Derrick Lewis Is a PTP'er*. "Dick, you're here even when you're not here," Harry said. The best part was that my buddy Jimmy Valvano had to stare at that banner all night.

Ed Broida, my stockbroker in Michigan. I used to have Augie Borgi doing my portfolio. He was a sportswriter with the Bergen, New Jersey *Record* who covered my East Rutherford High School teams. Augie went on to the NBA beat for papers in New York and Portland before becoming a broker. After I got to ESPN, out of the blue he called me and got me involved with the market. The trouble is we'd get to talking so much hoops we never got around to buying and selling.

Six media guys must have called me to ask for a Super Bowl pick. Super Bowl? Football? Hey, I'm a basketball man. I told them all the same thing: Denver. When Mr. Elway gets through fast-breaking all over the field and hurling those rainbows, it'll be all over and Mr. Manley from Washington will be on his knees begging, "*No mas, baby, no mas.*"

Bob Gibbons, another high school ratings-service expert, based in North Carolina. Gibbons and Garfinkel and Bill Cronauer down in Florida are always at each other's throats over their different player ratings. Sometimes I think I'm a liaison shrink between 'em all. Gibbons had heard me say on TV that Crawford Palmer, a Duke recruit out of Virginia, was in the long line of tremendous centers from that state: Malone, Sampson, Robinson, Reid; now Alonzo Mourning and Palmer. But Gibbons is not a Palmer fan. "Don't let Garfinkel sway you so much, Dick," Bob said. "The kid isn't that good." Hey, we'll see. I just get a kick out of this ratings warfare.

On a happier note, a fan club for Danny Manning at Kansas sent me a sweatshirt in the mail. It says *Easy D*. Gee, I hope they haven't heard me lately plugging Hersey Hawkins of Bradley over Manning for player of the year.

Know what makes me uneasy? Kid drivers. I finally saw my daughters when they came home for lunch today. Terri got her driver's license this week and now she thinks she can just roll down the highway or drive in New York City traffic with all the confidence in the world. I can't believe these state laws that let kids drive at sixteen. I told her I want her to wait another month until after she'd practiced more with her mother driving back and forth to school. I'm such a scrooge. I guess the memory of our accident last summer is still too fresh.

Tonight Lorraine and I went out to dinner at the same restaurant where we were the night of the accident. Was it good to get away from basketball for a moment? What can I say? A junkie is a junkie. I got home just in time to see the end of Wake Forest's 83–80 upset over North Carolina. What a shocker!

MEMPHIS
FRIDAY, JANUARY 29

Today I entered a real den of lions, uh, Tigers—Memphis State Tigers. I haven't been too popular in Memphis for a few years now, ever since I questioned their team and its ranking back in 1985.

It all started when Jim Simpson and I were doing the North Carolina–Virginia game for ESPN. Carolina was undefeated, number one in the country, but Virginia was playing a great game in Charlottesville and they had a big lead. "Whoa, they're celebrating in Memphis, Tennessee, right now," I said. "They're getting ready to proclaim the Memphis State Tigers as the number-one team in America. But you know what? There's no way. Memphis State is not my number-one team. I'll tell you right now, there is no way that team down there in Memphisland is the best in the United States."

It was one of my typical, low-key, purely on-the-fence pronouncements. Boy, did it hit the fan after that—literally, as we'll see in a minute. I got lambasted from one end of Beale Street to the other. Some disc jockey took a poll. He got ESPN's address and had everybody in Memphis who disagreed with me write in. That was a bundle. Others tore up the phone lines. Then this deejay supposedly collected sacks of manure to send to me. "Tiger manure," he called it. Luckily, I never got the stuff. Lorraine would have had a heck of a time cleaning that up.

They even had tee shirts made up in Memphis about Vitale saying the Tigers weren't number one. You know, I should talk to my lawyer about collecting residuals on all these tee shirts people make up about me.

Remember now, I didn't even knock Memphis State. I said there was no question they were a Top Ten team. I just didn't think they were number one. I went into schedules and personnel and picked three or four teams better than the Tigers. But people get so wrapped up in being the best; you should have seen the vicious letters.

The Memphis State coach at the time, Dana Kirk, certainly promoted the issue. He's always been anti-Vitale in a sarcastic way. I think this time he said if there were seventeen basketball announcers, he'd rate me number twenty-four. At the end of the year, he was saying he wanted to go on the air with me as part of the ESPN package. A couple of seasons later he could have, too; he was out of the coaching job at Memphis and under a cloud.

The bizarre thing about this whole scenario was that Memphis State lost its very next game, at Virginia Tech. With a chance to solidify that ranking, bang! Right out of the box an L.

A short time later I was traveling to do a game at Mississippi and flew into the Memphis airport. All kinds of State fans were there and they were great to me. They had no argument now because they had lost. Of course, they liked me for one thing: I always tempered my comments about Memphis because of their pom-pom girls.

The Tigers may not be top-ranked, but the Memphis State song girls are number one in my book just about every year. And that's an NC'er.

I have one very sad memory of Memphis. I was watching an early-season tournament game here in 1982 between West Texas State and Tulane when Jerry Yarbrough, a referee from Meridian, Mississippi, had a heart attack and died right on the court. It was a terrible thing—it was a consolation game and we were waiting to telecast the championship—and I've always wondered how I possibly could have conveyed the sorrow or even if I could have continued if that had happened in the later game.

On a happier note, I met Ron Higgins of the *Memphis Commercial Appeal* at the Memphis State practice today, and he did his inimitable impersonation of my friend Joe Dean, the former Southeastern Conference TV color man. Joe had left his job as national vice president of Converse sneakers this year to become the athletic director at his alma mater, LSU. Higgins—"Mad Dawg" Higgins—was a Baton Rouge boy who had practically grown up in the Dean family and he had Joe down to a tee, discussing matters with his LSU basketball coach, Dale Brown:

"Dale," Higgins growled in that gnarly Southern, Joe Dean twang. "Dale, there is just no way I can get that three-legged

Brazilian midget recruit of yours in school." Higgins's impersonation of Dean is so good that Mississippi's coach Ed Murphy asked him to record a message as Dean that Murphy now uses on his office answering machine.

In an interview with the Dawg we were discussing the parity in college basketball this season and I gave him my biggest upsets of the year. Wake over Carolina just last night, of course, was one. And I had these others: UC–Santa Barbara at Vegas, Northwestern over Indiana, Auburn without its two best players over Kentucky at Rupp Arena and, my favorite, Lafayette beating Notre Dame. I think that was enough parity for Dawg.

My ESPN broadcast partner, Tim Brando, showed up at the practice just in time to renew some old acquaintances as well. He's a Baton Rouge boy too, and he used to work in Memphis. "You know Ron Higgins?" I said to Brando.

"Known the Dawg since he was a pup," said Brando.

Tim ragged me about being so unpopular in Memphis, but I reminded him I don't burn bridges. The season before this one I had named Memphis State coach Larry Finch my rookie coach of the year and had listed the Tigers' monster freshman forward, Sylvester Gray, on my Diaper Dandies team.

Meanwhile, parity was unfolding right before our eyes in Finch's practice as the Tigers' Marvin Alexander set a solid pick off of which Gray took two mighty steps and dunked. Finch turned around and said, "That's what makes me so sick."

The reason was that Gray and Alexander had been declared ineligible five games into Memphis State's season after they acknowledged accepting money from an agent in Atlanta. Add those losses to that of Vincent Askew, MSU's fine forward who had opted to go pro rather than play out his eligibility this season, and what could have been a strong contender for the Metro Conference title—and maybe even for the national championship—had turned into a worried team, 10–7 on the season, only 1–4 in the Metro race. Louisville, the other traditional power in the league, wasn't faring any better, being 10–7 and 1–2.

Finch still had a couple of terrific local products in Cheyenne Gibson—whose mother obviously was a big fan of western movies—and little Elliot Perry, a freshman guard who had been recruited by a lot of biggies such as Kentucky and North Carolina. I loved Perry, especially his enormous goggles that made him look like a frog boy. "The lead guard from Sea World," somebody wrote about Perry. I found out today his teammates call him "Chicken Hawk." You can bet I'd try to get that in the telecast.

At dinner tonight at Folk's Folly steakhouse, Finch gave me the interesting tidbit that he was about to sign a new four-year contract. The papers had been drawn up and sent to him and everything but he was hesitating. It wasn't the money but other considerations that were causing him to wait. Larry wouldn't say what they were. But I advised him to grab a pen and John Hancock that baby immediately. Four birds in hand is worth a flock in the bush. Especially in this day and age of instant firings. Look at Lefty Driesell. Look at Earle Bruce. It was disgraceful the way they treated coaches and you can mark my words . . . I went on and on.

Shortly thereafter Finch had to go home. Big game tomorrow. Do you think I talk too much?

Earlier that evening Brando had been on a radio talk show in Memphis, the main topic of conversation of which was yours truly and what it was like working with me. "I'm just glad I don't get paid by the word," Timmy said. "When Dick gets a day off, they should strap him in an Iron Lung."

Ah, friendship.

MEMPHIS
SATURDAY, JANUARY 30

This afternoon I taped a bunch of thoughts for this book; that's a tougher exercise than hopping planes or pumping microphones, if you ask me. Afterwards I took a long soak in my exquisite Holiday Inn bathtub. I'm a tub man, if you haven't already figured that out. Forget those quick showers, baby! Let me have a long, deep, relaxing, stress-relieving, thought-provoking session in a bathtub and I'm as good as new. There were a lot of games on the tube this afternoon but I just wanted to rest. Only caught a few seconds of the games. But scores—scores are different. Got to have my finals. In the immortal words of Memphis's own EP (and I don't mean Elliot Perry): Want them. Need them. Love my final scores.

The results this afternoon merely reflected what Dawg Higgins and I were talking about yesterday, the same subject that is on every basketball wacko's lips: parity. I think it's great. I think basketball made its leaps and bounds and giant strides into the national consciousness only after UCLA stopped dominating the scene and every city and town and campus had its own mini-UCLA with its own hopes and dreams of a national championship.

Downstairs waiting for a ride to the Mid-South Coliseum, I was scratching my head when I actually felt a hair out of place. Don't laugh. We bare-domers have our own problems with misplaced hairs. I knew I wouldn't be able to clip this one on my own since it was on the bad-eye side of my head, so I went to the front desk and borrowed some scissors. Brando clipped it for me; what's a broadcast partner for?

I usually get to the arena a couple of hours before gametime for our production meetings, promos, kibitzing with the fans and the like. Two years ago after I had made that remark about Memphis State not being number one, the Memphis State fans showed up at a game here with Vitale masks and tee shirts and banners, the works. And I wasn't even in town! This time I was really curious to see what the fans had in store. I wasn't disappointed.

Vitale Sucks was on several shirts, one of them worn by Jeff Welch, a senior who used to be the Tiger mascot. He said he made a mint selling the things year before last. "You're the antihero now, Dick," he told me. The older fans were more reserved. *I had dinner with Dick Vitale,* read a sign in the upper deck. Brando egged me on to shoot some threes for the crazies in the Memphis State band. I was waiting for the award-winning—they've won the national song girl championship three years in a row—mind-boggling, sweat-inducing Tiger pom-pom girls to arrive, but I made a few shots anyway.

That night ABC had arranged for me to take a charter prop plane to Louisville right after the game for my Kentucky–Notre Dame assignment on Sunday afternoon. Dick Paparo, one of the refs tonight, would also be working the game tomorrow. Paparo has the most amazing voice: like gravel being scraped across a chalkboard. No wonder he's called "Froggy." With Paparo and Perry on the same court tonight, we had Froggy and the frog boy. Too bad Clarence (Frogman) Henry couldn't sing the national anthem.

"Hey, Froggy," I said. "I haven't seen you all year. Let's have a quick game so I can get out of here. I've got to make that plane. No overtime or I'll bury you like I did in Boston."

I was busting his chops. A couple of years ago in a Boston College–Syracuse game Paparo made the key call that decided the game. Down by one point, BC's Michael Adams dribbled across midcourt, flew into the air and desperately launched a no-prayer. As he crashed forward into Syracuse's Andre (the Claw) Hawkins, who was stationary with his arms held high, the whistle blew. Out of nowhere Froggy came running, waved off Hank Nichols (who at the time was considered to be the best college official in the land) and called the foul. On Hawkins. Adams made both free throws and BC won the game.

"Adams still jumped into him," I kidded Froggy.

"Naw, Hawkins jumped into Adams," Froggy said, smiling. The strange thing is, Froggy was from Syracuse. He doesn't ref games in the Big East any more. "Laugh all you want," Froggy said tonight. "I'm the best in the business."

Before the game I met the new commissioner of the Metro Conference, Ralph McFillen. I asked him why South Carolina and Virginia Tech were being allowed to play in the Metro Conference tournament when they were ineligible for the NCAA playoffs. The league did the same thing last year with

Memphis State when the Tigers were on probation, and they got burned badly; the Tigers ended up winning the tournament and so no representative from the Metro was invited to the big show.

As McFillen pointed out, the bottom-line reason was the bottom line: money. Revenues from the basketball tournament are used to run the league office. Without a full slate, the tournament wouldn't draw nearly as many fans. The Metro felt they shouldn't penalize USC and Tech when they didn't penalize Memphis State last season. But I told him two wrongs don't make a right and I was going to rip the league again on this issue. It was just preposterous.

In the Louisville locker room, coach Denny Crum agreed with me. He was trapped with an 18–14 record last season against the strongest schedule possible, and when a nothing-to-lose Memphis State tore apart the Cardinals 75–52 in the Metro tournament, the 'Ville's tournament chances went begging.

"What we should do is declare our regular season champion the league's representative to the NCAA," said Crum. "That way the conference tournament wouldn't matter. Since anybody on probation can't be the champion, we'd be guaranteed an NCAA bid."

Crum was more concerned, though, with his game tonight and the fact that his young team was struggling again. "Tougher schedule. Tougher conference," he said. "I think the Metro top to bottom is stronger than it's ever been."

Louisville's backcourt problems were continuing unabated. There were no guards among last year's Cards. And though Crum brought in an extremely athletic jumper, 6-3 La-Bradford Smith, this season, I'm not sure he can play guard, either. Certainly he's not a point guard, and Keith Williams, another lean sophomore, has struggled at the lead guard position himself. Crum argues that traditionally Louisville has lacked a true point guard even on his Final Four and national championship teams. But, hey, he had Jerry Eaves in 1980 and Milt Wagner in '86. Come on. Those guys could *play*.

Sometimes Louisville's Never Nervous Pervis Ellison and Superb Herb Crook look like two of the best inside guys in the game; other nights they're AWOL. Like tonight. I couldn't understand it. Ellison scored the Cards' first 7 points in the opening two and a half minutes, sat out the last ten minutes of the half and scored only 7 more the entire game. "We wanted to bang him around," Memphis State forward Steve Ballard said. "He's not the most physical guy." Crook was 3-of-11 for 8 points. Worst of all, they looked bored, like it wasn't very much fun anymore. They didn't have the same aggression, joy and simple energy normally associated with Louisville teams.

All the excitement was on the other side. Start with Kellye Cash, the former Miss America, Johnny's niece. She sang the anthem. Wow! She did it in a plaintive country 'n' western wail. Dynamite. Then there were those pom-pom girls. Whoa! "I'm hypnotized," said Brando. Those honeys just about melted the makeup we're always teasing Tim about clear off his face. Next, Elliot Perry lost his goggles on one play, flung them off the court and scored anyway. I loved the frog boy!

"We're going to talk about the Final Four, Dick," Tim said at one point. "That copacetic with you?"

I thought to myself, copacetic? Who does he play for? Or she? Brando also used "embryonic" on me one time. I know one thing. I know Elliot Perry wasn't very embryonic at the end of the game when he wanted the ball. I really think the little 6-footer will be an impact player in the college ranks before he's halfway through his sophomore year. He reminds me of Johnny Dawkins, he has that kind of potential.

The difference in the two struggling teams was that Memphis had the point guard in Perry; Louisville did not. After closing to 68–71 in the last thirty seconds, the Cardinals missed a trio of three-pointers. Crum never called time-out. The Cards never set up to run something for Ellison in the paint—a drive and perhaps a free throw?—or for LaBradford Smith on the wing or even a screen for their best long-range shooter, Kenny Payne. Payne took two of the last three shots, but Memphis State defenders were all over him.

"This guy (Crum) is going to the Hall of Fame and he can't recruit a point guard or call a time-out?" somebody said later. I wondered the same thing. Some Memphis fans had a final, cold word for Crum. They had concocted fake gold medals and were wearing them around their necks on red, white and blue straps. "Hey, Denny," their buttons said, reminding Crum of his Pan Am Games defeat, "we've got our gold medals. Where's yours?"

Meanwhile Perry scored 19 points and handed out 6 assists in the Tigers' 72–68 victory and as he dribbled the clock away at the end, I couldn't resist. "Look at him go, everybody," I shouted. "Elliot Perry. The Chickennnn Hawwwwwk."

LOUISVILLE
SUNDAY, JANUARY 31

The less said about last night's cold, bumpy, claustrophobic, stomach-pummeling flight across the Tennessee-Kentucky border, the better. What a way to begin Super Sunday! It was good to see the crew from ABC this morning, though. Since Keith Jackson was hosting the Super Bowl pregame show from San Diego, Gary Bender was my broadcast partner today.

Gary might be the nicest guy in TV; he sure as heck is one of the best-looking. Some critic once said Bender was sports television's answer to Edd (Kookie) Byrnes. Kookie, Kookie, lend me your mike. But I want to tell you, the guy is a real pro who knows his stuff. I always kid our technical people to make sure they use a two-camera shot when Gary and I are together so we don't have to appear on the same camera together. I don't want my wife seeing me next to this looker.

In the car on the way to Freedom Hall, Gary said that when he got in a few days ago, Joe B. Hall, the former Kentucky coach and his usual ABC partner, took him to Claiborne

Farms to see Secretariat and Spectacular Bid and Nijinsky and all the other great athletes Seth Hancock has there. Yeah, we're talking real athletes. Eddie Sutton wishes he had that many thoroughbreds for the stretch run in the SEC each year.

Cheryl Miller, the former legendary women's star at Southern Cal who also now works with us on the ABC telecasts, filled me in on all the gossip out of LA. Seems the media already have UCLA alumni buying out Walt Hazzard's contract. The UCLA program has been shaken to its foundation in the last few seasons; when Greg Foster quit the team recently it caused a few more tongues to wag, and now Trevor Wilson is also talking about leaving. Hey, Walt's had some players out there; as Cheryl said, "When you recruit the big names, you've got to win or else." Pooh Richardson was our Pan Am team's point guard. He should be a much better player. And he's not the only one. I've got to believe that for whatever reason, they've never played up to their potential under Hazzard; with the UCLA rep and exposure behind him a coach should have them in the Top Twenty year after year.

As for job openings, there's a real good one at Detroit, my old school, which I think would be perfect for John Shumate, the Notre Dame assistant who I saw today talking to Bob Lanier for Mutual Radio at courtside before the game. Shu is one of my guys; he was one of my frontline stalwarts with the Dobber at Detroit. Shu knows the school and the area. He's a helluva recruiter, too. But Shu's loyalty right now is to the Irish and the rest of their season, and he was heavily involved in ND's recruiting of LaPhonso Ellis, a 6-10 intimidator who'll be an instant impact player for the Irish. But I still think Detroit would be a great spot for him. [After the end of season, Shu accepted the head coaching job at SMU.]

"Larry Brown really got on me for my All–GQ team," I kidded Digger Phelps during the pregame warm-ups. (Of course, Digger made my team.) "He said he wouldn't want to be on any dress squad that included any of you guys."

"Who won the game?" snapped Digger, alluding to Notre Dame's 80–76 victory over Brown's Jayhawk team a week before, a win that probably guaranteed the Irish an NCAA tournament berth. "Just ask Brown who won the game. I was wearing a nine-hundred-dollar suit for that one."

Digger nailed me for a recent opinion. "I see where you don't have David Rivers starting on your Olympic team," he said. "It's Gary Grant this, Gary Grant that." Later he politicked for Rivers as Player of the Year. "Beat Danny Manning head-up. What else do you need?"

C'mon, Digger. Your guy was having a great season but I thought at the time that Manning was a lock for the award. Sometimes they give those postseason honors for career achievement rather than a one-season effort. For my money, Hawkins of Bradley and Sean Elliot of Arizona were having better individual seasons than Manning, but still Danny has had to struggle without much support around him.

Everybody in Kentucky was talking about the recent downturn of the Wildcats. Ed Davender, the point guard, was in a horrendous shooting slump and Rex Chapman was said to be having a tiff with his coach, Eddie Sutton. Seems Sutton had criticized Chapman's shot selection in the last couple of weeks, so in response Rex had gone into a funk and stopped shooting early in games.

Chapman may be the most popular Kentucky player ever, which is saying a bundle. People tell me he's already bigger than Sutton, bigger than Kentucky governor Wallace Wilkinson, bigger than Kentucky basketball itself. King Rex. When rumors hit the Bluegrass, they're whoppers. One story even had Chapman moving out of the Wildcat Lodge in anger at his coach and living in a motel.

After Vanderbilt beat the 'Cats last week, hitting 13 of 20 three-pointers (to Kentucky's 1 of 4) Sutton came out and said the new shot was making such an impact on the game he might have to change his recruiting strategy and go after more long-range bombers. I'd say maybe Eddie was a couple of seasons late coming around, wouldn't you?

I talked with Sutton before the game and he dispelled the Chapman rumors and stories—Rex was still ensconced in the

Lodge—but he did admit he was afraid he had hurt Rex's feelings with his remarks.

On the day before Kentucky plays its annual game in Louisville, one of the more fantastic scenes in basketball takes place: more than twelve thousand people crowd into Freedom Hall to watch the Wildcats *practice*. I don't think that would happen anywhere else in the country, and nothing was different yesterday. At one point Kentucky and Notre Dame had played for twenty-four years straight, but Phelps got tired of always facing Kentucky in "neutral" Louisville—Freedom Hall is about as neutral to the 'Cats as the briar patch was to B'rer Rabbit—and he cancelled the series after 1982. This was their first game since.

Several weeks earlier when I saw Sutton in Tuscaloosa, Alabama, before an ESPN game between Alabama and Kentucky, I urged him to go with his kids—LeRon Ellis and Eric Manuel. Ellis isn't the keenest of practice players; he's a Californian with a kind of laid-back attitude. Further, he had languished in Sutton's doghouse after missing curfew one night because he stayed up to watch the Clint Eastwood movie *Heartbreak Ridge* on cable. But Kentucky's veteran players weren't getting the job done and the freshmen had to get more minutes to be effective. I wasn't the only one with such advice; Sutton has upwards of thousands of unpaid assistant coaches out there in the Bluegrass.

Against Notre Dame, Kentucky came out of the box hyped and ready. And Ellis went over the ridge to break the hearts of the Irish with a career-high 14 points. Even though Rivers scored his basic 21, first Davender then Chapman played him tough; David looked spent three-fourths through the game. Rivers is the closest thing to a one-man team on campus. Today he was John Elway against the Redskins and like Elway he was destined to lose.

Kentucky took a 38–30 halftime lead by shooting over 60 percent. Though Notre Dame whittled away, the best chance for an Irish tie came with about six and a half minutes left when Rivers picked up a loose ball and sped by Chapman toward an unprotected basket. Instead of laying it in, though, David tried for the dunk and *kaaang*ed it off the back rim.

Another time Phelps screamed something at his star senior guard and Rivers turned away as if he didn't hear the coach. Oh, was Digger hot then. His nine-hundred-dollar suit might have burned instantly had he not whirled around and ordered in a substitute for Rivers, after which he set fire to David's ears for a good minute. Man, I remember when my players avoided my orders—they were on the bench so fast it made their heads swim.

In the Wildcats' youth movement, Manuel added 8 points and 4 assists in twenty-one minutes of Kentucky's 78–69 victory. Still it was what I consider the best backcourt in the nation that clinched the victory. Davender and Chapman combined for 13 of their team's final 15 points; Chapman especially was tough in the clutch. After scoring but 7 points in the first thirty-six minutes, the sophomore guard nailed 7 more on three straight possessions to make it 70–65 Kentucky inside of two minutes.

In my postgame interview with Ellis, LeRon thanked me for some things I had suggested to him a few weeks ago. "You told me to play like I was still in high school and I remembered that," he said.

It was raining afterwards as we drove downtown to the hotel. A couple of the ABC production assistants were going to keep going all the way to their homes in East Lansing, Michigan, where, ironically, I had to be the next morning for a telecast tomorrow night. I probably would have gone with them but I had my national call-in radio show to do in just a few hours. And I needed some rest. Ohio State at Michigan State tomorrow night. Georgia Tech at Duke on Wednesday. Hmmmm. Durham, North Carolina. Isn't this where you came in?

LITTLE RICHIE: COACHING AT LAST

You think that was hectic? Routine, baby, routine. On the go? That's the story of my life.

I got the supreme work ethic from my father, and the motivation to strive and overcome long odds from my mother, neither of whom ever went to college or even high school. They had an elementary education at best, but what they passed on to me from a lot of pain and suffering and simple sweat and toil was a doctorate—a doctorate of love.

My parents, John and Mae Vitale, were hard-working, second-generation Italian folks who worked all their lives in a factory. My dad was a presser for the Rex and Silvio women's clothing companies. He pressed coats and got paid by the piece. However many coats there were for him to do each day, that's how much money he made. He brought me into the factory once when I was little, and I tell you, there was no way I wanted that to be my life.

Once, when I was in my late teens, my father tried to make a go of it with his own women's clothing company but he ran into financial problems. He didn't make it, and it was a very depressing time because he put every dollar he had into the business. It was a tough period, but he had the strength to get through. He would work from 7:00 A.M. until 4:30 P.M. pressing coats, then come home, eat, and go out again till midnight as a security guard at the plaza in Bergen County. That was his way of life: to be able to raise us, put some money on the table, give us a start toward an education, provide the things we needed.

My mom used to sew the coats in the factories. Then she got ill; she was ill a lot in her life. Right after my parents got married, she contracted tuberculosis, and the doctors told her she would never be able to have any children. She was laid up in the hospital for a full year on a solid board mattress. You want a big-time comeback? Naturally, she went ahead and had children, three of us. And she worked like you wouldn't believe, sewing those coats, doing piecework at home.

They worked like this all the while I was growing up: grade school, high school, college. But when I was twenty-two, my mom had a stroke. It was a shock to her. It was difficult for all of us to deal with because she lost a lot of her speech. She kept having fevers and the flu, and the doctors said there was no way she would make it. They gave her the last rites three times, at least. But she fought back again and beat that. She had an operation to relieve pressure on her kidneys, and that was the key; she made a second major recovery. Talk about a PTP! From that point on, she was like a new woman and she lived a couple of decades longer before she died in 1983 at age seventy-two after another long illness. At least she did get to enjoy some quality time with her children and grand-children.

This little mouth of mine first came roaring out of St. Mary's Hospital in Passaic on June 9, 1939. I was the oldest of three kids, six years older than my sister Terry and eight years older than my brother John. Terry is a go-getter whose energy and enthusiasm make me look like Perry Como. She's feisty and, man, the women have to love her because she's a real libber—whoops, maybe I shouldn't say that. She's the president of a publishing company in Minneapolis, the City Business Corporation, after working for several years on *Denver* magazine. Terry lives in Englewood, Colorado, with her husband, Don Grimsrud, and two children, Todd and Piper. She commutes back there on weekends. Sort of like me during basketball season, only my commute's on week*days*.

When my nephew, Todd Grimsrud, was a freshman at Lehigh, in Bethlehem, Pennsylvania, he went to class for the first time and then went back to the dorm. He was sitting around with some other new kids when the subject of basketball came up. Todd said, "My Uncle Richie knows a little about the game."

They said, "Who's your Uncle Richie?"

He said, "Dick Vitale."

They said, "Get outta here. You don't know Dick Vitale."

So my sister called me right away and said I had to phone up Todd and talk to his roommates. I called a few times but nobody was home. But I'm going to surprise him one of these days and just drop by. Although I don't know about going to Lehigh. You know who came from Bethlehem, don't you? Besides Him. None other than Billy Packer, that's who. But I'll show up. I won't hold that against the whole town.

My brother, John Vitale, is probably 180 degrees different from me. A tremendous husband, father, and family man with a nine-to-five job at Sharp Computers in Paramus, New Jersey. He and his wife, Dee, have two children, Christopher and Pamela. John is always home for dinner, home for rides with the kids, home for all of it. I do so much traveling, I have to look like a real wacko to him.

In Garfield we lived upstairs in the house of my grandmother Josephine Scarpa, my mom's mom. My other grandparents, Carmen and Josephine Vitale, lived nearby, in Clifton. I can still remember helping my granddad pick the grapes in the vineyards of their backyard in Clifton; they made their own wine there.

I started my sports career in Garfield, bouncing a rubber ball off the front steps of the house. If it hit the upstairs porch it was a home run. Top of the ledge, triple. Wall, double. Window, trouble. If I hit the window, my grandmother would come screaming, "Richie, what-a you doin' always-a bangin'-a da ball?" I'd always be the Red Sox against the Yankees because I loved the Red Sox: Billy Goodman, the slap hitter; Bobby Doerr; Johnny Pesky; the Splendid Splinter himself, Ted Williams. My cousin and buddy, Johnny Scarpa, would be out in the field as the Yankees. If he caught the ball three times, I was out. My job was to hit the sharp edge of those steps. Hit it just right and that sucker went flying. "Going . . . going . . . gone." I'd always do the announcing just like Mel Allen. Always talking, even then.

I think I picked up my love of sports from my mother's brothers: Tom, Frank, Joe, Mike, and Sam. Five of them. And all sports nuts.

Every Sunday without fail the brothers would come to the house after Mass and my mother would have coffee, bagels, doughnuts and the newspaper ready for them. They would sit there with my dad and just shoot the breeze about every team in the area. Uncle Tom was the ticket man, the king in terms of getting seats for any game the others wanted to see. I never understood how they could sit around in the morning, decide they wanted to go to the big Giants–Dodgers game that afternoon, and then get in.

"Don't worry about nothing. We'll get the best seats," said Uncle Tom. And inevitably we'd end up near the dugout or at courtside or around the 50-yard line. I think Tom might have had a little con man in him—remind you of anybody?

My Uncle Mike and I used to argue football, follow all the high school teams; Garfield, Clifton, and some others made big football news back then. Thanksgiving dinner always had to wait on a high school football game. My Uncle Frank used to take me to Yankee Stadium. It was unbelievable: the Mantles, Berras, Howards. I became a Yankee fan. I got tired of the Red Sox getting beat, so I converted.

I was also a fanatic about horses as a kid, probably because of the horse track just up the road on Route 46 in East Paterson. There was one three-year-old there, a golden palomino we called Trigger after Roy Rogers's horse. I couldn't sleep at night without dreaming of Trigger. I would go over to the barns each day to help wash the horses and I convinced the boss there to let me go to work. Once he left my friend and me alone to walk the horses over to the track. "Screw this," I said. "That's boring. I'm not going to the track. Let's ride the horses around town."

Which, much to the chagrin of much of the town, we did. I didn't even know that horses needed special shoes to run on cement. We took Trigger out on the street, rode him over to my house and tied him up. If Trigger hadn't gone potty all over our lawn, we might have gotten away with it. As it was, my grandmother almost lost her mind, she was so mad. And then, when the boss came back the next day, the horses were still all sweaty; we didn't even know enough to wash them down. The guy wanted to break my leg. That was the end of my horse career.

I didn't really get into much mischief as a kid, except for moving Volkswagens and stuff like that on Halloween. Sports was my mischief. I played all the sports and devoured all the information about sports I could get my hands on.

Oh, yeah. Then there was the Eye.

When I was about two years old, I accidentally poked my left eye with a pencil, causing some infection. My mom and dad dragged me around to all kinds of doctors to fix it up. I remember the New York Eye & Ear Hospital. I remember crying. I had to wear a patch on my eye while it was supposedly repairing itself.

Still, I played sports in grade school even though I had practically no vision in that eye. I could just barely see peripherally. It was weird. But hey, I just had to make the most of it. I never knew what it was like to see well, to have great vision, so I never missed it.

In Little League I couldn't play the field because I couldn't judge the ball, so I became a pitcher. But I could never pick off anybody at first base because I couldn't see them over there. It was a good thing that runners weren't allowed to take a lead off base in Little League. Of course, I couldn't hit too well either because of the eye. I batted righty, which meant that my bad left eye was always facing the pitcher. It was frustrating. Throw the curve ball at me and forget about it, I was blind.

I started basketball in elementary school, and football, too. Football? I was a quarterback, but I didn't throw much because of the eye. Lots of roll-outs. Mostly keepers. It wasn't really a formal, organized team, and I kept it quiet so my parents wouldn't know. But then some writer for the local paper did a story mentioning that Garfield might have to change from its single wing offense to T-formation because of this one-eyed quarterback who was developing in the eighth grade. When my mother and father read that I was playing football, they went nuts. That was it for me on the gridiron.

I could still play baseball and basketball, though, and I wanted to do it for Garfield. But in my freshman year we moved to Elmwood Park, which was then called East Paterson. They didn't have a high school in East Paterson, so all the kids went to East Rutherford High. But I kept playing for Garfield, which wasn't too cool, or really legal, as it turned out. Athletic hanky-panky wasn't exactly unheard of then, either, and somehow the Garfield coaches had worked it out, giving me a make-believe address or something. I didn't really know or care; I was just happy playing with all my buddies from grammar school.

Happy, that is, until I got frustrated in the middle of my freshman basketball season. I had been scoring real big: 18, 19 points, a few 24-point games. I had this tiny coach, Chick DeVito, who had been my mother's teacher in grammar school. He was a legend at Garfield, a mini-legend. Chick was about 4-10, and when he came over to our house and sat on the couch, his feet never touched the floor.

Chick loved me. And he really kept on top of me. It was "Richie, when you going to do this? When you going to do that?" He always told me, "Don't pout or sulk when I get on you." I think that was the first time I realized that when a guy got on my case, it meant I was something special, that I had potential—the dreaded Mr. Po. But when I had a couple of awful games, going into a bad slump, I quit the team, just flat-out quit like the spoiled brat I was; I used to get so frustrated with failure. Chick just came over to the house to talk to my parents, dangling his feet off the couch and talking with so much affection and sincerity about me that I went back to the team and finished the year.

The Garfield varsity was having a great season and was the toast of the area. Their coach was a guy by the name of John Misko, a junior version of Bobby Knight. He was dynamite, a screamer. He would glare at you. I remember one time he came out to evaluate the rookies. He stood in the corner, but I knew he was there. I was trying to impress him. We had a big game and little Richie was taking the ball to the hole, stroking it, piling up the numbers. This was my chance for the big time, baby. I knew I had been great so I made sure to walk off the court right by him, hoping he would say "good game" or something. As I strode by, big-britches as all get-out, Coach Misko tapped me on the shoulder. "Hey, kid," he growled. "When are you going to learn to pass the basketball?"

I was devastated. But I kept working on my game, staying late after practice, getting home late every night, and finally one day Misko came up to me and told me to get dressed for the varsity practice. I was on cloud nine. I put on that varsity uniform as fast as I could. I literally skipped up the steps to the gym to get in the shooting lines. I was jubilant.

This was such a thrill. I was doing lay-ups right behind Paul Szcech, the Garfield senior superstar; "the blond bomber," the newspapers called him. Szcech was all-state, and he would earn a scholarship to Seton Hall and play for Coach Honey Russell. Szcech was such a hero of mine that when he was in college I would go to all of his games, and if he didn't get enough PT I would leave the arena, run to the nearest phone, call the Seton Hall postgame talk show on WSOU radio, and demand that Coach Russell give my man more minutes. So you can imagine how I felt to be in the same lay-up line. It was Fantasy Island time. For as long as we live, we never feel moments deeper than we felt them in high school. The Four Lads might as well have been singing, "We'll have these moments to remember." This was one of my moments.

But soon the Eye was to strike again.

By my junior year at Garfield I was finally ready to shine with the big fellas. It was all so exciting I tried not to notice that my eye had become badly infected. It started getting worse and worse, always bloodshot and weeping. I couldn't go out in the sunlight without squinting. I couldn't read or study or go to school. I couldn't do a thing. My family took me to specialists everywhere for help and advice. We tried to get opinions and treatments, tried to find out what was possible and what wasn't. Several doctors told my mother they had to remove the eye, but she wouldn't accept that. Finally, Dr. Bernard Samuels in New York—the Dean Smith of ophthalmology, a giant in the eye biz—told us what we wanted to hear.

"Don't ever let anybody operate on your eye," he said. "Don't let them get rid of it. I'll be able to give you some treatment. You're never going to see out of the eye normally, but you'll have some peripheral vision. Just don't remove it."

This was in December, and I had to sit out the entire school year. But I made up for it when I went back, this time to East Rutherford High School, where I repeated the eleventh grade.

Since all my buddies back at Garfield were ahead of me, I figured I'd start meeting new friends where I lived in Elmwood Park and finish my last two years of high school there.

That's where I met my friend and running mate, Frankie DeLauro, the Hoboken Hurricane. He was a cocky little son-ofagun, a transfer who had come in a year ahead of me and lit up the baskets. All-city. All-state. Frankie went on to play at Utah with Billy (the Hill) McGill, and ended up transferring to Hawaii, where he scored like crazy and broke some records. Frankie was sharp-looking, like Sal Mineo, with a dimple. And cocky? When he heard there was another player transferring into school, right away he hunted me down.

"I heard you're Richie Vitale and you're baaaad," Frankie said. "I'm Frankie DeLauro. Let's get it on so I can check out your game."

I can't say I didn't know what I was getting into. An all-time M&M'er, that's all. We played to eleven baskets, winners out. I don't think I touched the ball. After it was over he just looked at me and said, "Let's get this straight. You're not in my league, baby."

Naturally, Frankie and I became best buddies. The girls loved Frankie. They didn't fall in my lap, but I figured I'd get his leftovers.

I was the kind of guy in high school who was very talkative. Surprised? I always felt I had to compensate for my eye with an aggressive personality. I tried to be everybody's friend. Under my senior picture in the high school yearbook, in fact, the caption read, *Everybody's Buddy*. I really liked people, but I used to be frightened of getting in front of my classes for oral reports. I'd shake in my boots, terrified. I'd even cut class, get out of school to avoid those orals. I remember one teacher telling me I could get an A on written material, an F in orals and I'd still be okay with a C average. Boy, was I relieved.

Nobody can believe this, but I had hair back then, a thick crop. I used to wear a crew cut all the time. Oh, yeah, I'd wheel around in my red and white Ford convertible with the continental wheel on the back. My "red machine" was the only car we had in the family, and my parents never saw it— I was the taxi man, I'd drop them off at work and away I went. Forget the weather; I'd ride that baby all year round with the top down and the music blasting. The Platters. Dion. The Everly Brothers. Rock 'n' Roll with Alan Freed. Murray the K. You think I'm loud on the tube, baby, I was a volcano back then. You could hear me coming from miles away. Everybody knew when I was around. Here came Richie and his convertible.

So Frankie DeLauro had the looks, and I had the car. Were we baaad? We were so bad, I think Michael Jackson stole the expression from us. Michael's video producer is a guy named Bob Giraldi, right? Well, when we played Paterson East Side High they had a helluva jump shooter named Bob Giraldi. Same guy. He directed the Miller Lite commercials, too. Think we deserve a few royalties, Bobby baby?

We used to hang around Paterson Plank Road, Frankie as cocky as could be. I'll never forget one time he got in trouble. The opening game of the year was against Hasbrouck Heights. Frankie was a football player, too. All-state again. Great hands. Anyway, Hasbrouck had a great player named Danny As-trella, and Frankie wanted him bad. There was a big dance at Hasbrouck the week before the game so Frankie said, "We're going."

I said, "You're crazy. If we walk in the place, it's an instant riot."

Frankie said, "You in or out?"

We went walking into the dance. The word had gotten out. Nobody knew me from Adam, but here I was walking in with the big star. Frankie went sliding in there with his hands in his pockets, shades on, all cool and slow. He walked up to Astrella and pointed at him. "Big Fella, I'm going to take you apart. It's all over."

And it almost was. When the fight broke out, I headed for the exit sign. I broke all of Carl Lewis's records churning for the parking lot. I'm a lover, not a fighter, baby. Sure enough, the next week in the game Frankie caught a couple of long passes and we beat the hell out of Hasbrouck. Then he went up to Astrella on the field and started singing, "Oh, Danny Boy." What a wacko!

The summer before my senior year I was still trying to get my game back, playing every day down at the playground, but word came from the New Jersey state high school association that I was ineligible. The doctors produced papers proving I had been legitimately sidelined with my eye injury, but they still ruled this was my fifth year and I couldn't play. Again, I went home devastated. But this time I'd had it. I quit school.

That didn't go down too well with my parents. "How could you be a quitter?" my mother demanded. "Where are you going to end up?" But I just didn't want any part of school anymore.

I don't think anyone but my coach, Ken Sinofsky, could have talked me into going back. He was big and tough, the coach of both the football and basketball teams, and he was my all-time coaching idol. Most guys emulate players, but I wanted to be Ken Sinofsky. He was a heavyset guy who smoked cigars like Red Auerbach. He had the Auerbach aura about him, too. You could see in his walks through the halls, his mannerisms, his confidence and control, that he had so much respect in the community. He was really like a god at East Rutherford, and I'd probably be out on the streets today if he hadn't put me up against the wall and ordered me to shape up and get back in school.

I couldn't play high school ball, but I could still play for St. Joseph's Church in the CYO league. I averaged 20–25 points a game in CYO competition, but it wasn't exactly the best league around. Still, I wrote to all these colleges asking them to come take a look at me—Cornell, Colgate, Bucknell, Lehigh (my nephew Todd's friends would have believed him then). Can you imagine recruiters going after a guy in CYO ball? Man, did I have nerve.

I followed college basketball and all the players and teams

as if they were the subject of an honors thesis or something, and I would always notice Roanoke College when that school would make its Eastern swing. Roanoke would consistently get beat 40–50 points by NYU and Seton Hall and that bunch. "They must need some players, maybe they can use a guy like me," I thought.

So I went down there as a walk-on and found out I wasn't good enough to play for Roanoke, either. I had a roommate there who didn't know the first thing about sports. He would sit at his desk all night studying some kind of science. I was totally bored and homesick, and not burying my J, besides. I had been going steady most of that last year in high school with JoAnn Smith, who would become my first wife, and I missed her very much. When I realized I wasn't going to make an impact on the court, I knew I had to get out of there and go back home.

I really lucked out when Seton Hall's Paterson division had a vacancy and took me as a transfer right away. I didn't lose any semester time at all, and better yet, I got some quality minutes on the basketball team right away because we weren't Division I.

At Seton Hall–Paterson we were cupcakes for cupcakes, if you know what I mean. The Trenton States and Montclair States would eat us for breakfast, lunch and dinner. But I was able to keep up on things in East Rutherford, particularly the basketball career of Louie Ravettine, who was a couple of years behind me in school and a great friend of my family.

Louie was an excellent football, baseball and basketball player, a fierce competitor. He'd get in your face, and never backed down from anybody. He was always getting in fights. I kept going to the East Rutherford games and watched Ravettine get better and better. I think he was my first broadcast subject–guinea pig; I'd sit in the stands and do play-by-play of his games for all my friends: "Ravettine from the corner . . . Ravettine drives and scores . . . Ravettine steals in the backcourt . . . going all the way . . . it's in. My man, Louie. Take it down, Rav." It was a riot.

I got so attached to Louie I wrote letters about him to big-time coaches all around the country. When he didn't play well, I got all over his case. I guess I was coaching before I ever became a coach. One night against Paterson Central he was dogging it. There were media there and lots of hype about the game. I was always trying to build up this guy by sending out newspaper clips and getting coaches excited about him, and here he was laying down. I was furious. I roared into the locker room at halftime—I wasn't even on the coaching staff, remember, I was just a college kid back at his old high school—and got him up against the wall. "Louie, you're blowing it; get your butt playing." Or words to that effect. I think he went for about 30 in the second half.

Ravettine finally made it to Fairleigh Dickinson University, where he had a fine career. He could really stroke the J. Had a great game against NYU and their All-Americans Barry Kramer and Happy Hairston. I even tried to get Louie a tryout with the 76ers once when I was at the Wilt Chamberlain camp up at Kutscher's in the Catskills. Went right up to the Philly owner, Mr. Ike Richmond, and told him the Sixers needed this guy. In retrospect, I think Louie Ravettine must have been the athlete I had always wanted to be. And the way I threw myself into his career should have told me something about what I really wanted to do with my life.

As it was I plowed through four years at Seton Hall–Paterson searching for the answer to that question. As much as I loved sports, I didn't know where I was going or what to do in sports. I thought about the law as a profession. Everybody was always telling me I was such a persuasive talker. At home they said, "You should be a lawyer." So I used to skip classes to study the trial lawyers over at the courthouse in Hackensack, and I followed their careers in the newspaper. I was intrigued by what performers they were. Just watching their styles and deliveries helped me in developing my own way of communicating.

Ultimately, I received my BA in business from Seton Hall–Paterson in June 1962, but not before getting my first experience with coaching and recruiting—in baseball. A guy named Chick DeFranco, who sold chickens for a living, got the Benigno Tire company to sponsor a baseball team in Garfield for sixteen-to-nineteen-year-olds that would play in the All-American Amateur Baseball Association. Chick called me to round up a team. Naturally, I went after the best players. We had Jack Grasing, who later signed with the Giants, a left-hander reminiscent of Bobby Shantz; Kenny Huebner, who would have a cup of java in the majors; Johnny Briggs, a basketball player out of Paterson East Side High who played ten years in the bigs—just an unbelievable cast. I recruited and coached them for two summers. We won 90 percent of our games, and represented the state in the nationals in Johnstown, Pennsylvania.

The tournament in Johnstown was in August of '63, right after I married JoAnn. We had a lousy honeymoon in Johnstown: My team lost to Baltimore Leone's. Dave Boswell—the guy who later got into a brawl with Billy Martin—pitched against us. Ron Swoboda also played for Leone's and killed us. JoAnn and I then went on a real honeymoon to Provincetown on Cape Cod. Boswell and Swoboda couldn't get us there.

I took a job right out of college working at the accounting office of McBride Brothers in Paterson, but I knew after three days this was no place for me. I kept looking at the clock. I didn't want to spend thirty, forty years looking at a clock unless it was the game clock. Finally, the boss nailed me. Instead of doing my balance sheets, debits and credits, I was on the phone all day calling my baseball players to get them ready for the big games, or calling people to tout my players. Once I called Ralph Houk, who was managing the Yankees, from the office. Rang him up right in the Yankee clubhouse. "Ralph," I said. "You got to take a look at this kid, Kenny

Huebner. He's the next great hitter in baseball." Houk knew all about Huebner. He didn't know Richie Vitale from Richie Valens.

I took a big cut in pay when I quit McBride to go into teaching. My first teaching contract in 1962 at Mark Twain #3 School in Garfield was for $4500, and that included coaching the seventh- and eighth-graders in football. We went undefeated for two years. I didn't know a split-T formation from a banana split, but I could read the scoreboard; if they had 6 we better get 7. And I knew how to coach.

In my second year I was named head coach of varsity basketball. It was a late, last-second thing and I couldn't believe it. Here I was, twenty-three years old and the head coach. Of course, Garfield had lost all its players from the year before, when the team got drilled every time out anyway. Then for my first game, when I saw who we were playing, who I had to coach against, I swear my knees began to shake. Al LoBalbo was a legend in New Jersey. He had won numerous state championships at St. Mary's of Elizabeth, coaching Hubie Brown, among others. He was the master of defense, the genius of pressure man-to-man. How good was LoBalbo at defense? Bobby Knight hired him to be his assistant at Army. He ranked near the top of the nation in D a couple of times as head coach at Fairleigh Dickinson. Lou Carnesecca has Al working for him now at St. John's. The Ball-You-Man theory? The one that says a defender should always keep himself between the ball and the man he's guarding, the defensive strategy everyone now learns as a toddler? LoBalbo originated it. He's an absolutely dynamite guy, an innovator and motivator, and yet we played his Bellevue team tough all the way before losing 53–52 in my very first game. And afterwards, I was sitting in the office when Al walked in and shook hands. "Let me tell you something," he said. "You're going to be a good one." Cloud Nine City, baby.

Politics intervened and I was forced out of Garfield the next year, but I ended up with the head coaching job at East Rutherford, my old school. I was a sixth-grade teacher at

Franklin Elementary School, making about five grand, and
the coaching paid an extra six hundred. What could be better?
I was back in the city I loved. Many of my old buddies were
around. I was in my element—a coach. And right down the
road was the original landmark of *the* coach, Vince Lombardi:
St. Cecelia's in Englewood.

I came on like Lombardi in those days. I used to tell everybody we were going to do it like the Coach. We weren't going
to win tomorrow, we were going to win today. Winning isn't
everything, it's the only thing. I'd even drive over to St. Cecelia's and walk up and down the steps and through the halls.
To imagine that Vince Lombardi used to walk through here
and teach in these classrooms! Man, it was an inspiration.

Over the years I amended the Lombardi philosophy a bit.
I tried to get it across that the pursuit of excellence, the pursuit
of success, was the main thing. If you do your absolute best,
you're ultimately the winner. The scoreboard sometimes doesn't
reveal effort. But you can't tell me those kids at Wisconsin
and Northwestern, when they play their guts out against the
Indianas and Iowas and Purdues, aren't winners, too, whatever the scoreboard says.

We had quite a coaching clan back in those Jersey days.
There was Rollie Massimino (now the head man at Villanova)
over at Hillside High; Lou Campanelli (California) at Jefferson; Dick Tarrant (Richmond) at Passaic; Richie Adubato
(Dallas Mavericks assistant) at Our Lady of the Valley in West
Orange; Hubie Brown (formerly of the Knicks) at Fairlawn;
and Mike Fratello (Atlanta Hawks) playing at Hackensack.

I coached at East Rutherford for seven seasons and we
rolled up some impressive numbers. But I'd have days when
I'd leave home at seven in the morning and not come back
until midnight. I'd go to school, teach, coach, and then take
courses at night toward a Master's degree in education, which
I ultimately received from Paterson State College (now William Paterson College).

I wasn't taking very good care of myself. That drive to excel
in basketball bore a deep hole in my marriage. I ended up

being completely negligent as a husband. JoAnn and I had no children. She was working at the Sears Roebuck in Passaic, and while I was struggling through the East Rutherford years we weren't really sharing each other's lives.

One Thanksgiving weekend comes to mind vividly. Coaches go through such mood swings, and this one year we had a three-team scrimmage on the Wednesday night before Turkey Day. Both JoAnn and I have fairly large, close families who get together for the holidays and really put on the dog. When I came home that night from the scrimmage JoAnn was all ready to go to her sister's house to start preparations. She had the pots and pans ready and everything. "C'mon, let's go," she said.

"I'm not going," I said. "I'm down. I'm depressed. I'm aggravated. We finished worst of the three teams there."

JoAnn started crying. She went anyway and faced her sister. She always made excuses for my missing these occasions. "Richie isn't feeling well tonight," she would say. I put her in some awful predicaments. But this was the last straw. Finally, while I was in practice one day my brother-in-law and good friend Peter Murray arrived and told me JoAnn had left me. I went through practice like nothing had happened. It was only when I went home and found JoAnn gone that I knew it was over. We got back together twice more and tried to make it work, but it was no go.

So my marriage was breaking up. And there was the buildup and the tension of the games. Maybe it was the hours that I kept. I wasn't eating right or sleeping much. Everything was just building up inside me.

I was always a stalking maniac on the sidelines. Always in referees' faces. More technicals than anybody. "Get his butt out of the lane," I'd scream at the official, "or your butt is out the door." The worst thing about high school ball is that you hire your own officials for home games, so if the refs want to return they know they'd better give you some of those three-second calls. Oh, I was wild. I made Bobby Knight look like *The Sound Of Music*. I don't know if I was trying to

intimidate; maybe I just felt that was part of the job. But I
was up and down all the time. Every basket was life or death.
And then a headline following an East Rutherford–Lodi game
told the story: *Lodi Wins, Coach Faints.*

I had been rushed to the hospital after I collapsed in the
locker room following that game. That was a warning, but I
didn't slow down. And then, about a year later, I went home
after a game, got dizzy and passed out. I started throwing up
blood. It was coming out of my mouth and nose and everywhere. That was the first time I realized I had a bleeding
ulcer. In the emergency room at the hospital my hemoglobin
count was down to six. I lost about five pints of blood. Fortunately, I came out okay.

But I wouldn't let the ulcer cramp my style. "Calm down,
coach. You're ranting and raving but we've got it under control," one of my players, a great kid named Billy Kesgen, told
me in one game. "We're up by thirty and you're worrying
about finding something to be worried about."

One time I brought my East Rutherford team over to Fairlawn High to scrimmage Hubie Brown's team. Bill Kunkel,
the late major-league umpire, refereed the scrimmage. There
were the three of us future pros in this little high school gym
and we were all really going at it. In scrimmages, when the
whistle blows everything stops so the coaches can correct things.
Well, Hubie and I were whipping these kids like you wouldn't
believe. We might have even whipped some words on Kunkel
as well. It was awesome, languagewise, if you know what I
mean.

Anyway, there were these two Marines who happened to
be standing in the gym watching all this. They were on leave
or something, local guys back from boot camp. And there we
were, tearing these kids' rear ends off. I'll never forget it. I
ran past them and heard one Marine say to the custodian of
the place, "Man, I just got back from Parris Island, but I've
never seen anything like this."

I used to work my players' butts off, I'll tell you. Sometimes
I had practice at six in the morning. John Chaney of Temple

got a lot of press in the last few years for working out the Owls at dawn, but I was way ahead of that. We'd sweep the snow and ice off the cement and do it. Just a little practice in dealing with adversity. The kids thought I was crazy, but it's surprising what the body can do if we make it. I didn't want excuses or alibis. Hey, we're out here, let's practice. It's tough hitting the J when it's 15, 20 degrees out. But just imagine how easy the stroke will come when we're back in those 70-degree climes.

I was a maniac. I'm not proud of it, but I definitely lost control a few times. Once, we were playing North Arlington in the sectionals of the state tournament, and they were a monster. But we had a good chance at a major upset. I was in the locker room, hollering as usual, when I took a towel and started snapping that sucker around. One of my kids, Charlie Grillo, was in the first row, and I smacked him right in the eye with the towel. Oh man, you can imagine what went through my mind. I was dying inside. But what could I do? I couldn't stop the harangue and lose the effect. I couldn't show anybody I was concerned. "Don't you have any guts, Grillo? Forget that damned thing in your eye and let's play ball." I thought I'd put the fool eye out, and here I was screaming at the kid to forget it. We won the game, and Grillo was okay, but I sure never slapped kids around with a towel again.

The town of East Rutherford really loved the Wildcats. The whole community supported us. We practiced in a bandbox gym about 40 by 70 feet and had to play all our games over at Garfield High School my last four years. We were a small school, about six, seven hundred enrollment, in Group I, the smallest of the divisions in the state. But we felt we could play basketball with anyone. And when we got Leslie Cason, Big Les, the most important player I ever had in my coaching career, we really could.

I always had tough, hard-nosed kids, competitors, over-achievers. But never had I coached a talent like Les Cason,

a genuine, franchise-type PTP. He was a local guy, from right
there in East Rutherford. We called him "Pee Wee" because
he was so big, even in the fifth grade. By the time he was
twelve he was 6-2, throwing bullets from the pitcher's mound
even though he couldn't find the plate. In basketball, though,
he had all the control you could ask for. He'd come to the
school gym after varsity practice every day to drill. Right
hand, left hand, lay-ups, post moves, shooting exercises, rebound practice; I'd work with him all the time. He was a
fanatic about work. He wanted to be a player. You could see
it all over him. An only child, he also had great love, caring,
and guidance from his mother and stepfather, Mary and Bob
Johnson.

Even in the ninth grade Cason was a McAdoo-type player.
He wasn't your basic post-up, inside, low-box center. He could
play the wings, handle the ball, drive, dish, slam. He loved
the game. Anytime I wanted to find him I would get into the
car and go to the Clinton playground where he'd be scrim-
maging with the guys or practicing his jumper for hours.

I monitored his progress from day one. I watched him improve his skills, his quickness, his ability in all phases of the
game. Les did have a problem with academics, however, and
no love for school. It was a constant battle to get him to hit
the books. Often we would ask Willis Reed, whom I had
befriended through basketball camps and clinics, to talk to
him. Reed was an enormous hero in New York basketball
then, and Cason responded to him. Willis had Les over to his
camp. "I've never seen anything like this kid at his age," Willis
once said to me. That's how good Cason was.

I love to tell the story of how I snookered Freddy Barakat,
who is now the assistant commissioner of the ACC but at that
time was coaching over at Hasbrouck Heights. He wanted to
have a little scrimmage between our junior high teams, so we
scheduled one at his place for eleven o'clock one morning.

Freddy hates to lose, whether it's marbles, checkers, or a
bet on who picks up the fork first. He especially hated to lose
to Dick Vitale. So when my little kids walked in that morning

trailed by Cason, who was about 6-6 and a monster, Freddy went nuts. "Who is this?" he said.

"Oh, him," I said. "Didn't I tell you? That's my seventh-grader, Pee Wee."

Cason amazed coaches in junior high with his quickness and agility. By the eleventh grade he had become a complete dominator. He had grown to about all of his 6-10 then, and in a regional playoff game against Mountain Lakes we just ran away and hid. Leslie had a colossal game. I missed it, being confined to St. Mary's Hospital with one of my major ulcer bleeds. But Hubie Brown, at the time an assistant coach at William and Mary, was there along with Howard Garfinkel, the guru of high school scouting services. Garf is the guy who founded the famous Five-Star Camp in the summertime for outstanding prep players, and when he gave a kid a "five" rating, that meant he was the ultimate, the numero uno, the top gun. As Cason was dominating this game, Hubie looked over at Garf and flashed a palms-up sign: "Five." Garf looked back at Hubie and shook his head no. Then he held up both hands, signaling: "Ten."

That's also how good Cason was.

I signed myself out of the hospital for the state Final Four in Atlantic City and sat on the bench with a quart of milk next to me as we played in the finals. In an unbelievable game, we came from 12 points behind to beat Burlington Township by 1, 67–66. You know what Cason did? Just 45 points, 27 rebounds and 9 blocked shots, that's all. He put on an incredible show, baby. And what coaching, too!

College recruiters were coming out of the woodwork by this time. Tennessee invited me to speak at a clinic. I felt real proud. But I was so naive. Part of the deal was that I had to bring Cason with me in order to get paid for speaking. It wasn't cheating, it was just the deal. I didn't go. Jerry Tarkanian was after him to go to Long Beach State. I thought Tark would be the perfect guy for Cason; Tark could always communicate with guys like Les.

Early in his senior year, Cason announced he would go with

Tark. Long Beach had Eddy Ratleff and Leonard Gray and the Trapp brothers in that era. They were a national contender every season. There was a big press conference and the rumor was that I was to go along in the package and be Tarkanian's assistant. There was never any deal made, but I was ready to leave for a college job; still, I was torn because I wanted to do it on my accomplishments, not Leslie's.

To this day I don't know what happened to Cason in his last season at East Rutherford, 1970–71. Outside people got to him: so-called "advisors," agents, general riffraff. Somebody really got to him about his relationship with me and made it a black-white conflict. "Here's this white coach trying to use you to get ahead, Les." That type of thing.

"I woke up one day white and I can't change it," I said to Leslie one day, "and you woke up black and can't change. But we're both people. I happen to think the world of you. There is no question you've opened doors for me. But I like to think that it's been reciprocal and that I've poured out my best to try to make you into a better player and person."

But nothing worked. Cason slacked off even more in class. He became a problem in practice. He abandoned his work habits. I even had to suspend him for a game and risk our 32-game unbeaten streak. It was like our relationship had burned out. The last straw was when Reed was going to come out to East Rutherford to see him and Cason didn't show any interest. I knew all the good things were over.

Oh, we won another state title, beating Gloucester in the finals in another one-pointer. But Cason wasn't the same player. He was fumbling the ball, messing around, not playing hard. I heard rumors about drugs. I questioned him about it. "No, no, no," he said. "I thought you believed in me, Coach."

Then came two major downers. First: These were the days of the 1.6. A kid's grade-point average and SAT score had to balance out in the formula to 1.6 for him to be accepted to an NCAA four-year institution, and Cason's weren't going to, so he couldn't go to Long Beach. Second: Les positively bombed out in Sonny Vacarro's Dapper Dan high school all-star game in Pittsburgh. I was shocked. Garfinkel was stunned—and Vacarro still calls Cason's performance the worst in the game's history. (Garf didn't hold any fingers up this time.)

Cason wound up at San Jacinto Junior College and later I helped him get back East, into Rutgers. But he was never a force in college ball. It's one of the sadder stories I've ever been associated with. Les had a gift; he was something special as a player, but he let his talent drift. He didn't use the ball, he let the ball use him. Cason should have been a major star, a multimillionaire—I know that in my heart—but he took his size and talent and gift for the game and virtually committed it to oblivion.

As for me, there was a long period when I was bothered by the rumors and accusations that I was in a package with Cason. I had been in control of the program at East Rutherford, so everybody just thought it was a given that if you wanted Cason you had to take Vitale. This demeaned me and all the years I put into the coaching profession. I knew I had talent. I'd been preparing for a college job before Cason ever came along. I wanted to make it on my own, but if I had to latch onto Cason to get a good assistant's job somewhere, well, it wasn't like I was a leech and had nothing to offer. I knew I could do the job.

I had maintained a lot of contacts and relationships with college assistants. I had the feelers out. George Raveling, then an assistant at Maryland, was helping me. I felt I had ability, that I could contribute. Down deep, though, I just didn't think anybody would give me the shot. I was considered too ambitious, and people resent ambitious, aggressive guys. This had been going on for several years. Pounding and pounding away at advancement, I drew a blank. *Nada.* The Ballantine Blast. Three rings: Zero. Zero. Zero.

I spent hours in the teachers' lounges in East Rutherford composing letters to the John Woodens and the Ara Parseghians and the Bear Bryants, to all the great coaches, asking them to share some of their wisdom. Everybody used to laugh at me: "Dick, you're not a name. You're going to be a junior high teacher all your life. Forget it."

But my mother always taught me never to think small: Don't be afraid to reach for the stars or chase your dreams. So I kept chasing. And when my chances came, I was ready.

BUYERS AND SELLERS

The summer of '69 meant the Miracle of the Mets. The summer of '70 meant the Miracle of McGrath. That's how I remember the year and how much I think of the girl who changed my life more than anything in basketball ever could. In fact, I don't know which was more amazin': Ron Swoboda making those catches for the Metsies in the World Series, or me coming out of nowhere to make the grab on the fantastic Lorraine McGrath the very next year. If ever an angel walked the face of the earth—or at least into the parking lot of the Blue Swan in Rochelle Park, New Jersey—it was Lorraine McGrath.

I've never been a drinker—the folks at ESPN call me Mr.

Cranberry Juice—but during this period of my life I did tend
to hit the singles places with grenade force. Every Friday night
during the school year, and in the summertime a few other
nights as well, the coaches would hang out at the local clubs—
guys like myself, Tommy Ramsden, and Richie Adubato, my
longtime Jersey pal who would later be my assistant on the
Detroit Pistons.

When Adubato was single he was a real ladies' man, with
a different date every night. I can't tell you how many of
Richie's "fiancées" my wife has sat next to at our games over
the years. Back when we would all be out talkin' hoops and
ogling the beauties at the same time, Richie would always be
the one to put a stop to basketball talk. "It's 1:00 A.M.,"
Adubato would say. "We've been on basketball time for four
hours. Now it's Adubato Time, and I got one hour to make
the play. See ya around." And he'd stroll away to the vicinity
of the nearest skirts.

This particular night, though, we were all out at the Blue
Swan and basketball couldn't have been further from my
thoughts. It was summer and I was stylin'. That afternoon I
had just bought a brand-new limelight green Bonneville convertible. It was a knockout, a dream—big, long, sleek lines.
Kind of built like me. It had a dark green leather interior to
go with that lime green glow on the outside. I can still see it.
That thing was shining when I pulled into the lot, the top
down, Chuck Berry rockin' on the stereo at the Blue Swan.

Understand, I didn't park just anyplace, now. I didn't want
any part of the regular spaces because I was afraid somebody
would pull up too close next to me and scratch the doors. It
was one of those gorgeous summer nights with the stars as
clear as can be, and I pulled right up to the entrance where
everybody who would walk by had to see Dicky V's new
Bonneville.

Shortly after we went inside here came this attractive redhead with great long hair, blue hot pants and white boots.
"That's the one," I said to the guys.

The redhead was with a girlfriend at the time, obviously

there to dance and have fun. But when I went over to ask
her to dance, she shot me down. I want to tell you, it was a
long, long walk back to the table where I knew my coaching
buddies would be all over me. It was like taking the big L.
The guys were just busting me: "Hey, Richie, baby—the Ri-
fleman. Are those gunshot wounds in your chest? You just
went down for the count, on the deck, Marciano-style, my
man. Want us to get Cus D'Amato?"

But I wasn't discouraged. About a half hour later I went
back again. But it's a definite no again. Now I was really
ticked off. This was a slap in the face. All I wanted to do was
dance and she kept turning me down. Then after a while I
looked out on the floor and she was dancing with some yo-
yo in white socks!

Now the guys were really in my face, and I was steaming.
There was no way I was going to take a called third strike. I
went over and grabbed the redhead by the arm. "I'm not
asking you to dance this time," I said. "I'm telling you."
Whoooaaa. Sly Stallone himself.

"Boy, are you aggressive," she said. "Okay, we'll dance."

To this day Lorraine teases me about my outfit that night.
She says I looked like some goofball nerd with my milkbottle
glasses, my royal blue jacket and my shocking orange turtle-
neck. Plus I had the green car outside, of course, and I was
dancing with the redhead in the white boots. And they said
Vitale would never be a color man!

Of course, I just happened to be carrying some press clippings of a charity basketball game I had put together and she
seemed impressed by that. By the end of the evening the guys
had finally let up on me, and I thought I was getting somewhere when Lorraine let me walk her to her car.

"Uh, could I have your phone number?" I said.

"No way. But it's in the phone book if you really want it,"
she said.

Women. I thought for sure I had been blown away again.
But as we walked out the front of the Blue Swan to go to her
car, I said, as cool as can be, "Mind if I drop my jacket in

my car?" Then I strolled over and suavely deposited my royal blue sportcoat in my limelight green Bonneville convertible there right in front of the entrance.

Lorraine told me later that, sure enough, the car made the impression. Earlier when she and her girlfriend had arrived, they had spent ten minutes out in the lot inspecting the hot new wheels and wondering who owned them. Anyway, I called her up over the weekend to invite her to a Dionne Warwick concert at the Garden State Arts Center. Second row seats. *What's it all about, Alfie? Do you know the way to San Jose?* All that jazz. After some serious Vitale rap, she finally said, "We're on." And the rest, as they say, is HB: History, baby.

We dated for about ten months, and then in May we were married. Tommy Ramsden had been my best man when I married JoAnn, but this time he begged off. "I gave you away once; I must be bad luck. I'm not going to do it twice," he said. So another friend of mine named Mooney Kurnath stood up for me this time, Mooney and my entire sixth-grade class at the Franklin School.

My first wedding had included all the bridesmaids and groomsmen and limousines, the whole schmeer, and it was a spectacular show. This time Lorraine and I were hitched in the mayor's chambers at the municipal hall by Jimmy Plosia, the mayor of East Rutherford himself. It was on May 22, 1971, and we invited my sixth-graders and they all showed up at the mayor's place with these beautiful little gifts they had made in shop class: crooked little bookshelves, birdhouses, the works. It was a riot. We have a picture of Lorraine and me surrounded by these sixth-graders just after the ceremony. I have my grey plaid jacket on, one every bit as loud as anything Bob Knight or Wimp Sanderson ever wore on a basketball court. But at the time I was Mr. GQ in that outfit.

We had the wedding reception in the cellar of my mother's house and partied till midnight, then took off on our honeymoon. We drove four hours to Atlantic City, where we learned we couldn't get into our hotel room until 8:00 A.M. So we had approximately four hours to murder and murder

them we did. We adjourned to Rocky's lounge near the board-
walk, a tavern that was not exactly uncharming in a sleazy
sort of way, owned by a former journeyman boxer in the
middleweight division.

Actually, Rocky still seemed a bit punch-drunk, because
when he heard any kind of bell, he immediately snapped to
and went into his crouch, fists up, ready to rumble. The gag
in Rocky's was to clink glasses or bottles to simulate the ring
alarm. Immediately, Rock would be on his toes sucking air
and punching shadows.

That's how Lorraine and I spent our wedding night. We
toasted our wedding, clinked our glasses, proclaimed ever-
lasting love . . . and watched Rocky jump to his feet snapping
jabs and hooks and promising to go the distance just as as-
suredly as we were.

It's funny how the turning points in your life coincide. About
this same time I had realized that I couldn't go on coaching
high school basketball. We had built up the program at East
Rutherford and we won two state championships. Cason was
leaving. We were hardly going to do any better and we would
be pressed to do nearly as well. Bottom line, I really wanted
a college coaching opportunity.

Moreover, East Rutherford was about to become a regional
high school called Becton Regional. The rules said that because I taught in the elementary school system in East Rutherford, I couldn't be the head coach at Becton; I would have
had to switch to teaching high school there. And I didn't want
to do that. If I was going to be a teacher, I preferred working
with the sixth-graders, with whom I felt I could have such an
impact. But coaching was the main thing, so I decided to look
elsewhere, and that meant college. That also meant, as I mentioned before, Nowheresville.

I wasn't making a ripple anywhere. I was trying to hook on
with the local universities, but guys like Billy Raftery, who
was coaching at Seton Hall then, couldn't use me, and Fairleigh Dickinson couldn't find a place for me. Here I was,

thirty-two years old, what I would consider a success at my level, but I wasn't getting a chance to make the next step.

Until the Garf.

I have to explain the circumstances of my first meeting with Howard Garfinkel to show what an impact he had on my coaching career. The original connection obviously came through Les Cason, whom Garf wanted for the Five-Star Camp. Leslie didn't really want to go there, so Garf came down to convince us one day. I had only heard about him and talked to him a few times on the phone, but I pictured this tall, distinguished, strong, power guy.

So here he came into the gym, and the guy had on his horn-rim glasses, he was smoking six thousand cigarettes a minute, and his black hair was slicked back all greasy like some motorcycle jockey. I thought he was the lead singer for Sha-Na-Na. He was my number one, best-of-all-time character. But let me tell you something: the guy knew his basketball.

Garfinkel started talking that quick talk out of one side of his mouth and rattling off names and numbers and stats so fast I didn't know what hit me. He shocked me—not so much with all the information but with how technical the info was. I thought the guy was either the biggest con artist in the world or a basketball genius. If you're reading this, Garf baby, rest assured I mean it as a compliment when I say I finally figured out that you're a combination of both.

Garf started right in on Cason, whom he had seen play before. He delineated Leslie's quickness, his hand-eye coordination, his strength, his shot. "He needs a little more hand," Garf would begin. "A little more upper body. I don't like his drop step down in the lane. He wants to go perimeter too much. But we can refine all that. I'll get Hubie [Brown] to teach him the drop when he's at camp. I'll get Chuck Daly to talk to him. Rave [George Raveling] can work with him on rebounding. We'll get so-and-so on this, so-and-so on that. No problem." He just went on and on. I thought it was great. Totally impressive.

Of course, I was trying to impress him, too. I wanted him

to know that this guy knew his hoops as well. The two of us
went after it, two wackos trying to con one another, New
York–style. But we hit it off so well. Some guys have always
been down on the Garf—he's extremely sensitive and he over-
analyzes everything to the point where reality sometimes takes
a back seat—but I have always trusted him. And if he's in
your corner, the guy is the most loyal of backers, which he
proved back in 1971 after a banquet at East Rutherford.

When it was common knowledge that I was going to leave
my job coaching at the high school, some community leaders
got together and held a banquet in my honor, chaired by my
former wife's sister, Darryl Murray. That night was very emotional for me and I poured out my heart in a kind of valedictory
speech in which I spoke for several minutes about each kid
who played for me. I talked about what all the players meant
to me and my family and how it was the greatest seven years
in a community a guy could hope for. I almost broke down
but I hung tough.

The response was overwhelming, if I do say so myself. And
I was so pleased. I sincerely wanted to communicate my feelings and I meant every word. Garfinkel, whom I had invited
to the banquet, said later, "It was electrifying . . . unbelievable . . . I've never heard a speech come across like that."
We were sitting in the Park Diner on Paterson Plank Road
after the banquet and rapping on hoops until about 3:00 A.M.
"You've got to get a college job," he said. "I'm going to see
to it. You belong in college coaching."

I thought Howie was just being nice; I mean, I knew he
had contacts and all but we were just shooting the breeze and
sympathy was in the air. And then a few days later I was about
to present the state championship jackets to the East Rutherford team at a special school assembly when I was called to
the telephone. "The coach from Rutgers wants to talk to you,"
somebody said.

Sure enough, it was Dick Lloyd on the other end of the
line. Lloyd was a famous name in Rutgers athletics. His brother,
Bobby, had been an outstanding guard for the Scarlet Knights.

Played on a very good NIT team in backcourt with somebody named Valvano; Valvano passed the ball and got out of Bob's way. Dick Lloyd had just replaced Bill Foster as coach at Rutgers. "Coach Vitale," he said, "I've been talking to Howard Garfinkel, who's a big fan of yours. I need an assistant coach. Can you come down for an interview tomorrow?"

Could I? I didn't say the word "wow" but I was feeling it ten times over. Right after I made an appointment with Coach Lloyd, I called Garf and he gave me the whole scoop: how Lloyd had interviewed his final six candidates and wasn't going to talk to anybody else; how Garf pleaded with him just to chat with me; how Lloyd was doing this almost as a favor; how my chances were about ninety to one against (I had never interviewed for a college job before); how I would have to go in and do the selling job of my life; how Garf believed in me so much he told Lloyd, "This guy is so dynamic, if you have an open mind about this, after you talk to Vitale there's no way you *can't* hire him."

Since I really didn't know much about Dick Lloyd, I did a little research in the time I had, made a few calls—about ten hours' worth. I knew this was my big shot even if it was a long one.

When I got to Rutgers, Lloyd took me around the campus. I met some of the administration, and since Lloyd was a family-oriented guy he took me to meet his wife, Marian, and left us alone so she could give me a once-over. It was all very quick but thorough, and it wasn't as if he was saying okay, I gave Garfinkel's guy his hour, now he can get out of here. I knew I was in the running.

I especially knew he was impressed with what I told him about recruiting. Look, recruiting is the lifeblood of a basketball program. An assistant coach who can recruit is a good assistant coach, period. Lloyd and I talked about players, about loyalty, about job responsibilities, but mostly about recruiting. I told Lloyd of my experiences with the Benignos baseball team, about the phone calls and contacts, the letter-writing campaign, the follow-ups. When I had Cason I had watched some of the great college recruiters come in and do their thing. I was always trying to learn. I was prepared to develop questionnaires and card files on players and schedules for visiting potential recruits.

One great thing about the interview was that never once did Cason's name come up. Never once did Lloyd say, "Well, Dick, Leslie's going to San Jacinto but maybe you can get him back here in a couple of years." It felt terrific to be wanted only for myself.

I've always known this: Selling is selling, even if you're promoting yourself or a university. It gets down to aggressiveness, personality, desire, a constant work ethic. I kept telling Lloyd I could do the job. I think he was impressed when I insisted that Rutgers could and should go after the great player, not just the soft medium-level guy. The school was a state university with a lot to offer. We could turn the small fieldhouse, the Rutgers "barn", into a positive: a rollicking, in-your-face, Deaf Dome with 2500 fans breathing down the necks of visiting clubs. Make it a happening. To tell the truth, I was selling my butt off about a place where I had never seen a game.

Did I get the job? Hey, it was an NC'er. Only later did I find out what I would be making (eleven thousand a year— Lorraine and I rented a little three-room apartment; she was pregnant with Terri, who would be born that January) and that while other assistants were out scouring the nation for players and scouting upcoming opponents, part of my job was to hand out towels a couple of days a week.

That was okay. I'd issue all those Cannons again to have the chance to bring a kid like Phil Sellers to Rutgers. I remember the first time Lloyd and I sat down after school started in the fall to talk about recruiting. We looked at Garfinkel's list of prospects: the five-stars, fours, threes and on down. Lloyd was talking about some of the less-talented guys, saying, "We have to go after this kid," or "We'll have a shot at that kid."

I took a deep breath and interrupted. "Wait a minute," I

said. "What about Sellers? What about Mike Dabney? These are seniors, practically local guys. I can get these guys here. Please, Dick, let me go after them." And, lo and behold, he did.

If the present recruiting rules had been in existence then—three home visits, three other contacts, and visits to just five schools—there would have been no way Richie Vitale could have made an impact, no way Sellers or Dabney would have enrolled at New Brunswick, no way Rutgers eventually would have made the Final Four.

As it was, everybody mocked our effort to go after the name players, especially Sellers. He was one of the best high school players in the country, on everybody's top five, and some had him number one. He would be chosen MVP of the Dapper Dan tournament in Pittsburgh. Nobody around Jersey believed we could get him to Rutgers. "You have to face reality," people said. "He'll never choose Rutgers over the heavyweights."

But I knew a couple of things. One, we had a minorities program at the Livingston College branch of Rutgers that was geared toward academic success without the student having to compete against the 1300-SAT-score geniuses. And two, I had become friends with Sellers.

Initially, Phil and I had met at Garf's Five-Star Camp. Then he came to a benefit game that I helped put together with some NBA All-Stars. That summer I told him I was going to recruit him for Rutgers. He looked at me, laughing, "Rutgers? What's a Rutgers?" He didn't know where the school was or anything about the place.

But I knew about *his* place. It was Thomas Jefferson High School in Brooklyn. Phil used to tell me, "Coach, you can't come to my house, not a white guy by himself. This is not a comfortable place." And he was right. But I came anyway. Sellers lived in a section where guys would sit on the outside stoops right next to piles of garbage. Sometimes the stoops would be piled with guys. One day I went up the elevator in his building and four fellows got on wearing shades, blasting those blast boxes and smelling of an all-night wine-tasting party. Whew! Did I do some fast talking? "Hey, dudes," I said. "You seen my man, Sellers? I come to get my man for some hoops."

All of a sudden right there in the elevator car these guys started with their fake-dribbles and switch-hand moves and their jumps and drives and body-checking, a mini-game in a box. "Hey, look at my jumper, man," they wailed. "Take me. Take me out of here, too."

Over at the school gym I was the only white face in the place and I could read the question on everybody's lips: Is this guy a coach or a narc? The young teenager sitting in front of me turned around. "If you're here to see Sellers, forget about it," he said. "If you want to see the real king, come over to Madison [High School] and check me out. I'm the Fly. Fly Williams." What a scorer he was, eventually leading the nation in scoring for the Governors at Austin Peay.

Sellers and I always used to walk by a place somewhere in the deepest part of Bedford-Stuyvesant called The Badass Club. Whenever I wanted to stop and check out the action Phil said, "Be cool, Coach. You don't want to *ever* go in there!" Phil told me that the baddest dancer in the Badass moved just like a close buddy of his who also played basketball. Phil said I should try and recruit this guy. "My buddy might want to come to Rutgers with me," he said.

"Who's your buddy?" I said.

"Lloyd Free," Phil said.

Now I ask you? You think Rutgers would have scored a few points with a trio of Phil Sellers, Fly Williams, and Lloyd Free? Forget about enough balls, you think there'd be enough rims and nets to go around?

Back in reality, I told Sellers I was going to follow him every step of the way, that Rutgers wanted very much for him to come. He was pretty skeptical. First he looked at my card, "Assistant coach?" he said. "*Assistant?* I've got head coaches coming by—McGuire, Phelps—and you guys I've never heard of send an assistant?" But he never completely brushed me off, so I started a campaign almost like a teenager with a crush on a girl. Writing. Showing up. Telephone calls. I ended every day with a phone call to Phil Sellers. What I had to do was convince him that he could be a marquee name even while playing at a low-profile school. Jim McMillian did it at Columbia. Julius Erving did it at Massachusetts. If a guy is that good and talented, he'll make it anywhere. I thought I had Phil convinced, until he broke my heart and announced he was going to Notre Dame.

Actually, the fact that we finished number two to the Irish didn't bother me that much. A great school, the image, the prestige—you're really up against it when you recruit against the Golden Dome. Down deep I felt that Phil would really rather stay closer to home and go to Rutgers, but the peer pressure was too great, the name Notre Dame too big to turn down.

One of the ironies of this whole thing was that one of Notre Dame's top alumni who helped recruit the New York metro area was Aubrey Lewis, who had been the first black football captain ever at South Bend. Lewis was from Jersey and helped Digger Phelps with Sellers. And Lewis was working for the Meadowlands, where the big boss was Sonny Werblin, a graduate of none other than Rutgers.

We had never used Werblin to recruit in basketball, but that didn't stop me. "I'm going to call Werblin for some help," I told Lloyd one day.

"We can't bother Sonny Werblin," Lloyd said. "We need clearance from upstairs."

So I got clearance. And I called up Sonny Werblin: "Hello, Mr. Werblin. This is Dick Vitale. You don't know me but I'm an assistant coach at Rutgers . . ."

Werblin broke me off right away. "Sure I know you," he said. "I've read your name in the papers. You're the guy going after the kid, Sellers. How are you doing?"

"We'd be doing a lot better if we had some help in terms of doing something legal and legitimate like getting the kid a job in the summer," I said. "Everybody's after him, but it looks like Notre Dame. And your man, Aubrey Lewis, is doing a great job in that direction."

As soon as we got on equal footing in the Meadowlands, I felt better. Sellers would later get a summer job in the office of the New Jersey state commissioner of banking in Trenton where he was playing in a big-time summer league and living with relatives. Werblin became heavily involved in the Rutgers program, and everything expanded from there.

Meanwhile, even though Rutgers was not a member signator of the National Letter of Intent rule, we honored and respected Sellers's decision and did not pursue him any further. However, I soon heard that the guidance people at Thomas Jefferson High were having second thoughts about Notre Dame. They felt the college had put Phil on hold academically, that Notre Dame wasn't sure he could handle the load there.

A short time later Phil called and asked me to meet with him after an All-Star game in New York. He said he sincerely did not want to go to college so far away, he was bothered by the potential academic problems at Notre Dame, and he felt more comfortable about our program at the Livingston campus. He said he had changed his mind and wanted to come to Rutgers.

I was sky-high when he said that. I was so excited I completely forgot that we only had money in the budget for five scholarships, and all five were already committed. Panic set in. Buttons had to be pushed. Luckily, a prominent alum named Herb Goodkind came to the rescue and promised the athletic department money for one more scholarship. Hallelujah! I could do my dance for real now.

All the ducks—or future Scarlet Knights—were in a row. The signing of Sellers climaxed an unbelievable crop for all of us in New Brunswick. We had already nabbed the marvelous Mike Dabney, the best player in Jersey, the kind of 6-5, 6-6 monster athlete Rutgers never got before. I thought Mike might go to Dayton or Southern Cal but after I challenged him for an answer one night in Joe Patti's restaurant right by the Rutgers campus ("I got to know now, Mike. We're going to get Sellers and the rest. But you'll be the pathfinder") we got him. A classy kid from a classy family in East Orange, New Jersey. In addition we had commitments from 6-8 Mike Palko out of Hackettstown, one of the best big kids in the state, and 6-8 Bruce Scherer from Parsippany. We also signed Jeff Kleinbaum, 6-2, from Martin Van Buren High School in Queens, who was coached by one of the best basketball minds and funniest men alive, Marv Kessler. Kleinbaum was a lefty, a high draft choice of the Mets, but he passed up baseball to play hoops for us.

Whether Sellers was attracted by this crew or whether our going after Sellers gave the others confidence that Rutgers was a program on the rise is a moot point. Players want to play with players. When we locked up a guard from Washington, D.C., 6-1 Ronnie Williams, who had been a sensation at Admiral Farragut prep school in south Jersey—actually flat stole him from the clutches of Penn and the Ivy League—we had the six players who would be the nucleus of a Rutgers team that four years later would go through an entire season undefeated on the way to the Final Four.

That, baby, is recruiting.

My entire first year at Rutgers centered around the recruiting rather than any coaching duties. But there was a downside to our success, and it showed the next season when Dick Lloyd started feeling the pressure of overwhelmingly high expectations for the team. By midseason we were on our way to 15 victories and an appearance in the NIT, and he was a wreck. The freshmen were playing like typical freshmen, up and down, yo-yoing all over the premises—Dow Jones city. Sellers had some good games, some bad. Dabney contributed plenty as well, but the task of mixing the veterans and rookies was a tough one. It was hard for the older guys to accept the new kids with all their notoriety and ink. The presence of Sellers alone brought a lot of pressure on everybody to do well.

In the midst of all this, Lorraine and I had purchased a new home in Franklin Township, our first house together, and we were very excited. Then, in February Dick suddenly an-

nounced he was resigning as head coach, effective at the end
of the season, and I didn't even know if I'd have a job to pay
for the house.

Even though I knew Lloyd would try his best to get the
administration to hire me as his successor, I never counted
on it happening. At the time Fred Gruninger was the new
athletic director, and it was obvious he wanted an established
name to coach all this developing talent. Every day I'd read
in the newspapers that coaches like Pete Carril of Princeton,
Frank McGuire of South Carolina, and George Raveling were
popping into the picture. Never me.

This hurt me deeply. I felt I was right there. I was ready.
I had done my time in the trenches of high school ball, at the
camps, in clinics, scouting, and recruiting. Recruiting? I had
been personally involved in all these kids coming to Rutgers
in the first place. I had won state championships in Jersey. I
could tie into all my contacts around the state. I deserved the
shot.

I went into Gruninger's office and told him I'd work for the
same assistant's salary I was making already. Just give me one
year. If I couldn't handle the heat, fire me out of the kitchen.

He had stacks of applications on the desk. I mean, *stacks*.
He asked how I was more qualified than anybody else on the
list. I told him he could read all the applications he wanted,
I had these kids' respect. The program was successful, we'd
just been to the NIT. I'd represent continuity. The alumni,
the players, the coach—everybody was in my corner. I just
couldn't make a dent. He never encouraged me to feel I had
any legitimate shot at all.

You can imagine how down and depressed I was. It was
early spring and I had made up my mind I absolutely would
not stay as an assistant to a new guy. If I hadn't earned my
way at Rutgers by now, I would make it my goal to be an
assistant elsewhere. I actually had it in mind that I could end
up at Chapel Hill, assisting Dean Smith. An opening on the
staff had just come up, and though I didn't fit the Tar Heel
image, I thought I might try for it. If I could sell Rutgers and

a bandbox 2500-seat gym I damn well knew I could get the job done at a big-time program.

Friends later told me that if I had just been a little more patient, I might have gotten the head coaching job at Rutgers. Today Gruninger and I are actually good friends, but back then I felt like I was backed against a wall so thick it would take a truck to knock it down. Or something else from the Motor City.

ROCKIN' IN MOTOWN

When I picked up the phone I thought it was a joke. The voice at the other end said he was Bob Calihan, the athletic director of the University of Detroit, and that he would like to fly me in to interview for the head coaching position at U of D. I thought one of my buddies was playing games with me.

Really, now. Why would Calihan be calling me? This was ridiculous. It had to be a gag. "Tell you what," I said to the caller. "You want me to pay my own flight and expenses?" (I was always suave on the finances.) No, he said, he would fly me into Detroit and pick up all the bills. I was so convinced this was a put-on, I called "Calihan" right back to verify that it was really him.

It was.

To this day I don't know what's true and what's not about how Detroit happened to add my name to the list of candidates for the coaching job there. I know I was getting a lot of favorable press in the New York area for the Rutgers job. Scarlet Knight players were helping me, and my friends in the NBA were talking me up. Willis Reed, whom I had befriended through charity games and clinics, was a big supporter of mine. Ultimately, I believe it was through Willis—and then through U of D's all-timer, Dave DeBusschere—that Detroit heard of me.

That spring the New York Knicks were on their way to another championship. I remember hanging around the locker room during the playoffs and Willis introducing me to all the guys. DeBusschere jokingly said his alma mater was looking for a coach and that I should apply. That's always stuck with me. DeBusschere still denies any involvement, but Calihan had been Dave's coach at Detroit and maybe he did call his old mentor.

I still don't know. But back then it really didn't matter. There I was, having landed in Detroit, psyched up, rarin' to interview at U of D, when I grabbed a taxi and started tooling downtown. I had never been in Detroit in my life. I opened one of the local papers, and saw an article in there that the coach at Grand Valley State, Tom Villemure, a former teammate of DeBusschere's, was about to be named the new head coach—at the University of Detroit.

Well, I was just about blown out of the water. I said, what am I doing here? I went for the interview anyway and it turned out to be a big, formal deal. Boardroom. Round table. The committee treatment. I had never been in anything like this before. Steve Wall, the dean of students, coordinated the whole thing. Peter Roddy, the dean of admissions, was there. Ken Elliott, a key alumnus. Calihan, of course. I came walking in with all this paraphernalia: letters to Sellers, articles about my recruiting, programs, pamphlets, a mound of organizational material on how I thought a basketball program should be run.

Anyway, I set all that aside, rose to speak and started in on a tear. "Gentlemen," I said. "I came out here . . . I don't even know why you guys flew me in . . . I read where the job is a lock for someone else . . . It's all over with"—They started laughing—"but I'm gonna tell you one thing. Rather than you interviewing me, I'm gonna tell you why I should be the next head coach at the University of Detroit. I'm probably not going to be, but I should be. And even if I'm not going to be, let me tell you why somebody in America is about to give me that chance."

From there on I was rolling, baby. Anybody who's heard me in coaching clinics knows I can flat-out talk. I mean, I can handle the case verbalizationwise. People think I just came out of the woodwork with this TV role and started stringing the words only when the red light came on. Let me tell you, this career was a long time in the works. Speaking was my gig long before TV was. And here in that Detroit boardroom in front of an audience of college administrators and with my future on the line, there was no stopping me.

When I was finished, Wall said, "If we want to name you coach right now, would you take the job?"

Now that floored me. They also asked me what salary I would need. I said fifteen thousand a year sounded great. They said fantastic, they had eighteen thou budgeted and I would save them three. (I thought they were joking.) This was all so mind-boggling, I said I would have to talk with my wife, get her out here, look over the situation. What the Detroit people were concerned about, as it turned out, was that I might be using U of D as leverage to enhance my position with Rutgers. They didn't know how disappointed I was back there and that the situation looked hopeless.

I was honest with Wall and the others. I told them I wanted the Rutgers job. I was from Jersey. I had lived there all my life. All my friends were there. If I had a choice, I would coach at Rutgers, but Rutgers hadn't offered me the job. "Make me an offer here," I said. "Let me make the tough decision."

Well, they didn't do it then, but I went home feeling good about the situation. Calihan had shown me around the facilities and I was impressed. Here was a large urban school, but unlike the Marquettes and DePauls and St. John'ses, which have to go into city-owned arenas to draw their big crowds, it had its own nine-thousand-chairback-seat facility right on campus. Still, I definitely wanted to stay at Rutgers. We had built the house. Lorraine was expecting again, this time Sherri. And it was not a good time to move away to a strange place.

No sooner did I get back to Jersey than Lorraine told me Steve Wall had phoned with a message to call U of D right away. When I did, he offered me the job on the spot. Multiyear contract, a few more thousand than what I asked for. (They weren't joking.) A car. Recruiting budget. The Big Time. "We want you here," said Wall. "We'd like you to fly out for a press conference tomorrow."

I explained to Wall I still had to tell Rutgers about this. I owed it to myself to see what they would do. Detroit understood everything; they just didn't want it out publicly that they had offered the job only to get turned down. I promised secrecy, and they gave me a few days. Then I started making calls.

Among others, I called Dick Lloyd, Garf, and Chuck Daly, who was then the head coach at Penn. They all gave me the same advice: Forget about Rutgers. Take the Detroit job. Daly was especially adamant: "Here is a place that wants you. It's a sure thing. The city is full of good players. You might be able to get it done there."

Still, I wavered. When I finally got another audience with Gruninger, I told him about the multiyear contract offer from Detroit and practically begged him to hire me. I said I'd take the same money for just one year. That's all I wanted, a chance to mess up. But the best he could do was promise an interview with the Rutgers search committee the following week.

I couldn't wait. I rolled the dice and started off to Detroit. Naturally, on the way to the airport, we ran out of gas on the New Jersey Turnpike and barely made the flight. On the airplane the only seats available were in the thirteenth row. All the signs said turn back and I broke down crying on the plane, wondering what in the world I was doing. But Lorraine convinced me to go for it.

So I was going to be a head man at last. It all happened so fast I was still a little stunned, but I was finally getting the respect I deserved. Or so I thought. I showed up at the Detroit Press Club for my first press conference as a head coach, and was greeted by Vince Doyle of WWJ Radio with the following: "Ladies and gentlemen, let's meet the dynamic new coach at the University of Detroit, Dick Vitooli." And then Al Ackerman of WXYZ-TV asked me, "Coach, how does it feel to be in a job where you don't belong? This job belongs to a black guy." Nice greetings from my new city. Welcome to the big time.

Detroit was not going to take a back seat to Michigan, Michigan State or anybody else while Vitale was on the watch. We won 17, 17, 19, and 25 games in my four years at the U of D, beating both the state schools and doing it with Michigan kids.

I knew that if we were going to have credibility, we had to take on the state schools and take it to them. In my first year, I got all geared up for Michigan, which was going to be our fourth game of the year. We loaded up with three cupcakes to start out the season. If you're listening, Bill Frieder at Michigan or Cliff Ellis at Clemson or John Thompson at Georgetown, recipients of my Pre-Conference Cupcake Awards, let it be known that Dick Vitale started his career at U of D with Hillside, Cleveland State (pre-Mouse McFadden) and St. John's of Minnesota.

The night we had Michigan coming into our fieldhouse, however, it was put-up-or-shut-up time. We made sure our players didn't see the maize and blue outfits and the leather bags and other classy stuff the Wolverines bopped in with. All the pro scouts were on hand to see Campy Russell of Michigan. They were ranked in the Top Ten. But we played man-to-man pressure down the court and then dropped into a 1-2-2 zone with our 6-8 Owen Wells on the point to discourage perimeter shooting. We matched up with Campy all over the place, shut him down, released Wells on breakaways in the opposite direction—he went for 38 big ones—and we won, 70–59.

The president of the U of D, Father Malcolm Carron, called me into his office the next day. What a terrific man. I was really thrilled. I called home and told my wife this was it: four games on the job and I was getting a new contract.

"Dick, we're all so happy," Father Carron said in his office. "The alumni are excited. The game is on the front pages. The campus is alive. You're doing such a great job I've decided to say five Hail Mary's and five Our Father's for you and your beautiful family every single night."

"Father, that's great," I said. "But I'm living in West Bloomfield with four mouths to feed on seventeen thousand. Our Father's won't get the job done. I need some Uncles. Some Uncle George Washingtons."

Well, at least I got a good story out of it.

We were doing some great things. But how can you top beating Michigan? I was hoping the season would end with that victory. From that point on the Wolverines wouldn't even schedule us anymore. Hey, people joke about schedules, but when you're an independent it's tough. If you're on the brink of being pretty good, the way we were, people won't give you a shot, won't even schedule you.

That first year we got out of the box like gangbusters. Three . . . Five . . . Seven . . . we were 10–1, along the way beating Minnesota at Minnesota and Michigan State with Terry Furlow and Lindsey Hairston. We finished 17–9 but we lost four of our last five, including Marquette at home. That probably killed us for an NCAA bid, that and getting blown away by Southern Illinois, 95–52. I don't even want to remember it. We didn't make the NIT, either.

What we did do that first year, however, was stir up interest. Let's face it: I wasn't hired because Detroit was losing games— the Titans were 16–10 under Jim Harding the year before. What the school was losing was fans. So we came in with a campaign and at my first team meeting I went into my whole routine about how we were going to win and how we were going to promote and market and sell, and that the goal was to walk into our UD Memorial Building and have the signs say SRO.

We redid all the facilities and pulled out all the promotional stops that season. We built locker rooms; established coaches' clinics; held "Days with the Titans" for the fans; printed flyers, leaflets, and posters with a fabulous picture of the two most famous U of D players: DeBusschere going one-on-one with Spencer Haywood. We got cars donated to the staff in the Titan colors of red and white from Bill Packer Pontiac—geez, I couldn't get away from that name even back then. And paint! We painted just about everything that didn't move. I tried to hire a painter but we didn't have any money, so I got the students to volunteer their time to come in and paint all the chair backs inside the area. It was beautiful. And then we remade the locker room into individual stalls. You would not believe our locker room. Each kid had his own area for locker and stool plus his name and picture and lights. There was plush carpeting, a stereo system and pool table, the works. I had to go directly to the alumni for the money to pay for new uniforms, billboards, a floor and a club room. I'll bet the Dean Smiths and Bob Knights never had to personally hit up alumni for the goodies needed to put on a first-class program.

We wanted spectacular teams to warrant our spectacular new look, and I vowed to go after all the great high school kids hard and heavy. I focused most of my attention on the local players, but Smokey Gaines, my assistant, successor, and prime-time recruiter—I called him "Mr. Ambassador"

in Detroit—went out hunting big game and got involved with
the kind of national recruits Detroit had never approached
before. I remember having Kenny Carr over to the house,
but he wound up at North Carolina State. We talked to Butch
Lee, but he went to Marquette. We even thought about Bill
(Poodles) Willoughby—remember him, the phenom out of
Englewood, New Jersey, who never played college ball and
hopped right to the NBA? He was from my old stomping
grounds. Smokey and I went to the young man's home, but
there was another fellow sitting there with his parents.

"I feel very comfortable telling you about the benefits of
Detroit, Mr. and Mrs. Willoughby," I said, "but I'm wondering who this gentleman sitting here is."

"Oh, just an advisor to the family," they said.

But Dick Vitale can smell an "agent" from several time
zones away, and I quickly bade farewell to Willoughby and
his family. I wasn't about to put Detroit in the NCAA doghouse, no matter how great Poodles might have been.

Speaking of high school–to–pro prodigies, how about Moses
Malone? Smokey insisted he could crack Malone, that he
could get him to Detroit.

Hey, we had a lot to sell—especially for the black athlete.
There was no football at U of D, so basketball was king. We
had the Pistons and all the other big-time pro sports. Great
media coverage. The corporate world of the auto industry was
right there. The airport is easy to get in and out of. Our game
was dominated by inner-city kids. For any black guy who
ultimately wants to make his life and career in a city, Detroit
is a great town. Mayor Coleman Young is black. So is the
superintendent of schools and the police chief. Other key
positions are also controlled by blacks.

Anyway, Moses had a great visit in Detroit. He was so
impressed that I was invited to speak in his hometown of
Petersburg, Virginia, when they retired his uniform at a cel-
ebration in a public park there. Gaines had arranged all of
this, of course. Smokey was a hero in Petersburg by then;
everybody in town knew him.

So I went out to the park and got to talk with Moses for a few minutes before the ceremonies. Then we hit one of the hot spots in town, a huge, barnlike club called the Mousetrap, where we danced the evening away. When I cut an incredibly mean rug with Moses's mom, Mary, the crowd went wild. But soon it got down to prime time, the time to leave the Mousetrap and to meet Moses at his house, where we had planned to lay all the Detroit recruiting cards on the table.

Moses lived in a tiny little shack outside town with holes for windows and a pot-bellied stove. Smokey had developed a secret code with Moses because Big Mo had gotten so tired of all the recruiting and publicity and hype. He probably did this with other coaches, too, but with Smokey the code was two-one-two: Two knocks, then one, then two again. That let Moses know it was Smokey.

I thought this was the wildest thing going, until we arrived at the shack and tried the code again and again and again. Nobody answered. It was obvious Moses wasn't home. And, boy, was I ticked.

"Gaines," I told Smokey, "I can't believe this. I've had it with you. We fly all this way, kill all this time and spend money we haven't got from our recruiting budget, and I don't even get to talk to the guy."

"We aren't leaving yet, Dick," Smokey said. "Our plane's at 8:00 A.M. tomorrow and we'll wait him out."

Which is exactly what we did. Outside on the street. In our rental car. We worked shifts: I would sleep and Smokey would stay awake to watch for Moses coming in, then we'd reverse roles. In the middle of the night these huge dogs began to gather. German shepherds, police dogs, humongous, vicious creatures. They began to bark and then they started jumping all over the car. I was terrified. Finally, about four in the morning—the dogs had exhausted themselves by now—here came Moses.

Smokey jumped out of the car. "Big Mo, where you been, baby?" he said.

Right there on the street, in the middle of the night, Moses

Malone told us he was fed up with all the attention and he was going to Maryland. We thanked him for his honesty and his interest in Detroit. I told him he had really helped the school by keeping us in his top three or four schools and giving us all that ink. I also remember one other thing Moses said. I'll always remember this. He said, "Coach, someday I'm going to get my mama a house where the rich people live."

Several years later, Smokey was invited to Moses' wedding. By that time, of course, Big Mo *was* the rich people. And he didn't forget his mama—she lives in a palace.

Another one that got away was a terrific hotshot guard, a Michigan all-stater out of Saginaw named Tony Smith, who ended up starring at UNLV. I was sure we had him locked up when I went to his house for one last visit, but still you're never secure until the paper's signed, and so I was giving him one last sales pitch, and Tony was acting really down for some reason. Finally, he said to me, "Coach, I'm sorry to say . . . "

"Sorry to say what, Tony?"

"I think I'm going to Houston."

Just one of your everyday recruiting losses, but I didn't get the punchline on this one until ten years later. Flash forward to the spring of 1988. I'm sitting around a table with Sonny Vacarro from Nike, Freddie Barrakat, the ACC director of officials, a couple of other coaches and little Ray Jones, a guy about five-foot-nothing, a recruiting fanatic who's worked at Minnesota, South Carolina, Duke, LaSalle, Houston, and is now with Wyoming. Somehow Tony Smith's name comes up, and Jones starts looking at me and laughing. I asked him what he was laughing about, and then he told me that the whole time I was getting the goodbye speech from Smith and giving him my spiel, *Jones was upstairs in the kid's bedroom, hiding under the bed!* (I've had some recruits, too, who made me want to find a bed and hide under it, but usually not until after they started practicing for me.)

Of the recruits we did get to come to Detroit, I guess Tyler and Long—"Thunder and Lightning" we called them—made the most impact. John Long from suburban Romulus, Michigan, was all-state, a great shooter, a real thoroughbred who would later be drafted by the Pistons—by me, actually—against a lot of expert opinion and turn in a ten-year career in the NBA. Terry Tyler was simply a tremendous shot-blocking monster. Jim Boyce, another of my assistants, had coached him at Northwestern High School in Detroit, giving us a big edge. There was no doubt he'd come to U of D. Until . . .

"Mr. Vitale," Terry's dad said to me one day, "Terrence wants to come with you. But before you sign him, Mr. McGuire would like to talk to us."

"Mr. McGui-ah?" I said, scared out of my mind. "Wait a minute. That's wonderful. Let him come and talk, eat here, whatever. But let me sign Terry *first,* then you talk to Mr. McGui-ah."

"No, no. We'll just talk to him first, then get back to you. Don't worry," said Mr. Tyler.

Here's how much I didn't worry: Terry's house was about ten minutes from our campus. The day Al came to talk, I spotted his car and drove around Tyler's block with Smokey time after time after time to see if Mr. McGui-ah was still parked outside. An hour, two hours went by. "What the hell's going on, Smoke?" I said as I kept driving around and around the block. I'd probably still be driving if Gaines hadn't gotten me to relax and insisted we get back to school.

Six months later I saw Al at a clinic somewhere and, to show what a class act he is, he came up and congratulated me for signing Tyler. Then, to show what a one-upsman act he is, he also had to say this: "Oh, by the way, Dick, congratulate me back. We signed Butch Lee."

The University of Michigan didn't take such a cordial attitude toward our new recruiting efforts at Detroit. The truth is, Johnny Orr, the coach at Ann Arbor at the time, and his staff were taking a lot of heat from the Michigan alums about Vitale getting all these name local kids. We had Tyler locked up and we were about to sign Long as well; the Wolverines were getting shut out on the two best kids in the state.

So the Michigan people denied they were even recruiting

Long; they said he couldn't get into their school. Now I'll admit the kid was a borderline case academically. He was also shy, and wasn't the easiest kid in the world to reach. But John turned out to be a gregarious, loving person, and college was the thing that turned life around for him.

But for Michigan to deny they were after him was a joke. Worse, it was a lie. I know; I was in his home when the Michigan recruiters were calling him on the phone. I saw the letters written by Orr to Long. And I got so upset over the whole thing I went public with this information, saying, "If anybody wants to see one hundred letters from the Michigan people to John Long, I'll show them. If they aren't recruiting him, then Orr is wasting valuable taxpayers' money for a lot of postage on the kid."

If Michigan was going to come on like Goliath, you can bet I was going to play that David role to the hilt. We were the little guys trying to compete with the big state school, and if they wouldn't play us on the court, I was sure going to play up our victories in the recruiting wars.

When you're the new kid on the block, nobody wants to give you credit. So it was either our cheating or their academic standards being too high for these players. Well, that was bull-youknowwhat. We were hustling and building a program that was ready to kick some butt.

The thing I loved about college coaching over the job at any other level was the control I had. Both in high school and in the pros you have to coddle your players a lot more; you're at their mercy because you can't control who attends your high school—usually—and even if you can get rid of a player in the pros, you don't have that much say in what you'll get in return. In college you can recruit to meet your needs; if I didn't like my backcourt, the next year I could go out and get two or three guards I did like.

And I was one tough disciplinarian in college. I remember one time we were playing Wayne State, a local school, a rival but not really in our class hoopswise. We weren't getting the big effort, so I came in the locker room at halftime breathing fire. Back then our players' pictures were on the walls, and I just took all those pictures and started slamming them around the room. I think I broke every one of them. It was a wild scene. *And we had a big lead at the time!*

Well, that's what a wacko I was. I went after my college kids. Long will tell you. Tyler will, too. My second year at U of D we had a team meeting scheduled for 3:15. I always operated on Lombardi time, of course. If I called a meeting at 3:15, you better be there at 3:00. That was my philosophy. Learn punctuality. Learn how to respect discipline. I didn't expect any problems with that on the college level. I told my coaches nobody gets into this first meeting after 3:15. The door closes. Nobody. We started the meeting at 3:15. It was the first meeting Long—the big local star—was supposed to attend as a college player. So we started the meeting and the door opened and here he came sauntering in like nothing happened.

"Where are you going?" I said.

"To the team meeting," he said.

"The team meeting has already started," I said. "Get your ass outside and call me tonight."

To make up for being late, Long had to come in at six the next morning and run two miles. He did this a few times before he smartened up and got the message.

Then there were the kids from another planet. Like Ron Bostick from my first recruiting class . . . now there was a piece of work. Same high school as Long, ironically. A real Rip Van Winkle prospect. Suspect hands. And I wasn't too sure about his attitude either, though he did end up going the distance in school and getting his diploma. Once I was in the middle of one of my major rips; I was ticked off that one or two guys weren't going to class, and I was really jumping in their faces. Suddenly Bostick raised his hand. "Hey, Coach," he said, "Where did you get that yellow tie?"

Yeah, I loved every single, crazy minute of coaching college ball and every single crazie in it. I still believe the one really big mistake I made in coaching was leaving the college ranks.

I should have stayed at the University of Detroit. I belonged in college and I would have been better off if I had remained at U of D, had a little more success and then maybe the call would have come from a prime-time program like it did for Valvano at N.C. State or for Gene Keady at Purdue or for Bobby Cremins at Georgia Tech.

But I never coached in a situation where I had the surf and turf and carte blanche stuff available. At East Rutherford we didn't even have a home court. At Rutgers we played in an isolated band box, not one of your spectacular showcase arenas. I went to Detroit and, let's face it, it wasn't North Carolina or Kentucky or Indiana.

The people poured out their hearts to me and the university was beautiful and I loved it. But I never coached on national TV; I was too early for cable. Even when we played Michigan in the NCAAs my last season, when John Wooden broadcast the game with Curt Gowdy, it was just an NCAA regional telecast, a local game, no big national deal. And then when I went to the Pistons, they were in a terrible down cycle.

So I was never part of the upper crust, the high-tone establishment winners in the sport. I never had the big bucks. I was always going after the Rolls-Roycers with a Volkswagen budget. It caused me problems with the administration at Detroit—they held it against me that I spent more than I had—but I always believed that if you want to build for the big time, you've got to let the kids go first cabin.

At Detroit I was building a good record, fan interest, excitement, enthusiasm. And in terms of charisma in the Midwest . . . well, McGuire would be stepping down at Marquette, so maybe I would have had the center stage. But this is all hindsight.

What happened at the same time was that my old stomach problems were resurfacing. After my second year at U of D, I went to visit my family in Jersey during the summer and I started bleeding like a pig—blood out of my nose, my rectum, everywhere. They rushed me to the hospital and it was just in time because I lost six pints of blood. My hemoglobin count was way down, it was a bleeding ulcer and I was scared.

We kept all this very quiet because I didn't want it to hurt Detroit's recruiting—we had signed Terry Duerod but that wouldn't have prevented other coaches from breaking and entering. I was nervous as hell. If the recruiting sharks found out about this, I was through. So I was doing stuff from my hospital bed with my assistants on the phone back in Detroit: Do this, guys. Do that. Tell everybody I'm just visiting my family. I think some of the local Detroit writers knew about this but it was kept kind of quiet. Fortunately my recovery was quick and complete, but the memory of the ordeal lingered. I knew we were building a monster and in 1976–77 it all came together as the Titans went 25–4; Long, Tyler, Duerod and company finally led us to the NCAA tournament. The season was magic. As a matter of fact, Magic Johnson himself, a high school senior at the time, was in the audience for our first big win: at Michigan State, even though his future buddy Greg Kelser had a huge night against us.

We were really excited about the season. We had been blown out early in our second game by Minnesota's Who's Who of college stars—Mychal Thompson and Ray Williams with Kevin McHale off the bench—but then we came home to face an Arizona squad that had beaten us by 30 points the year before. This was that terrific team of Detroit-area kids coached by Freddy (the Fox) Snowden, an old Detroit guy himself. He took no mercy down in Tucson the year before, and he really thought he would smash us again in the return engagement.

The night before the game they had an unbelievable banquet in Detroit in honor of the Fox, like they were celebrating another victory already. But we needed the upset if we were going to make any impact on the national scene. And we got it when Dennis Boyd hit one of his clutch jumpers at the end. We were so excited the players threw me to the floor in the locker room and we rolled around on the carpet in there, my glasses flying off and everything. We knew it was the beginning of something big.

Try a twenty-one-game winning streak. Included in that run was a victory at Dayton where I did my first dance—Joe Namath–style, I had guaranteed I would dance at center court if we beat the Flyers—and became known as "Disco Dick."

Then there was that other small victory at Marquette.

You remember that Marquette team: Butch Lee, Bo Ellis, Jerome Whitehead, Bernard Toone. A month later the Warriors would win the national championship. But this night they were second best.

I've got to go back to two years before, when I had last coached in the Milwaukee Arena against Marquette. Against the god, McGui-ah. It was Intimidation City. The home team was trapping and pressing and banging our guys into submission. I mean, it was a Forty-second Street mugging and I was all over the officials from the beginning. "Hey! You don't have to let them get away with this. They're good enough already," I screamed. "Hey! Make it respectable." I went on and on, I kicked my chair, and I got bounced from the game before halftime. I was livid. On my way out, I ripped off my coat and tie and threw it at the ref. "You been choking all night, baby. Choke on this!"

Al McGuire, with his great compassion, came over, put his arm around me and uttered those immortal words: "Take it easy. It's only a game."

Hah!

Now two years later we were back, riding our own win streak this time. And it was a war. Twelve seconds left on the clock, we're down by a point. Marquette's in the half-court spread offense and Butch Lee has the ball. We go to a half-court trap, pop the ball loose, and Boyd takes off the other way. While I'm jumping up and down, screaming and signaling for a time-out so I can devise a genius play to get us the W, Boyd shakes and bakes, jukes and jives, and throws one up as the buzzer sounds. The ball goes in the basket, Detroit wins, and Vitale goes . . . absolutely . . . stark . . . raving . . .

mad. But on the run out, I didn't forget one thing. No sir. On my way racing past a stunned Marquette team and a shocked McGuire, I bellowed: "Al, Babeeeee, Only A Gaaaaaame!"

Later that night I rescinded all curfews for the team and we stayed up till dawn celebrating. Of course, in our next game, at Duquesne, we got beat in overtime, a game that stands out in my mind for three reasons: It ended our twenty-one game winning streak; it was "Norm Nixon Night" at the school and Norm was sensational; and it was the worst homer job in the history of organized basketball. I didn't get thrown out by the refs this time, but my assistants had to drag me back to the dressing room after I got into a screaming match with some Pittsburgh fans.

The NCAA couldn't deny us a tournament bid this time, and after we beat Middle Tennessee in the first round down at Baton Rouge, we had what we had been desperately seeking for three years: another game against Michigan. The fact that the Wolverines, with Ricky Green, Phil Hubbard, Steve Grote, et al., were ranked number one was just icing on the cake. We knew we could beat them. For a week I hyped the contest like it was World War III. Which it was.

I called Orr Muhammad Ali and myself Chuck Wepner. I said we'd take our pounding and our cuts and scratches and come back for more, just like the Bayonne Bleeder. I said they were the majestic maize and blue, and we were just the little city kids trying to make a score. The papers said I was really getting under Orr's skin, but I was just having some fun. When I came out for the game dressed in a maize and blue outfit and ran over to shake Johnny's hand on the court in Lexington, Kentucky, the crowd went into a frenzy.

The closeness of the game, the nip-and-tuck intensity, the emotion and setting and stakes involved, everything combined to make this event into one of the truly marvelous sporting engagements of my life. And I would have appreciated it even more if we had won. As it was, Hubbard had a great game inside for Michigan. This was one game where Kevin Kaseta, who didn't play for us basically all year because of injury, could have been a tremendous help. We lost 86–81, but a shot either way could have meant the ball game. And the best thing about it was afterward, when all the players hugged and showed such great class and sportsmanship.

I tell you, the game was great for the city of Detroit, for the state of Michigan, for all basketball. I'll always believe, too, that we set the Wolverines up for their grand fall in the next round to UNC-Charlotte. Emotionally, I think our game cost them that Mideast Regional title and with it probably the national championship that Marquette won over North Carolina in Atlanta a week later. I think Michigan was the best team in the nation that year and we weren't far behind.

Seriously now, wouldn't you like to have seen—and heard—me at those Final Four press conferences? Baby, they wouldn't have had enough typesetters to get my stuff out that week.

Ironically enough, I didn't know it at the time but not only was I out of the tournament with that loss, I was out of coaching as well.

Before the next season I was in my lawyer's office one day when I started having pains again. After about a week I still didn't feel well. It was the same kind of ache and pain that had preceded my major bleeds of the past. By this time I had been named athletic director at U of D as well as coach. The boosters had given me a brand-new Lincoln and a trip to Florida. I was making some extra change from the Bob Lanier—Dick Vitale summer basketball camp. We were returning a powerful team and a potential national contender. I was in the best professional shape of my life.

But physically I was tearing myself up inside. The doctors said I had lost so much blood during my other traumatic attacks that if I had another I'd probably have to have my stomach removed. I had a lovely wife and two daughters, five and seven years old, who needed me around. Why take such a risk? Plus, I knew if I got out now, right before the start of the season, the job would have to go to Smokey Gaines, who deserved it. And I would be leaving Smokey with a mother lode of talent. I decided to resign my position as coach and remain solely as the AD at Detroit.

The good news about the following year was that Smokey went 23–4 with the Titans. The bad news was that we missed out on an NCAA bid again. I couldn't believe it; I was back to the old feisty, bitching, moaning Vitale again. I was feeling so perfectly healthy, in fact, that . . . well, this will show you how deeply coaching was ingrained in my soul.

One night I was sitting in the stands as we played Harvard in the Motor City Classic. We were behind by about 10 points and playing awful. It was a joke. So I went to the locker room at halftime. I never should have, but Smokey asked me to talk to the team. I should have known better, but there I went. And it was like the Vitale of old. In short, I went nuts. Totally wacko. I jumped all over the players. No heart. No guts. No pride. I didn't tear any pictures down this time, but I think I must have screamed a few obscenities. "I don't want anything more to do with you quitters!" The routine stuff. And I stalked out.

In the second half I was in the stands playing the crowd like an orchestra, too: shouting, waving, getting them to stand up, to clap, to cheer the Titans to victory. There are pictures of this. I was a maniac. The crowd went nuts. The team took off and just blew Harvard out of the place.

The next night in the finals U of D blew away Eastern Michigan. The losing coach that night was Ray Scott, who a couple of seasons earlier had been the NBA Coach of the Year for the Detroit Pistons. From the pinnacle to the pits in a couple of easy steps. You'd think I would have learned. You'd think I could read an omen. You'd be wrong.

THE CONS OF THE PROS

Deep down inside, I was never happy in an administrative position, pushing the pencils and papers, stacking the paper clips. Are you kidding me? Can you imagine me doing that for the rest of my life? With only secretaries to talk to? Gimme a break.

Looking back, getting out of coaching was a panic move on my part. My ulcer attack, the bleeding, had scared me to death. I was hearing all about stomach cancer and the like. Certainly, I realized a long time before this that I had resigned too quickly. But after I regained full health and the doctors cleared me of any serious difficulties, I really wanted to get back to the action.

The irony was that a national spotlight had become available right at my doorstep: When the Detroit Pistons fired Herb Brown as coach in the middle of the season and gave the job to GM Bob Kaufman on an interim basis, it was obvious where my next challenge might lie.

I mean, just imagine! I was the kid who grew up with the coda "A boy, a ball, a dream." I used to stand outside Madison Square Garden in awe as the Knick players and coaches walked in and out: the Harry Gallatins, the Joe Lapchicks, the McGuires. The NBA! Broadway. Showtime. The big time. The University of Detroit people didn't understand when I started letting hints drop that I would be interested in getting back into coaching with the Pistons—professionally, they couldn't comprehend that I would be willing to subject my body to the stress and travel of the pros. They had some hard feelings about it, too. But given my background and my dreams, there was nothing physically that could stop me from going after a job at the highest level of the profession. A job in the NBA.

My chances? Hey, remember, I had become a little bit of a cult figure in Motown. I knew I could communicate with the modern athlete. I had a close relationship with Bob Lanier, the Piston star, from the camp that we ran together in the summer. The one thing the Pistons needed was what I could best provide: Enthusiasm. Color. Energy. I knew I could create some excitement about the team, and when it became obvious I was a candidate, I became the people's choice. Everywhere I went, into restaurants and out shopping and to the movies, people came up and encouraged me to go for it: "Dick, we want you to coach the Pistons."

I had preliminary discussions with Kaufman, and I knew that Herb Tyner, a minority partner in the Pistons' ownership, was pushing hard for me. But my big chance occurred on a cold, icy, snowy day when Bill Davidson, the majority owner,

called to ask me to a meeting at the Maple House in Far-
mington.

You talk about exhilarating! There was a blizzard outside,
the schools were closed, the roads were nearly impassable.
But the guy wanted to talk to me! I would have cleared our
driveway on my hands and knees to get to that meeting. As
it was, Lorraine and I shoveled our driveway as if we were
digging out from under an avalanche, and then I started creep-
ing across the white wasteland to my destiny.

If this sounds dramatic, understand how much I hated driving in winter weather. I once had a major accident in Detroit,
spinning 360 degrees off Highway 10, hitting a concrete abut-
ment and totaling a U of D official school car. Film at 11:00,
pictures all over the newspapers. Joe Falls, the renowned
Detroit columnist, wrote, "My man, Dick. He'd do anything
for publicity."

But seriously, folks.

This was a treacherous journey for a job interview. And
when Davidson and I talked, all he seemed to be concerned
about was how I would handle the referees. It was a great
meeting even though nothing was offered, but it drove me
crazy that Davidson had stressed the coach-officials relationship so much. Could it have been because I was a certified
wildman on the sidelines? That he was afraid I'd humiliate
him with my wackiness on the bench? That I made most of
these zanies coaching today look like bankers? That once I
had taken my tie off and threatened to strangle a referee?

I shouldn't have worried. A few weeks later—the snow
having finally melted—Kaufman called, and at a subsequent
meeting they offered me the job in a three-year package at
about a hundred grand a year. Don't whisper this to a soul,
but I would have jumped at the job for about a third of that.

Right here I want to point out the neat irony in Dick Vitale
finally making it in the media after all those years of the media
making Dick Vitale. Yeah, quoting me, helping me, rooting
for me. In all honesty, the media was probably most responsible for my getting the coaching job with the Pistons. It was

1

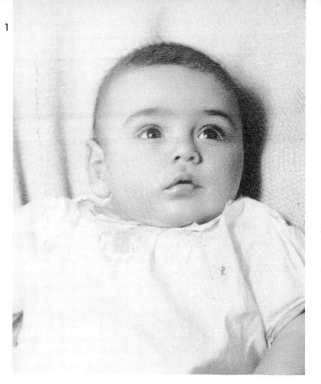

The apple of John and
Mae Vitale's eye. Of
course, I hadn't learned
to talk yet.

Christmas morning,
1944. Believe me, the
pants-under-the-armpits
look was *very* stylish at
the time.

3

My high school yearbook picture.
I told you I used to have hair!

2

Meeting the press in Lexington
after my Detroit team fell to top-
ranked Michigan in the 1977
NCAAs. I still think our battle may
have cost them the national title.

4

6

Dancing at midcourt with a couple of my friends after we beat Al McGuire at Marquette—no wonder they called me Disco Dick.

An intimate wedding portrait: just me, Lorraine, and my sixth-grade class from Franklin Elementary.

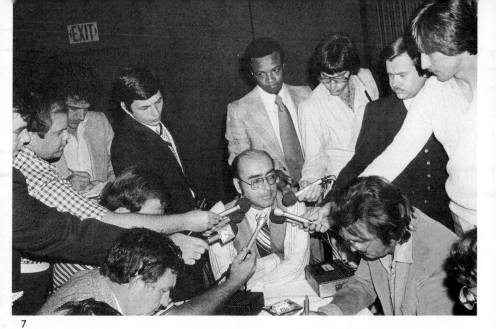

The Detroit press corps crowds around me in my days with the Pistons. I like it a lot better on the other side of the microphone.

Rockin' on the side-lines—I was always a ranter and a pacer. I made Bobby Knight look like Mother Teresa.

9

I probably owe more to Jim Simpson than to anyone else in broadcasting. He's a complete pro, and his patience with me was a godsend.

No, that's not me in the '88 Kansas victory parade, just a couple of imitators dogging Larry Brown (seated), in the days before Larry swept himself out of town.

10

Backstage with the General: Bob Knight gives me the benefit of his experience before Indiana's shocking defeat at Northwestern in 1988.

11

Dicky V and Jimmy Vee—as usual, we've both got our mouths roaring.   12

A summit meeting in the studio, as Bob Ley hosts basketball's answer
to the Three Musketeers—or is it Stooges? From left, me, Al McGuire,
Billy Packer, and Ley.

13

The Vitale family, 1988: clockwise, it's Lorraine, Terri, Theo, Sherri, and one very lucky ex-coach.

14

Here I am hanging around at the Austin Peay banquet. The players really flipped after I promised to stand on my head if they beat Illinois in the 1987 NCAAs.

15

My favorite spot—here I'm at Duke, but it could be anywhere there's a college, a crowd, and a little game of hoops.

a real campaign all over Detroit, and I know that the attention was key; the Pistons needed someone with a flair for pro-motion.

It's hard to believe looking back, but I was really supposed to be a big hero for the Pistons. You should have seen the opening press conference. Billboards. Fireworks at the Sil-verdome. "Vital-Ize The Pistons." "Re-Vitalize." We put on clinics and gave speeches and did shopping-center openings. I used to go around to restaurants in the Detroit area and hand out tee shirts and throw souvenir basketballs to people. "Come out and watch the Pistons." I don't know how many times I screamed that phrase. I just loved to meet the people. I would get so emotional, I'd cry about the Pistons.

We had videotapes and Q-and-A sessions for kids at malls. We set up baskets and shot free throws and challenged people as they walked around to support the Pistons. Boy, was this my strength. I loved being interviewed, appearing on radio and TV, selling tickets, coordinating the whole promotional deal. Plus I was finally going to get to coach in the NBA.

Even before my first Piston training camp I had the ex-traordinary feeling of ecstasy. *I was coaching in the pros.* Vacationing again down at Wildwood on the Jersey shore, I took a week's break from all the buildup in Detroit and had what felt like the greatest joyride of my life. Walking around with my friends, speaking at a few clinics, my wife and daugh-ters with me—I was a man satisfied with life, on a high with the universe.

Then back to Detroit, where the press was banging out articles that said, "Vitale is the guy for the job," and "Vitale can change things." And I started to believe I could come in and actually be a savior. I used to do everything on emotion, and before that first season even started I fell into the trap of changing the makeup of the Piston team with a move totally based on an emotional reaction.

When I first got the Detroit job I heard a lot about Eric Money, the young Piston guard from the streets of Motown who'd played at Arizona for Freddy Snowden. The word around the league on Money was "trouble." He was a problem to handle, quick mouth, nasty, no discipline. I made up my mind ahead of time that the first time he opened his yap to me about anything I would jump in his face. So I called a luncheon in the Silverdome to set the tone.

There I was with my assisstants, Richie Adubato and Wil Robinson, and Money. I presented him with my philosophy and expectations, and I just didn't like the way he reacted. I mean, I was really burned up because this kid was not taking to what I was saying at all. Looking back, this was probably ·a big mistake on my part. I didn't give him a fair shot. But right then I got up from the table and told Money, "I don't like your response. I don't like the way you act. I'm going to trade your ass."

I turned around, walked out, went upstairs to the office and got on the phone to New Jersey. We made a deal late that summer to bring in Kevin Porter and to ship Money to Jersey. The Nets were upset with Porter and I knew he wanted to come back to Detroit, where he had played his best years.

Obviously, I was showing how tough a guy I could be by dealing Money that way. I was taking over, assuming command. And it was very immature, because I never gave the kid a fair shot.

Of course, nobody should have expected me to come into the NBA on my tippytoes. But it didn't take long for me to get my feet so thoroughly wet I nearly drowned. Things looked so terrific at first; it took much longer for me to realize that coaching in the pros was a horrible mistake.

We had such a great training camp that first year, 1978–79. We lined up with Lanier, John Shumate and M. L. Carr on the front line, Porter and my captain, Chris Ford, in the backcourt. Leon Douglas and my two local University of Detroit kids, Long and Tyler, were coming off the bench. It looked like we had a nice team, a nice attitude. To this day M.L. tells everybody it was the toughest training camp he ever went to.

And man, was I psyched the whole time! I'll never forget

my first day. I was so nervous right before my first speech to
the players. All the owners were there and I was juiced up,
flying. I told Adubato, "I'm going to lay down the law like
it's never been laid down before. They think I'm this fun-
loving, fast-talking happiness guy. Wait till they get a load of
my notebook."

I had this thick notebook that I passed out on the first day
with plays, rules, goals, dreams if you will. I'll never forget
that notebook. Guys used to ask me, "Why don't you sell the
book? Tape the stuff in here. Copy the speeches. Make them
available for motivational seminars."

Then I realized who the guys were I was talking about. Bob
Lanier, an all-pro center, a legend in Detroit. John Shumate,
whom I had watched play at Notre Dame against Bill Walton.
M. L. Carr, a wily vet who would become a celebrity at the
end of his career. Chris Ford, the established captain. All
these big names. I started sweating my socks off. But I went
in and gave one of the most emotional speeches of my life,
all about pride and the sense of mission we were going to
develop with the Pistons. I talked about Shumate's magic at
South Bend. I challenged Lanier on the fact that people said
he wasn't a big winner. "What's going to stop us from bringing
enthusiasm, desire, character, all these elements that have
made you great players in the past at all the levels to your
game in the pros?" I asked them. "It was your work ethic
that got you here in the first place. And it's that same work
ethic that we'll need to climb to the mountaintop."

Afterward, I felt like a million dollars because I had really
reached these guys. They all came up to me and said they
were raring to go.

Maybe I was naive, but I really thought that we had a chance
to make a mark in the NBA. I thought we would be together;
I liked our camaraderie. I thought there was mutual respect.
I firmly believed all the parts were there.

In Porter, the Pistons had a point guard who was willing to
give the ball up because he knew that was his role. We had
a power forward in Shumate who could score around the boxes

and do some serious damage inside, get us 16–17 points and 10 rebounds a night. We had a superstar in the middle in Lanier. I've always believed basketball efficiency starts offensively and defensively in the lane; if you're solid down there, you've got a chance to win every night.

Chris Ford was a winner, a guy who would do anything to get the W. Our bench was young and capable of great things— Tyler and Long and Leon Douglas spelling Lanier. Then we had Carr, who would eat the basketball if a coach asked him to. He personified the intangibles—play the minutes, do the dirty work, grind it out on the glass, take the charge, practice like you wouldn't believe. M.L. had the great work ethic, and optimistic? He was basketball's Ernie Banks. Didn't Ernie come to the park each day and say, "Let's play two"? Some of my guys would be bitching about practicing for two sessions a day, and M.L. would say, "You guys should try life in the CBA. Two sessions? Two? Let's have three! Let's go for the triple!"

I actually thought that with this cast we could win 41 games and break even. With that record I would have been a hero in the city. I knew we would break all the attendance records anyway. I had done that wherever I'd coached.

Everyone responded well and we were 4–2 in the exhibition season, with our two losses coming when Lanier didn't play a minute. We came into Madison Square Garden in New York and everybody wrote that the Pistons were heading in the right direction.

Then all of a sudden the team just dissipated. Shumate developed a serious blood clot right before the season started. We were told he'd be out for the year, and there was some question as to whether he'd ever be able to play again. Lanier went down soon after that with knee surgery. We were just wiped out. Finished.

Let me say this about the Dobber. Bob Lanier and I have had our ups and downs throughout the years, but I never had a bigger supporter in what I was trying to do as a coach than

Bob-A-Dob. He gives you the big tough-guy stare, that mean look. But he's just a softie inside.

The first time I met Bob was years ago when I worked the Jack Kraft basketball camp in the Poconos in Pennsylvania. He was a big college star at St. Bonaventure at the time. He was, a counselor at the camp and all the little kids looked up to him. Even to us high school coaches just starting out, he was a celebrity. But he was just like a little teddy bear, too. He was always running around having water fights, stripping beds, playing pranks, going bananas. He was supposed to be leading the kids, but there he was, in the middle of all the chaos.

I only met him briefly there. But when I got the U of D job, Smokey Gaines brought Bob around to the office and we started rapping and spending a lot of time together. For some reason we seemed to hit it off and we decided to form our own summer basketball camp together.

The first year we had the camp a problem cropped up. Lorraine was doing all the paperwork, typing letters and sending out materials. There was a lot to do, of course, but the Dobber thought you merely showed up and the kids came because your names were on the camp. It doesn't work that way. There's a lot of other camps out there working their buns off.

At first I didn't say anything to Bob. I wasn't coaching him yet and I didn't know him that well. But on the first day of camp I was there bright and early at 8:00 A.M. It was a day camp. We were signing all the kids up, registering them with medical forms and all. I wanted to do everything professionally. We had a great staff of coaches to work with. But at 8:00 there was no Lanier. 8:30—no Lanier. 9:00—no Bob-A-Dob. 9:30—Bob Lanier was nowhere to be found. Now I was hot. The camp was going on and I had parents all around looking and wondering where Lanier was. About 10:00 here came the big fella strolling into the gym with his shades and his cool look like, "What's happening, everybody?"

Well, the first chance I got I took Bob aside and told him right then and there, "Let's get one thing straight. The billing says Bob Lanier and Dick Vitale. It doesn't say Dick Vitale. If you want to run the Bob Lanier camp, that's cool. I'll run the Dick Vitale camp. But as long as our names are together, if I come here at eight o'clock in the morning, you're going to be here at eight, too. We're doing this for the kids. They've paid the money and we owe it to them. If you can't deal with that, let's find out right now."

Enough said. Our camp went on for seven years and I think the Dobber missed one day. And that was because he was president of the NBA Players' Association and he skipped a session to be at one of their meetings.

It was beautiful to see the big guy get so involved with the kids in their drills. Bob also brought to the camp a bunch of his friends from other pro sports. Jim Rice of the Red Sox, Roy White of the Yankees, Mark (the Bird) Fidrych of the Tigers. The baseball players would come into Detroit for a series and when there was nothing going on at the hotel we'd pick them up and bring them to the camp to talk to our kids.

I felt kind of guilty asking these famous pros for their time, so once I had Lorraine write out a check for a hundred dollars to Jim Rice, and when he went to lunch I gave Jim the check. Lanier would have none of that. Bob reached over and grabbed the C-note. "Screw that hundred," he said. "He doesn't get a dime. I'll do a favor for him sometime. Anyway, I'm picking up his lunch, too." Later the Dobber told me he didn't want to embarrass those guys by giving them chickenfeed. "A hundred is nothing," he told me. "If you're going to give them anything, give them five G's or nothing." Hey, what did I know? In my world a hundred dollars was big dough. Tell you the truth, it still is. But I should have taken that lesson to the, uh, bank, as far as pro sports were concerned.

So in my first year with the Pistons, the team I thought could win half its games went 30–52. All things considered, we did a helluva job without Shumate and with a virtually crippled Lanier. We created all kinds of excitement in the city; we broke all the Piston records for attendance, helped by the club's move to the gigantic Silverdome. Off the court, things didn't look as bad. But on the court, the losing was killing me.

The misery started in the very first game, opening night at the Silverdome. All the banners and anticipation. Everybody in the organization had on tuxedos. And we got beat by the Nets in the last few seconds—my first big L from Kevin Loughery, one of my favorite college players when he played at St. John's. I'm telling you, I wanted to crawl into a hole.

The next night, after we went to Atlanta and got blown out by the Hawks, I went to the hospital right after the game. The second game of my pro career and I think I'm in for the bleeding ulcer again. It turned out it wasn't the bleeder, but I was rushed back to Detroit anyway and hospitalized for about a week. We lost our first five games, and lost more games in a month than I lost in I don't know how many full seasons in college and high school ball.

I was, needless to say, going nuts. I got a technical in my first game—welcome to the big time. I got ejected from my first *victory*, if you can believe it. I had missed three games when I was in the hospital, and Adubato took over on the road. I left him in great shape, but the team got bounced three times. Now I came back out of sick bay 0–0–0 and I had to axe that Ballantine sign, X those 0's, get that big W.

My first game back was against the Cavaliers in Detroit and Bill Fitch was coaching them and he was on a roll. I'll never get over meeting Fitch in the hallway. Here I came walking in, just out of the hospital, and I figured the guy was going to be nice and friendly and sympathize. So what did he say? "What's the matter with you?" he said. "Can't make it in this league? I don't want to hear about this bull, you're upset, your stomach hurts, you got to stay in the hospital. Maybe you just can't handle the job."

Nice greetings, huh? I thought, man, I don't know this guy that well and he's reaming me. I figured that's the way of life in the NBA. But now I wanted to win badly. And I acted

absolutely wild. It was a close game which we ended up winning, and near the end I went positively bat-dip about a call
and the refs ran me out.

There was a security cop in the Silverdome, Walt Myers,
a big beautiful, three hundred-pound guy who sat behind the
Piston bench and made sure the fans didn't assassinate anybody. And when he saw me being ejected, he thought I was
going to punch the ref. I was that wild. Well, sure, I was going
to get in some final gems on the way out. If I was going to
pay the $250 fine I was damn sure going to get my money's
worth. So I was really letting the zebras have it when this
guard jumped me from behind. I was throwing my elbows,
swinging, I didn't know who it was. I was trying to throw
a three-hundred-pounder, my wife in the stands shrieking,
"I can't believe that's my husband!" and then she couldn't
look.

While I was flailing away, this guy was holding me and
carrying me across the floor on the way out of the arena.
People thought I was hysterical, ready for the loony farm. I
look at the tapes today and I can hardly believe it myself. But
several minutes later I was totally calm and composed. I felt
fine. The big first W was finally on the board.

Before a coach can stockpile those W's, however, he needs
bodies. And the Piston bodies were somewhat the same as
the year before—except for Porter and our rookies—when
the team went 38–44, healthy. And we weren't healthy.

Remember when I mentioned what a coach thinks he can
do? What I thought I could do? Forget it in the pros. You
can have all the coaching smarts and technical and motivational skills in the world in the NBA, but if you don't have
the 'breds, forget it. The thoroughbreds, the blue-chippers,
the winners.

Not only that. If you aren't lucky enough to stay away from
injuries, you can kiss any rings goodbye again. Because you
don't win with substitutes in the NBA, either.

Hey, you're not going to beat Dr. J or Kareem and Magic

or the Birdman and Kevin McHale down the stretch unless
you've got your best guys working to their ultimate and playing out of their minds. You just aren't. The NBA is a players'
league; with the twenty-four-second clock and the lack of
traditional zones, you can't negate the one-on-one abilities of
the Jordans or the Olajuwons.

I remember during one stretch when we had Lanier down
and Shumate down and a bunch of other guys out. And where
I was trying to win with Ben Poquette at center and Leon
Douglas and Essie Hollis in the corners. Try making a living
on that sometime. I could be the most brilliant mind in the
world, but here we came down to the last three minutes and
we had to go to war in a man-to-man defense because the
rules won't let you really zone. But we were playing some
zone principles, because we didn't want the Doctor to get 50
on us. So now we had Essie, who is on a fifteen-day contract
from the Continental league and who is happy and thrilled to
be in an NBA uniform, guarding Julius Erving when all he
wanted to do was hug and kiss him.

I mean, he wanted to take his picture or ask him for an
autograph, or at least he hoped his relatives in the crowd were
close enough to snap a picture of him playing against the great
Dr. J. And I'm telling you, we're just not going to win in that
situation. Then there's Poquette, who lasted a long time in
the league but who was really nothing but an All–Airport
player. Now we were going to war with him.

In one game against the Lakers Poquette was playing out
of his mind, shooting and scoring on this little pattern we were
running at the foul line. He would catch the ball, drill the
jumper, and look over at me on the bench like, "Hey, Dummy,
you've had me all year. Why haven't you been playing me?"

Here were Lanier and Shumate sitting in their eight-hundred-
dollar suits next to me and I got Ben Poquette out there
drilling the J. Kareem was taking the night off, of course, or
Poquette would be in the toilet. But Ben didn't know that.
Kareem was sitting in the lane, saying, "We've got Boston

tomorrow night," or whatever. And all of a sudden, when the game was on the line, Kareem decided it was time to play a little and earn his two mil. So *whap,* Ben went up for the last shot from the same position where he'd been scoring at will, and *splat,* Kareem flat squished it on the board. *Boom,* another big L for Vitale. And I took the long walk to the locker room.

Of course, now I had to deal with the media, and immediately I got a writer jumping on me about what happened down the stretch, why couldn't we win when it got tough? Jeez. I mean, you looked at the Laker front line of Kareem, Dantley and Wilkes, about four million worth of prime cut, and we got Poquette making about seventy G's and Terry Tyler making about forty and Essie Hollis on a fifteen-day contract. How were we going to win?

After I made the ride around the league, seeing and dealing with the egos and the megabuck guys and the lack of response to discipline and all the rest, I realized I just didn't like it. Maybe because we were losing so much I couldn't give it a fair shot. But it didn't take an Albert Einstein to realize that a ranting, raving, screaming maniac like I was would not be successful. Quite simply, nobody would put up with me.

As I've said before, the day of the dictator in pro sport is over, kaput, finis. You just can't control your destiny in the bigs. Guys like Knight, my buddy McGuire, trail-bosses like that would have a hard time dealing with the realities of the pro mentality.

Maybe winning makes up for all of it. I didn't win, so I don't know how beautiful it could have been at the top of the mountain when you get enough W's. But how tough is it to survive? Look at Hubie Brown. Hubie had some terrific years. Atlanta had one great season with Hubie at the helm, whipping and pushing and driving, but it caught up to him there. You can't get pro athletes to charge up the hill eighty, ninety nights a year.

I didn't exactly help the situation when I traded Chris Ford early in the season. A great guy. One of the most popular Pistons. Let me thank my buddy McGuire for that one.

What happened was the Lakers had a great athletic talent by the name of Earl Tatum who had played for Al McGuire at Marquette, where Al used to tout him as "the black Jerry West." LA had given up on him, but I knew this guy could play, and when I called Al he assured me Tatum was still capable of being a star in the league. It's taking advice like this that made a TV announcer out of me, if not out of McGuire. Because if Tatum was West—or even East—I'd still be in the NBA. But anyway, in October we went ahead and made the deal, Ford for Tatum.

You talk about a guy who didn't really want to be out there. I should have realized from the number of teams he had drifted to and from. But Earl was always off by himself. He wasn't a bad guy, just very inconsistent. He wanted to prove everybody wrong and have a great year, but for some reason Earl didn't think I liked him.

One day I pointed out something to him. "Let's figure this out, Earl. Don't you think I like myself?" I said. "If you do well, I look like a hero because we brought you here and made a trade for a popular captain. We took you in because you're younger than Chris, you have great athletic ability. You can run, you can jump, you can shoot. You think I'm against you. But I can't be because I'm not against myself. I happen to like myself."

Earl wasn't the most communicative guy in the world. Earl Tatum stories went all around the league. The most famous story they tell on Earl is about the time he fell on the court and was injured. When the team trainer came running out, he asked, "Where were you hurt, Earl? Where were you hurt?" And Earl pointed to the foul lane.

But to get back to losing . . . the losing flat-out killed me. A knife in the gut. And in response I let everybody down. I had never been through it like this and I couldn't handle it.

I was in desperate straits. I felt like a failure. I was complaining all the time, too. I was very depressed. I hated the travel and the lifestyle. I didn't like the job at all.

Bob Lanier would talk to me about my emotions. Other players would. My coaches, too. It didn't help much. Bill Davidson, the owner, came to talk to me once. "Dick," he said, "I've never seen anybody take it as hard as you. You've got to relax more. You've got to enjoy it. You have a lot of ability but you're not letting it show. You're getting tense."

When I look back on it now, I realize my actions were very childish. It was my own fault that when I got my cup of coffee in the bigs, I never got time enough to add the sugar. I envy guys like Red Auerbach, to me the father of the NBA; like John McLeod, Jack Ramsey, Chuck Daly, KC Jones, Pat Riley—the guys who have coached for so many years in the big league. They have personalities that are perfect for the way of life in the NBA. You can't treat it like life-and-death every game. You have to roll with the punches and come back tomorrow. I never could do it.

I took it out on everyone—my players, the officials, everyone. Besides my battles with the refs early in the season, I had one game where I jumped right on Earl Strom from the git-go. "Your shirt doesn't say CYO, Earl, it says NBA. Let's blow the whistle like you know you're in the NBA." He was laying for me, and he let me know it. "That's one," he said, making the big T. "I'm not taking any bull——from some junior high coach."

And did I give it to my players! At one practice I pulled everybody off the floor, got them in the locker room and roared myself hoarse. "Losers," I called all of them. "Lifetime losers." Here I was, looming over Bob Lanier, one of the greatest centers ever to play basketball, and I was ripping him as a lifetime loser.

Still, it would have been an effective moment, one of my all-time coaching coups. I had the team in the palm of my hand. They were stunned, shocked. I really felt I was getting across. Finally my effort, the constant harping and criticism meant something. I finished my harangue and started to stomp out of the locker room when . . . the . . . door . . . gh, ugh, wheeze, gasp, ugh . . . the damn door . . . wouldn't . . . open. The team broke up laughing.

As the injuries mounted and frustrations piled up, I became even more demanding, with more regimented practices to boot. Lanier led the players in telling me, "Look, Dick. This is not college. We play three and four times a week and here you are making us practice two to three hours a day besides. Drills, running sprints, agility series. This won't cut it." And the Dobber was right.

Of course, Lanier was out with the knee problems. I don't think he was ever at full force for us. In all my life in coaching I've never seen a guy go through such hell with his knees as Lanier did. Nine knee operations! I'd come in a few hours before gametime and there he'd be with ice-packs all over his knees. Then he'd go into the whirlpool and I'd see him sitting there shaking his head in pain and disgust.

One night before we played against Moses Malone, the young Moses, Lanier said, "Dick, get Leon Douglas ready tonight. This sonofabitch Malone never stops moving. He just grunts and groans and hustles and gets on you like you're his last meal. He never stops moving! My knees can't take it."

I think I knew it was over then.

Much earlier I sensed that with Shumate out we were in trouble down low. And we really had no strokers from outside either. That's why we had gone after Tatum. It was like our great training camp had never happened and we were in a season for which we couldn't have prepared. What else did I do? Well, I made overtures about getting Campy Russell from Cleveland. He was a local kid who had played at Ann Arbor for the maize and blue. A versatile player with a true flair for scoring. And he could handle the rock as well.

I came out in the press, kidding my owner, "Mr. D, get your checkbook ready because we're going after Mr. Campanella Russell!" That ticked off the Cavs' coach, Fitch, again because now Campy, who was going to be a free agent, had a much stronger position in the market.

We never got Russell because Cleveland wanted Lanier in return. In those days I lived half my life on the phone, proposing deals, dangling guys like Douglas, listening to offers of bow-wows you wouldn't shake a bucket of Alpo at. But while all this was going on, I knew full well I really didn't have much authority anyway.

First off, Bill Davidson is a very proud, brilliant, capital-B businessman. The team was his product and he did as he wished with it. But I always felt in my heart that most of the basketball decisions were always transferred over into the business sector; the ownership never allocated me the powers I would have liked. You better believe Davidson was calling all the shots and I was like a puppet on a string.

The six- and seven-game losing streaks piled up and just tore me to shreds. I was just pitiful. I wasn't drinking or anything like that, but sleeping was tough. And did I ever bring the losses home! I would sit in rooms and just diagram what I wanted to do and pout and sulk. It was extremely difficult for my wife and daughters to deal with that.

Then one night in Portland—we had been losing all these games, to Houston, to Seattle, to Portland—I called up Davidson and told him he should just fire me. I couldn't get the job done. I wanted to go home, I just couldn't take it any more. I told Richie Adubato and our director of scouting, Al Menendez, that I couldn't live this life anymore. I hated losing too much. I never saw any light at the end of the tunnel.

Davidson didn't fire me then, but I'm sure he filed that call away in the back of his mind.

The saviors of my second year with the Pistons were going to be our first-round draft choices. We had three of them. I'm still taking heat for passing up Sidney Moncrief of Arkansas and drafting Greg Kelser of Michigan instead, but I'm going to pass that buck to Davidson right now.

The truth is, I wanted Moncrief, and I thought we had him

locked. But on the weekend before the draft, when the owner called me at home and asked me who our first choice was, he said he'd heard Moncrief had bad knees. We talked about the knees, got the trainer involved and went over some hurry-up reports. I got word that Moncrief's knees really weren't a problem and I told the owner I felt we should still go with him. Davidson said we couldn't take that risk.

I will say this: I did think Kelser would be an impact player in the NBA. He was a local guy, great college career, won the NCAA championship with Magic Johnson. He was quick as a cat. You could check all the scouting services: he was rated the number-one small forward coming out of college, right at the top of the ladder. Best of all, he was healthy.

We heard that Milwaukee, drafting number four, one ahead of us at five, wanted Kelser. But remember now, Davidson didn't want Moncrief because of his knees. So we would get Jammin' James Bailey or Vinnie Johnson, somebody like that. We didn't want any of them at number five. We felt there was a big drop-off after the top five that year. It's the year Magic was number one, David Greenwood at number two went to the Bulls—a real genius pick—and Bill Cartwright at number three went to the Knicks.

Anyway, we decided to offer Milwaukee a switch in positions plus fifty thousand dollars so we could get Kelser. If you're going to invest a million dollars for a player, isn't it worth paying fifty thou to guarantee who you'll get? And that's what we did. We moved up the ladder, paid fifty G's and drafted Kelser. Later he ended up with knee surgery and Moncrief became a Hall of Famer. The NBA, it's FANNNNN-tastic.

About our other two first-round choices: Phil Hubbard, a medical redshirt out of Michigan, has had a solid pro career, despite injuries that have continued to follow him around. And Roy Hamilton of UCLA—well, I'm not copping any plea there. As a first-rounder, Roy was terrific associate-producer material. (That's what he is now at CBS.) But talk about a kid you had to love. He spent the day with my family. He lived at my house. I fell in love with him like I would a son.

The problem was that the first time Roy came down court, his left elbow flew out to here, his shot *kang*ed into Nowheresville, and we knew we had a disaster.

I'll never forget the look in Lanier's eyes when he saw Hamilton shoot at our first practice. Here was the Dobber having to battle three guys down on the blocks all his life, we had nobody to score outside and relieve the pressure, and we had finally got in position to draft some shooters so that Lanier could get some rest. And Hamilton showed up with that swandive elbow. Lanier didn't have to translate. His eyes said it all: "How in hell could you have gone and got me this brick thrower?"

And people wonder why it's so hard to win a championship in the NBA. Well, you know about mine, right? What? You never heard how I traded for a title? Of course nobody ever gives me the credit. But you can ask Mr. Red Auerbach, the man to whom I gave M. L. Carr plus two first-round draft choices for Bob McAdoo. Did I pull the wool over Red's cigar or what? Those drafts ultimately resulted in Robert Parrish and Kevin McHale becoming Celtics and in the Boston franchise getting back on its championship feet for good. So never say I didn't leave my legacy in pro ball.

What happened was that Carr had played out his option with the Pistons at the end of the 1978–79 season and signed as a free agent with the Celtics for over a million dollars. In compensation, we thought we should get somebody like Cedric Maxwell from the Celts. But we got scared we weren't going to get anybody good. In those days you had to go to the commissioner, state your case for compensation, and let him decide what you got. And we were frankly afraid to do that.

Instead, to solve the problem, the Detroit owners and I got together, looked at the Celtic roster and decided we wanted McAdoo. We felt that even though he'd been bounced around by a lot of teams, McAdoo had a lot left in his career. He was still only twenty-eight. We figured he'd be hungry to prove himself in a new situation, the pride factor and all that. Here was a three-time NBA scoring champion, remember, and we thought he could give the Pistons some needed adrenaline. And we knew he could still cash some points out of two positions, both at forward and in the hole when Lanier's knee got shaky.

The Celtics had given New York three first-round choices to get McAdoo, so their asking price was two first-rounds plus our waiving the compensation for Carr. And that was the deal we made. Michael Leon Carr still shows me his championship rings, holds them up and says, "Dick, I think about you every night, baby."

So McAdoo got loads of cash, the Celtics ended up getting loads of championships, the Pistons got loads of L's, and it all became a nightmare for a one-eyed, bald Italian coach who wasn't going to be a coach much longer. Did I say no compensation? Vitale got compensation. My compensation was the Ziggy. The formula basically read McAdoo equals compensation equals Ziggy for Vitale.

Mac and I have been down some roads since then. Actually, because I only coached him in the first twelve games of that second season, I never got to know Mac as well as I wanted to. Initially I was overjoyed that we obtained him for the club. I really thought he'd be our savior. I knew his Celtic situation was an unhappy one, but this would be a fresh start. Who could match up with us, trying to check both Lanier and McAdoo? We could interchange them, high, low, and in between. Both were great shooters and scorers. They had to be dynamite together.

Lanier told me later that McAdoo's first reaction to me was a bit different than mine to him. After one of my emotional locker room orations—with my head wagging and my bad eye wandering all over the place—McAdoo said to Lanier, "Dob . . . where is this guy from? I can't ever tell if he's talking to me or that window!"

I got upset with McAdoo for missing games with his supposed injuries and ailments. "Mac," I said one day. "Have

you ever asked yourself why you've been shipped around this
league so much? Buffalo. New York. Boston. Detroit. And
you're not even thirty years old. You've never had major
surgery. And you're a great talent. Well, I'll tell you why.
The word is out you're a malingerer. Players don't really
believe you care. You're a problem because guys don't feel
you put out."

I thought this would challenge him, but it didn't.

It was only later that I found out the series of hardships
that had marked McAdoo's NBA career. Agents had ripped
him off after he came out of North Carolina. He went through
a tough divorce. His father died just after he came to us. In
Boston his feelings had been severely damaged by his teammates' reactions to him and his play. He carried that over to
Detroit; I don't think he was ever comfortable or secure in
the environment surrounding his new team.

I just wish I could have known all of McAdoo's background
back them. Maybe I should have. We get so wrapped up in
the W's and L's, we don't realize these guys are human beings,
that they have other problems beside loose-ball fouls. Now
Mac and I have buried the hatchet. McAdoo even comes to
visit my house in Florida, and I helped his son get into my
buddy Nick Bollettieri's tennis academy. Mac's been going
great guns for Tracer Milan in Italy for two years and he really
loves being over in Europe. Of course, you don't have to play
every night in that league.

So here came our second opening day and we were playing
Indiana. It was going to be a new era: Lanier, McAdoo, and
Shumate across the front. We went out and played tremendous basketball. The three of them blended so well together.
Nobody could match up, sizewise. We had more M&M'ers,
mismatches, because their 6-6 forwards had to play either Mac
or Shumate.

We won easily and I wanted the season to end right there.
Why did we have to play eighty-one more? I was so excited
to read the papers the next day. Don't ever believe coaches

don't read the papers. I read everything ever written about me. I still do.

Anyway, the next day we went to San Antonio for the Spurs' opener. They had fireworks and the place was going crazy, and Doug Moe, the Spurs' coach then, was in full roar and we had no chance, right? What do you know, we beat them too and we're two and zip. McAdoo was like a little kid. I remember coming into the locker room afterward and McAdoo and Lanier were sitting there and Mac said, "Hey, Dick, this isn't all that bad." And we slapped five.

It looked like the Pistons were finally putting something together. And suddenly, whoa, reality reared its ugly head. We went to Cleveland and the Cavs positively blitzed us.

We came home after that and got to 4–3. Again, I thought we were really on our way. But then came the death knell: The ownership gave Shumate his unconditional release on October 29.

This was such a shocking blow that I can't even begin to describe its effect. Man, the team was crushed. I was crushed. During the exhibition season Shu had been nervous about being moved. He had the history of the blood clot. They had taken some exams to determine if it would come back, but I thought everything was worked out. By a certain deadline, I think it was December 1, if Shumate was still on the team he was guaranteed the full year, plus some kind of bonus. He was in the final year of his Pistons contract anyway, and he had told me he didn't know whether to invest in a house in Troy or not.

I told Shumate there was no way he was going to be waived, that he should go spend his money and do what he wanted. He was one of my favorites. And then this happened out of the blue.

I knew there was a lot of money involved, that the team would save something like a quarter of a million if we released him, but I was totally against the decision. Davidson and some others in management thought we could go with the younger

people, but this guy was our starting power forward, an inspirational leader. Not to mention I had advised him there
was no way the team would let him go. When it happened, I
was absolutely furious.

Because they thought I had a big hand in the decision, all
the players turned on me. Even Lanier and McAdoo blamed
me for the release of Shumate. I called a team meeting. I
believe in being a team player. When I work for a team, I
expect everybody on that team to be team-oriented, but what
happened destroyed my credibility and my relationships with
the players to such a point that I couldn't survive. I promised
them I was against the Shumate move, but I don't think they
ever believed me. And I know that after the meeting it got
back to ownership that I was blasting the move to the team.

That about did it. In the doldrums, we dropped our next
five games. After a loss to the Hawks in the Silverdome—I
had gotten run out again and I was waiting in my office,
listening to the end of the game—Davidson came up to talk
with me. We were 4–8 at the time, and the conversation was
basically about decisions, player personnel, the future, everything. And about attitude, personality, where I was headed
and how I would react to things. We had a nice long talk.

And then the next day the phone rang at my home in West
Bloomfield. It was November 8. I was in my coaching clothes
ready to go to practice. I had my pad ready and a new attitude
and I was excited because I thought the owner was responsive
to the things we had discussed. The call was from the Pistons'
secretary, Madeline Hazy (now Ward), who told me not to
leave for practice; Davidson was coming to the house.

Can you imagine? I didn't even realize what was coming.
Lorraine did, of course. Immediately my wife said, "You
better prepare yourself. He's coming here for one reason.
You're fired."

I didn't believe her. But Lorraine didn't stay around to find
out. She left the house and drove around for a few hours. She
obviously didn't want to be there when it happened.

I still didn't believe it. Even when the big stretch limo pulled up. Even when Tim, the chauffeur, let Davidson out of the limo and they came to the door. Even when the owner walked in and I invited him to sit down. But there was no doubt about it. This was strictly business. Gallows business. Davidson may have said hello first. I don't remember. But very quickly he said, "Dick, I made a coaching change today."

I think then I made us some coffee. Jeez. I never even made coffee for my wife and here I was making coffee for my coaching funeral. My dream was gone, and I started crying.

The Ziggy hit me real hard.

TELEVISION: THIS (WASTE) LAND IS MY LAND

It was over. The doors were closed. Professionally—at least in this profession of hoops, which was the thing I had devoted my life to—the Ziggy had dropped me with a roundhouse to the chops.

Initially I felt sorry for myself. I felt like a total failure. All the good things that I had achieved seemed to have been flushed down the toilet. I actually locked myself in a room at the house for hours on end. I didn't want to hear the radio or watch TV or answer phone calls—not that the phone was ringing. It was a very immature reaction to the Ziggy. But then, this was the most depressed I'd ever been. Here I was, thirty-eight years old, I should still be striving and reaching for the top, but instead it was like my life in basketball had come to an end.

I just knew nobody would ever want me to X and O or to run a team again. I wasn't a former great player or coach or a big name with a lot of famous, important contacts to fall back on. I had always had to jam my foot in the door so I could prove myself. I had always believed that one mistake and it would be over; that's why I worked so hard. I figured I would never be able to recover from a single setback, a fall, a failure. And now here it was.

I did a lot of sleeping. Then I read that sleeping is the first sign of running away from your problems. I thought about psychoanalysis, but then I cancelled that idea. Can you imagine me on the couch? They'd have to throw away the Official Shrink Guidebook, baby. I'd be terrified of what a psycho doc might find in the recesses of this wacko's mind. Part of the problem for me was that I was still picking up a check from the Pistons, so I had my own personal security blanket. I didn't have the incentive to go out and hustle for a job.

Lorraine really got on me for my attitude. She told me it went against everything I believed in in the field of athletics, all the positives I talked about in speeches at clinics and camps, all the encouragement and motivation and dreams and goals I had always preached about to youngsters. "Now here this happens," Lorraine said, "and you want to quit? You can't give up, Dick. You can't be a quitter."

Then, out of the blue, a representative of something called ESPN called me. I had no idea what ESPN was. It had just been invented up in Connecticut—a twenty-four-hour, all-sports cable television network?—and they inquired if I would like to do the color analysis on a college basketball game. My first reaction was, "ESPN?" It sounded like some spacey, out-of-body scientific experiment—which now that I think about it, where I was concerned, is precisely what it turned out to be.

It took me weeks just to be able to say "Entertainment

Sports Programming Network." But after doing a few games, getting out and seeing basketball people, rapping with the players, coaches and scouts all around the sport, I was totally rejuvenated. I got back energy I didn't even know I had. At the time ESPN was doing tractor pulls and full-contact karate exhibitions—is there *half*-contact karate?—and I figured it was just a fly-by-night operation, somebody's idea of a quick-bucks-and-out affair. But after I talked with Scotty Connal, the ESPN second-in-command who had been such a success at NBC, I felt much better. Scotty told me his former colleagues over in Peacock Land, Chet Simmons as president and Jim Simpson as number-one announcer, had left to be part of this, and I immediately realized ESPN would be more than an extrasensory perception gag.

My first game was in Chicago at Alumni Hall, DePaul against Wisconsin, for which my broadcast partner was Joe Boyle, a hockey guy and former voice of the Minnesota Twins. I thought this was great, here I am a novice in television about to do a game with a novice in basketball. But man, was it fun. I had no idea what I was doing, of course. ESPN planned all the transportation, met me at the airport, made all the hotel arrangements, furnished me with plenty of brochures and statistics. What a piece of cake. The game was at 8:00 P.M., so that afternoon at about 4:00 I had a bite to eat, read the papers, made some phone calls, shaved and showered and nonchalantly wandered over to the gym at about 7:40.

How was I to know there were these strange gatherings called *production meetings?* Nobody told me. The crew was in a panic at Alumni Hall. They had left messages at the hotel, they had tried to reach me all day; nobody knew where I was. I had figured TV was like coaching, where you show up a couple of hours before tip-off and do your thing. Uh-uh.

Before I knew it, I was on the air. One guy, Boyle, was talking to me live, and another two or three people, or so it seemed, were back in the truck screaming in my ears. I didn't know what to do. In the opening we talked about Mark Aguirre of DePaul and Wes Mathews of Wisconsin and how they

would be two of the better players in America that year; at
the end of the game I even did an interview with the Blue
Demons' Ray Meyer. Imagine this: I had to get *Ray* to shut
up. I don't remember saying anything off the wall or contro-
versial during that first telecast (although later in the season
Aguirre and I would have it out about his work habits). But
Meyer and I found plenty to talk about. This was the season
after DePaul reached the Final Four for the first time under
the legendary coach, and everybody was picking the Demons
number one, so we yapped on and on about that. But finally
I had to give Ray the "cut" sign—a sign I would soon become
thoroughly familiar with myself.

Following the game I went out for a drink with Rod Thorn,
the general manager of the Chicago Bulls, who was there
scouting. It felt so great just to be chewing the fat about
basketball again with one of the guys. I was tremendously
exhilarated from the telecast; I mean pumped, jazzed, rein-
vigorated.

I came home a totally changed guy. The game and trip gave
me a shot in the arm. Lorraine said I was like a little kid with
a new toy. I had a sparkle in my eye; I couldn't wait for Scotty
to call me for more games.

The next day Connal gave me his evaluation. Remember,
here is a guy who worked with both McGuire and Packer
when they were part of television sports' best threesome, Al,
Billy and Dick Enberg. He told me I had a long way to go
but that I had three things nobody could teach: enthusiasm,
knowledge of the game and candor. "But you have a lot to
learn, Dick," Scotty said. "You'll have to cut out the rambling."

Oh well, three out of four ain't bad.

If there is one person I could point to and say that's the
guy who put me in the comfort zone in TV, that's the one
who showed me it was okay to be myself and not be afraid
to be outspoken, who encouraged me to say what I felt and
to let the chips fall where they may, that guy would be Jim
Simpson.

Simpson took hold of me early in that first year at ESPN and I couldn't have been in the hands of a better guy. In fact, *my* hands were probably shaking when our relationship started—remember, I was such a novice and here was one of the giants of the business. I remember watching Jim Simpson on NBC do the World Series, the Super Bowl, golf, all the biggies. He had worked with John Brodie, Tony Kubek, McGuire, Packer, you name it and he did it. And now I was going to meet him in Chicago to work a college basketball game.

The first night Jim and I met, we wound up eating dinner at a place that was so little it had only three tables. We met at the hotel and walked to this restaurant, just the two of us, and I was very nervous. But Simpson put me at ease right away. "Scotty Connal wants me to work with you," Jim said. "He says you have a lot of potential. He says you have things we can't teach. But you're going to need more."

Jim doesn't mince words and he didn't then. Right off he told me the one thing about my delivery that annoyed him was how I always referred to myself as a one-eyed, bald-headed Italian as if there was no way a handicapped, average-looking, minority descendant could make it anywhere. "You're putting yourself down," Jim said. "Worse, you're implying a putdown of all the people out there who also might have one eye, be bald, or be of Italian heritage." He said I should be proud ESPN believed in me and what I could do, and not treat it as if I was some naive miracle victim.

I took those words to heart—but I don't necessarily agree with them. I *am* bald, I *am* one-eyed, I *am* Italian, and I am always amazed at the fact that I got to where I am today. But all that's a part of being myself, too, and that was what Jim was talking about in the first place. From that first meeting we built up a tremendous relationship founded on mutual respect. Jim Simpson's a class act in every way.

When he took me under his wing, Simpson was anything but easy on me. "A lot of guys with big egos can't take this. They wouldn't listen to what I'm going to tell you. They resist changing in any way. But you have to make the decision if you want constructive criticism."

Was Jim kidding? Want it? I was hungry for anything I could get. "Let me have it, give it all to me," I said. I knew I had to take the lumps if I wanted to get any better in the business. In the back of my mind I still had interest in an NBA general manager's job or even getting back into college coaching, but I was soon coming around to liking the TV business. I appreciated that ESPN was interested enough in me for Connal to get Simpson to help me so much.

Jim and I set up a schedule for when we worked a game together. We would meet for breakfast, then sit in his room and talk about the telecast. We'd talk about the teams and coaches and players, break down the rosters. We'd discuss tendencies and strategies and how the coaches worked a game and what players were likely to do with the ball in different situations.

Jim would say to me, "Okay, let's start with Kentucky: Kyle Macy." And I'd have to give him a couple of comments on Macy. Then we'd go to the next guy. We'd have a little byplay through here, a conversation about each guy so that Jim could get into the flow with me and know what I would come up with on everybody. I think he learned a lot about the individual personalities himself in here. Remember, I knew most of these fellows. I had probably recruited, scouted, or seen almost all of them play at some point.

We'd go over offensive concepts and defensive counters in these meetings. We'd talk about the meaning or importance of the game itself, maybe the rivalry of the leagues or the teams, the tradition of the game. We always got a sideline story angle going that we might have to develop in case of a blowout.

Jim and I broke everything down to the point where when the telecast came we were ready to roll. We flowed in and out with each other and really had fun.

After a while we also made up a list of about ten items for

me to comment on from time to time during a game. These could be anything from rules to injuries or from the building of a new arena to a philosophy in recruiting. Sometimes there would be news items to comment on. Anything that would be interesting to the basketball viewer.

The fact is, Jim Simpson became greatly involved in convincing ESPN to keep me working with him. He kept pushing me, teaching, cajoling and making me better. I'm very indebted to him for all of this.

At first I thought this TV gig would merely be something to tide me over for a little while. It would give me some identity, get me involved in areas where I'd meet people again and be able to solidify some contacts, maybe search for some good job opportunities. Remember, too, nobody knew what ESPN was back in those days anyway. My daughters thought I was a total fraud. Because we couldn't pick up ESPN in our home for several years, they'd see their dad go off to all these games and say, "Yeah, sure, ESPN. There's no such thing."

The network's identity was obviously a major concern of the company biggies, too. While I always wanted to know how I was doing on the air, the one thing Chet Simmons kept zinging me for was that my ESPN logo pin was always on crooked.

Looking back, the recognition factor must have meant a lot more to me than I originally thought. Even though it was cable TV—and people from the three older networks still use the word "cable" as if there's a foul odor attached to it—and I couldn't even get it in my own home, I knew people were watching because of the reception I'd get everywhere. It's amazing how deeply the slightest exposure on television injects a person into the public consciousness. I mean, if a weird-sounding oddball like me can become a "sports celebrity" in a few short years . . . baby, you know what I mean.

That was my obvious appeal, too. Average Joes, the guys in the street, blue-collar workers, *the people*—I think they saw a guy like me up there on the tube and figured, "Holy smoke, this man is us. He's talking to us. If he can do this, anybody can." Not to mention, the whole thing was so much fun! Going to games, sitting courtside in the best seat in the house, kibitzing with all my buddies in the coaching ranks, meeting the athletes and the other students on campuses all over America. And getting paid for it? Hey, was I stealing money or what? Even $350 a game, which is what I got the first couple of years, was grand larceny for that kind of labor.

How psyched was I? I used to go up to ESPN's offices in Bristol and try to use all my charms on Ellen Beckwith, their director of assignments, to get as many games as I could. Of course, I wasn't the only one; she was swamped with tapes from everyone in the business. "How many games do you want?" she would ask me. "You're already doing so many, what do you want—a game every night?" Well, why not?

I can't think of anything else that could have pulled me out of my funk. I was so excited. People would come up to me and say, "Hey, Dick, how're you doing?" Total strangers. "Enjoyed you on the tube last night. What did you think of that call? Who're your All-Americans this year?" I felt like somebody again. I felt I was doing something positive. Basketball fans were recognizing me everywhere I went.

Early on, players and whole teams began treating me like I was one of the family. After my first couple of games, I flew on New Year's Eve to Tucson to do an Arizona–Kansas game. and the Jayhawks happened to be on the same plane. Darnell Valentine came up and started rapping, mentioning he had seen me several years before at the Five-Star camp in the summer and now here I was on TV. He thought that was neat. This kind of thing happened all the time; I established more and more friendships with players and coaches.

The first couple of years at ESPN, though, I still hoped to get back into the pro game. I was writing to Joe Taub, the Nets' owner, to suggest myself for a job in his organization— as general manager. He sent word to me through Howard Garfinkel that he would hire me all right, but as the guy in charge of ticket sales. Yeah, I really wanted to be a ticket salesman.

Then I was also talking to Ted Stepien, the owner of the Cleveland Cavaliers. He was actually about to offer me a position. Listen to this deal: Stepien wanted me to convince Hubie Brown to come to the Cavs as coach and Stepien would bring me along as GM in a package deal. I would have jumped at that in a minute, but after meeting with Stepien, Hubie turned the job down in a hurry. Now that I look back, I can't believe how lucky I was. If that arrangement had gone down, today I'd probably be selling hardware door-to-door in downtown Akron.

I can't pinpoint the exact moment when I felt that TV announcing was something I could do better than anything I'd tried before, that it was right for me, that I should give up any ideas I had about coaching or managing another team. I know that when ESPN kept renewing my contract, I started to feel secure. The first couple of seasons my contract was on a game basis, but then it got to be two- and three-year deals and I was in a comfort zone and very, very happy.

As I grew in TV, I thought about what Wil Robinson told me when I was coaching the Pistons and Wil was a Detroit scout. Wil should be in the Hall of Fame himself; he was the first black head coach at the Division I level in college, coached Doug Collins at Illinois State, a legendary guy in his own right. He was the first to suggest that television would be my forte.

Back in my Piston days I would do a little play-by-play in the office, without even realizing it, you know, just joking around. Then I'd do these little five-minute speaking gigs at luncheons around Detroit to try and sell tickets. "You're unbelievable, Dick," Wil said. "Twelve of these lunches the past few weeks and you've got twelve different stories. The people eat it up. You're wasting your time. You belong behind a microphone."

I've never pretended to be able to follow all the rules of broadcasting. I'm a jock. I came out of the locker room to TV. I'm one of what Howard Cosell has referred to as the "jockocracy." But hey, I'm proud of that. I know I'm still a novice at this profession and it hasn't been easy taking all the shots from the critics over the years.

In the beginning, especially, there were some people in the sport and at the network who didn't appreciate my candidness. I'm smart enough to know that if I'm doing Indiana Pacers games and they're paying my salary—which was the case for a few years—you're damn right I ought to sing their praises. But once I began representing a national network, not being a local or provincial telecaster, I started out being up-front and honest about everything. I wasn't a homer except in the sense that I saluted the entire college game.

But there was some serious anti-Vitale feeling out there at first—and I'm not talking about the guy at the neighborhood tavern who disagreed that Pearl Washington whirled out of control on occasion. I mean people in the NCAA establishment, in the conference offices, some coaches who made it known they didn't appreciate ESPN foisting me on the listening and viewing public.

Simmons and Connal stuck with me through thick and thin, though, and when Bill Grimes—a real basketball fanatic—came aboard to head up ESPN, he backed me to the hilt as well. Let's face it; I was going to be different. I'm unique. I'm not out of the Razorcut School of Robert Redford Telecasters. Forgetting my resume's simple negative look—the shining dome, the wild orbs—I had a hilarious time coming to grips with the technical aspects of the trade.

All my buddies think the transition from coaching to television is so simple. Becoming an instant genius—that's the easy part. But try to keep your brain unscrambled and in working order while you are trying to talk on TV with a producer screaming in your ear counting down the seconds to commercial or to fade-out or to oblivion, wherever. I'm kind of proud of the discipline I've attained with producers, in that they can recognize something I might miss on the court, feed it to me, and I can incorporate it immediately into the broadcast without it seeming like I've broken down and wandered off into Gobbledygook City. The action is furious, the crowd is screaming, the band is blasting away, the play-by-play guy is referring to something on the air, and the voice in my ear is telling me to describe the activity in the replay we're about to see. It was really difficult to get used to dealing with all that.

Game openings on camera were also tough for me. Now the camera is my best friend; I'm an AT hot dog. That's Air Time, for those of you who may have thought I misspelled PT. I can be as down and deflated as can be, but when the red light goes on, I'm immediately on a roll. But back then just learning where to look and how to look into the camera was a major undertaking.

I used to tense up as soon as I knew the camera was on. It scared me, to tell the truth. Mainly, I think, because I was always concerned with how my bad eye would look. I used to call Lorraine at home all the time and my first question was never how was I or how was the content, did you think it was interesting? It was, "Hon, what about the eye? Did it wander? Did it lie off to the side? Did I look goofy?"

See, I had no control over the thing. My eye used to hitch-hike way out to the side of my face when I first started doing TV work and there was nothing I could do about it. In the opening of a live game situation, there'd be me and my partner, and the producer would tell me, "Dick, we want you to look at the play-by-play man, then turn back left to the camera, then turn back to him and talk as if you're in a conversation. When you want to answer his questions, turn back left to the camera again."

Well, I totally lost sight that way. I could see my partner okay with the right eye, but as soon as I tried to turn back to the camera with my left eye leading, it was Looney Tunes time. I finally figured out that I had to be on the play-by-play man's right side, so I could start off with my partner with the left eye and when I turned back to the camera, the right eye would lead the way there, my two eyes would function together momentarily and I could hide my disability.

Only one problem. A lot of play-by-play men have their

earpieces molded to a particular ear and sometimes it was the right ear, so they'd want me on their left. That would force me to remain in the very uncomfortable position of seeing virtually nothing!

Like with any other little handicap in life, however, I had to adjust. For a while, that is. Now, all my play-by-play guys understand the situation and let me set up on the right side.

Sitting at the broadcast table with the monitors, I had the opposite problem. There, I needed the monitor on my right side, my good side, because it's more important for me to see what's on the monitor than it is to look at the pathetically good-looking mugs of guys like Jim Simpson and Mike Patrick and Tim Brando on ESPN and Keith Jackson and Gary Bender of ABC.

I mentioned my rambling. Folks might think I still go on and on to the detriment of humankind, but let me tell you, they don't remember the way I used to be. Geez, Connal used to have to tell me all the time, "Dick, mention the two-three zone has gaps, point out where they are, then get the hell out. Finish it. End. Stop. Let's hear something else. Don't keep talking about the gaps. Nobody cares." And he was right. I used to start with the zone, then keep rambling about it. I think I'm much better now.

I also used to step all over my partner's play-by-play lines. I feel sorry for those guys in the early days. I'd see something on the floor and want to dive right in and explain it. Finally, I was taught a code system: the old "touch" game. Simpson and I had this one down pat. Whenever I wanted to say something, I'd simply touch him on the arm. At least, I thought we had it cold.

One night I was touching and touching and touching him so much, practically pounding his arm to get my AT, yet Jim knew he had to finish his own thought—he was right, as usual—so he kept waving me off and shaking his head no to keep me quiet.

Hey, it's a special art coming in and out with your partner. By comparison, baseball and football telecasts are as simple as taking candy from a diaper dandy. There's all kinds of time in which to point out strategems and tell stories. Basketball—you have maybe three to five seconds to make that quick point; it's such an emotional game up and down the floor, you have to let the other guy call the action as well. So I had a whole lot of room to improve in that regard.

Bill Fitts, a producer who came to ESPN from CBS, where he'd won a number of Emmies, suggested another improvement. He told me to stop using the word "well" prior to every sentence. "Well, Jim . . . Sampson's going low this time down the floor." "Well . . . there's no way Connecticut can keep up this pace." "Well . . . I don't know why I say 'well' all the time unless it's a crutch to gather my . . . well . . . thoughts."

After a while I wrote the word down and stuck it smack in front of me on the table during games to remind me not to fall back on it. Well then, imagine my surprise when shortly after I started at ESPN, a movie actor who used the word to begin just about every thought he ever had got elected President of the United States. So much for communication experts.

The key to any successful partnership in broadcasting is when the two people have a common comfort zone. In the early days I was so new to the business that all the old pros went out of their way to make sure it was easy for me. Connal used to liken the ideal partnership to a double-play combination: all rhythm and timing. "The two guys have to go in the same direction," he said. "We can't have one guy doing his game and the other guy doing his."

There were times, I admit, that I was doing my X's and O's and the other guy was going off like I didn't exist. Other guys I just naturally blended better with. Jim Thacker, the well-respected gentleman from North Carolina who used to combine with Billy Packer on ACC games, was a guy who had more than the usual knowledge about the game. At times he would be almost like an analyst. I found myself thinking, "No, I can't say that because Jim has already mentioned it." Jim knew the game so well he could be both the analyst and the play-by-play man. Learning the strengths and weaknesses of my partners was simply a matter of getting the feel.

But the whole thing was such mad, bountiful fun that any glitches were only dots on a landscape. "Paradise Lane," I called it. I was like a kid in an ice cream shop: every game was a better flavor than the last. Rejuvenated. Exhilarated. Pick an exclamation.

People asked me if I got the same turn-on that I used to get coaching. No comparison. It was better. My love for the job kept building and building. I felt I was bringing some innovation to the field. I was making an impact. I knew I was a character; critics said I was just turning into a wacky maniac for the cameras. My friends and loved ones knew better than that.

I even started to like doing interviews. Well, why not? I got to talk first. Seriously, I learned from Simpson to make my questions short. Initially, I had this habit of asking a question and answering it at the same time. "Why do you think the zone wasn't effective tonight, coach?" I'd say. And then I'd begin before he could get a word in edgewise: "I thought the reason was you guys weren't getting any movement inside."

Honestly now, I don't do that anymore. At first I was petrified doing postgame interviews. I sought out Simpson and the other partners for help: What should I ask? What are some good questions? When we would double-team a coach or player afterward, it was no sweat. That was like I was being interviewed myself. It was when I had to do the interview "naked"—in other words, all by my lonesome—that I got terrified.

I'd be standing alone and have to throw it back to courtside or the studio to someone on a count—ten, nine, eight, seven— and be on the money at zero. About two years ago when I started getting it right, there was cheering in the ESPN truck.

Then there was the time I totally panicked after the NCAA Division II championship game a few years back. Florida Southern won, but when coach Hal Wissel brought over three

of his players to be interviewed, sweat was pouring down my
back like Niagara Falls. I had no idea who two of the kids
were!

"You're thrilled about this, aren't you?" I said to the kids.

"Yes, it's a great win," Unknown Florida Southern Player
said.

"You're really thrilled. I can tell," I said.

Thank you and goodnight. I don't know if they ever ran
the interview, we were switching so much between live and
tape those days. But boy, was I stuck.

Another interview dear to my heart was following a big
Louisville victory when I grabbed Darryl Griffith, Dr. Dunkenstein himself. We got our ear pieces on fine, but all of a
sudden mine malfunctioned. I couldn't hear the producer from
the truck—they tell you *never* lose contact with the truck—
and there I was, live, with Griffith. To make matters worse,
the stage manager who was supposed to be shooting signals
to me and counting me down had disappeared. He was checking out the ladies in the crowd or something. What did I do?
Simply what came naturally. I just kept on talking to Griffith.
I had no idea when to finish, so we just kept on rapping.
Finally—I knew we should have stopped long ago—I threw
it back to Fred White at courtside. Of course, he had no
contact with me either except by sight. So I just pointed and
he leaped on the air and signed off gracefully.

Hey, asking Dicky V to count down an interview and break
for commercial does not exactly put me in my comfort zone.
But I'm not afraid of interviews anymore. Even naked ones.
In the past few years I've insisted on doing some interviews.
Last season after Lou Henson of Illinois won his five hun-
dredth game, I wanted the interview and nailed that sucker.
Not Henson, the interview. I even asked Henson about his
characteristic combed-forward, multicolored haircut, the "Lou
Do." I can get away with that kind of thing, possessing the
famous "Dickie Do" myself.

Color analysis. On-cameras. Interviewing. It was all part
of the job. Then there were the studio shows. These may have

been the most fun of all. One was Sports Center Plus on the weekends. I'd come in prior to the basketball season and we'd go over a few lists for the upcoming year, like Vitale's Five Best Point Guards or Vitale's Five Mystery Players. Stuff like that.

ESPN would bring in a slew of spokesmen from different fields to comment on their specialties on this potpourri show—Joe Frazier, Dick Williams, even Murray the K, the disc jockey of Swinging Soiree fame. But I remember being with Dick Williams vividly. They had a little room where we waited before going on the show—sort of like Johnny Carson's Green Room—and we could rap and eat and watch TV in there.

This was in October of the year that Williams had been fired by the Montreal Expos and he was between jobs. Dick was stunned that I was such a baseball nut. I knew he had played with the Dodgers as a reserve on those great teams with Duke Snider and Gil Hodges, and I was asking him dozens of questions about the old days. He was up there to comment on the World Series the day of the final playoff game between the Dodgers and the Expos for the NL pennant.

As we watched the game, Williams was analyzing the players and strategy for me, and I could see he was eating his heart out. I could tell how much he wanted to be out there matching wits with Lasorda. But I didn't really think his heart was with the Expos. There was something hard in his eyes as he watched them, and I could sure relate to that. I know how the Ziggy can hurt.

They called Williams to go on the air, and I was really curious to hear how he was going to handle it. There he is on "Sports Center" talking about the Expos: "Ohhh, I really feel for them in this tough game," Dick said. "I want them to win so badly. Those guys were great for me while I was there and I'd feel awful if they couldn't pull it out."

When I heard this, I thought, no way, baby—don't give me that old line.

Sure enough, when Rick Monday hit the dramatic home run to win it for the Dodgers, Williams nearly hit the roof with joy. Then they rushed him back out on camera. "Ohhh, I don't know what to say," Williams said. "I'm crushed. Rick hit a really good pitch."

Yeah, sure. But that's what getting the Ziggy will do to you.

My favorite studio gig was the College Basketball Review show we did once a week during the season. Bob Ley was my partner right out of the gate. That was the program where we'd review the week's big games and key news and preview the following week's stuff. We'd have Dick's Picks and commentaries.

Ley has a great way of getting things out of me, of pushing the conversation to the key topics. He's been every bit as important to me in the studio shows as Simpson was to me on the live telecasts. He's another Seton Hall guy, bright, a valedictorian of his class. I first spoke to Bob when I was coaching at Detroit and he called me to interview me for a local Jersey newspaper. He's also the guy who once said of me, "Doing a telecast with Dick is like taking the ride on Space Mountain with a case of nitro on board. It's not *if* but *when*."

Ley's almost too smart for me; some of his words went beyond my limited vocabulary. On this show he'd use terminology in questions and I wouldn't know what the heck he was talking about. He also had his little trick where he'd ask me a question and, after I started answering, he'd give me the cut sign before I could get a word out of my mouth—and you know how little time that is. The crew got a big laugh out of this, but once I just cracked up and said, right on the air, "Look, keep throwing me the cut sign; I don't care, I'm gonna keep talking."

The more I appeared on the tube, the more recognition came my way. This opened up new vistas, including dozens of requests to do radio talk shows around the country. Q and A's, rapping with the fans, getting into friendly arguments about teams and players and coaches—I loved all of it. It gave me great entree to basketball junkies.

Inevitably, too, I got my own television Q-and-A show on ESPN, "Dial Dick Vitale," which I did for a couple of years with Jim Kelly. You may know Jim from the America's Cup races from Freemantle, Australia. Forget those sailboats, baby. "Dial Dick Vitale" made Kelly everything he is.

At first the network wanted me to do the show by myself, but I chickened out on that. I didn't want to have to break away for those commercials and worry about the introductions and closes and all the rest. I'm much better playing off another guy, anyway. But basically, I didn't have the guts.

The only problem with the show was we could never get a locked-in time for it. My schedule was so zany, traveling all over for games, that we could never set it in stone: one particular night and time. But you talk about viewership! When we could bill it ahead of time, we got great response—the phones were always lit up.

One night Kelly literally had to put his hand over my mouth to stop me from talking because we had run out of time. Another night it seemed like we were just getting started, the phone lines were lighting up as if it was Times Square and we had to sign off. "For those of you who haven't gotten through," Kelly announced, "Dick will be staying tonight in the Bristol, Connecticut, Holiday Inn."

No sooner did I get back to the hotel than the phone was ringing off the hook. I ended up rapping with a dormful of kids from Louisiana Tech, home of Karl (the Mailman) Malone, until 2:00 A.M. from my bed in Bristol.

Then there was the classic show Kelly and I did from a tiny room off Alexander Coliseum on the Georgia Tech campus. We had to rush in there directly from a Georgia Tech–Duke game, but once we got on the air all the phones went on the blink. Oh, they would ring okay; our operators would hear the caller give his name and city, but then when the caller asked a question, we couldn't hear it.

The first few were funny. Kelly would say, "Here is James calling from Topeka, Kansas. Go ahead, James." And we'd hear nothing. "Okay, Dick, sorry. Now we have Katherine from Gainesville, Florida." Nothing. Finally, after this went on for several calls, Kelly got perturbed. "You callers would be better off filing your questions on postcards and sending them along to Dick. We'll get them quicker that way."

Inevitably, I went to my instincts. "No problem, Jim," I said when "Tom of Louisville" called in. "I know Tom wants to know why Denny Crum's Cardinals can't get untracked. I think the Cards blah . . . blah . . . etc." Then came "Jack from Detroit." I said, "Jack must wonder why Bill Frieder up at Michigan has benched so and so. Well, I'll tell you why. The kid is an underachiever blah . . . blah . . . etc."

I continued in this fashion, making up the questions, asking them, and answering them in one fell swoop. The phones never did get back to normal. So I kept asking and answering. I loved it. More than anything in my career, this was the essential Dick Vitale.

What I've always tried to do is to combine my expertise with my own personal shtick, because I realize there are a lot of people out there, insurance reps and office managers and factory workers, everyday individuals, who aren't into the technical game. It's the old KISS theory—Keep It Simple, Stupid. And yet I try to do it in a precise way.

I try to make the game interesting, exciting and fun. And in my description and analysis I try to be authoritative, too. Think about it. Isn't that what communication is all about? When you listen to the Dan Rathers, the Larry Kings, the Peter Jennings, the John Maddens—when they speak, they jump right at you. You believe what they're saying.

I try to be strong that way; above all I want to be enthusiastic. I just feel blessed that that's always been a part of me. A certain pizzazz. You get an identity early in life, whatever your line of work, and mine was always that I was a fiery guy, a promoter, a motivator. An emotional wacko, okay. However you want to put it.

The point is, I had that feel for communication and a voice for the game—remember my favorite review, *"He sounds like college basketball"*? I just had to be channeled in the proper direction.

Two young producers took over those duties in the last few years; I've been the player and they've been my coaches. The irony is that both are former basketball players—not Y-ball hackers, but players on the Division I level. Steve Anderson at ESPN, who now heads up all the production at that network, played at Holy Cross. Kenny Wolf at ABC came out of James Madison High in New York and played at Harvard with James Brown, now an announcer for CBS.

Small world. When I first started working with Anderson, he had just gotten out of coaching. He came to ESPN from being an assistant to Dick Stewart at Fordham, but I remembered him from even further back. Steve is the son of Dave Anderson, the Pulitzer Prize–winning sports columnist for *The New York Times,* and they used to live in Tenafly, New Jersey.

Steve stuck out his hand to introduce himself at the ESPN studios in Connecticut. I stopped him cold. "I know you," I said. "Steve Anderson. Xavier High School, Tenafly, New Jersey. Right-handed. Slow guard. A penetrator. Not much speed." I just broke his game down right there. "All-Airport. Looked great at the airport but never got any PT."

My first year as assistant at Rutgers I had tried to recruit Anderson. In fact, he reminded me of my visit to his school. He played with a kid named Billy O'Brien in high school. I was roaming Jersey looking for players in places where all they wore was pants and a shirt, and on the way to Brooklyn to see Phil Sellers I stopped by Xavier, which was a private military academy with uniforms, spit shines and all the rest.

Talk about out of my element. Anyway, I got in the room with Anderson and O'Brien and I didn't have much time. I got right in their faces and did my maniac routine. "Look, guys, I'm not kidding around here. It's either get on board at Rutgers or be left behind. We're building a national champion. We're getting the best. I'm not playing games. Know who I'm going to see now? Phil Sellers, that's who. From here I go straight to New York to nab Phil. Fellas, it's the big time. Hope you make up your minds, but I can't wait around. Got to go. Nice talking to you. 'Bye.''

Steve said he and O'Brien just looked at each other as if the Lone Ranger had just passed through their kitchen: "Who was that madman?''

Anderson and his counterpart over at ABC, Wolf, think so much alike, it's eerie. In the last couple of years both of them—without talking to each other—took me in hand and told me virtually the same thing: that my exuberant style, the shtick and pizzazz and anecdotes and the rest, was overriding my X and O communication of the game. Anderson and I went over some tapes together and he pointed out where I should have let the game action take center stage and left out the stories and slogans.

That's basically when we developed the "freeze it" concept, where in a replay I tell the producer to freeze it at the key spot of the action where I can point out what has happened or is about to happen. I recall I first used "freeze it" on a defensive-rebound-to-fast-break transition. Alabama–Auburn, Chuck Person was the player. We showed how the transition game is divided into three parts, the three P's: possession, penetration and points, which I learned from a clinic conducted by former Minnesota coach Jim Dutcher. We noted the attacking area, hash mark to hash mark, where a team created the advantage of numbers for the break.

Actually, a broadcaster almost becomes a teacher at this point; I'm teaching the elements of the fast break. As Kenny Wolf pointed out to me later in a similar situation, "After you break down the play, forget the funny shtick. Don't go right into, 'There's Jimmy Valvano, Mr. Lee Iacocca, the entrepreneur of basketball.' That overrides the analysis. Save that stuff for when it's related to a nontechnical part of the telecast.''

I think I really pounded the X's and O's last year because of our tape sessions. Actually, it was more that I realized the importance of timing. I recall a game several years ago as an example of questionable timing. It was a huge upset by Villanova over Georgetown in the Capital Center. I thought I had a great game, but the next day Connal called me. Scotty could be a firm, tough guy.

"Dick, you disappointed me last night!" he started off. "After all our talks, you took a step backward. You had a great event, a nail-biter down to the wire. Two minutes to go, the game in the balance. And you start talking about *linguini!* C'mon, Dick. I'm watching this unbelievable sporting event and suddenly I hear: 'Mrs. MASSIMINO! Rollie's comin' home with the W! You can stop praying now, Mrs. MASSIMINO! Get the LINGUINI ready!' "

Hey, Scotty knew my spirit was broken. I thought I had all the offenses and defensive changes. I was on top of the action. I had the players and the plays solid. But he was right. The timing for the linguini was all wrong.

That was then and this is now. Last year in another close ballgame, rather than dive into something unrelated to the action, I just called the atmosphere "Maalox time." We're coming down to the wire, thirty seconds left on the clock, everybody's stomachs are churning inside out. Baby, it's time for the Maalox. Nobody called to chew me out on this one. Instead, a week later I came home from a trip and a Federal Express package was waiting for me. Inside was a case of Riopan antacid pills with a letter enclosed from a spokesman at the company: *Next time, Dick, don't say Maalox. Say 'It's Riopan Time.'*

At least somebody was watching, right?

My audience increased quite a bit when I joined ABC for that network's coverage of weekend games. That all began with a call from ABC; they wanted me to come in for an audition. This surprised me—not because I felt I was too big for that or anything, but they had so many tapes. It's not as if no one knew what my style was like.

There are obviously no basketball games on in the summer, so what they wanted me to do was come into the studio and do an old game off a monitor. First they wanted me to do the Alabama–Auburn game. "You can have a week to prepare," ABC said. "Call up the coaches, get some anecdotes, whatever." I told the network that I was the original guy who telecast that game, so I could tell them everything that was going to be in it without even seeing the tape. So they came up with another game. I had done that one, too. A third game, a fourth. I had done them all. Finally, they asked had I done UCLA–North Carolina? I hadn't, but I'd seen it on ESPN. "I don't need a week. I'll do it right now," I said.

ABC had a local guy, Corey McPherrin, work with me on the audition tape, and he put me at ease right away. I did my all-time UCLA team and my all-time Carolina team, ran my shtick up the flagpole a few times and then I really hit the X's and O's solid. What really convinced me I had done a good job was when all the technicians complimented me afterwards.

"Dick! You were really rolling!" more than one of them said. If I've learned anything about television, it's that the guys behind the cameras know their business. There are no egos on the front lines. There's not an ounce of envy in these people's bones, and they tell you what they think. There's no airs, no bull. If my audition won them over, I knew I had the job.

I was a little apprehensive about working with Keith Jackson at first. I think I was intimidated by Keith, by his whole approach. Whether people like him or not, the guy is a giant in his profession. I was in awe of his stature and reputation. He's a flat-out superstar, Mr. College Football, and I remember listening to him as a kid.

In our first meeting prior to the Purdue–Louisville game, Kenny Wolf called Keith and me together for a production meeting. Immediately after we sat down, Keith let me know that this was ABC and that things had to be different from what I was used to in a cable operation. He talked about the little old lady out in Oshkosh who didn't want to hear about PT's and M&M'ers and all that.

Right away I got a little scared about the fact that they

thought I had to change. All I wanted to do was have a good telecast. But Keith is a pro's pro and he got me relaxed before game time. Except right after the game started I really panicked because we had monitor problems. This was on top of the fact that we didn't do an opening standup, because the previous game, Kentucky–LSU, had run over into our time. I had prepared an opening and was really excited, but there went that opportunity. Then, with the monitor jumbled, I was a nervous wreck.

Eventually, though, everything ran smoothly, and I thought I was myself, especially as the game loosened up. Dennis Swanson, the president of ABC, called me the next day in my hotel room and said it was a great beginning. Of course, I thought it was one of my buddies playing a joke on me.

As we progressed through the season, Keith and I had our difficulties, but I think as we learned to work together our coverage became more sharp and focused. Once, prior to our Michigan–Michigan State game, he said it wasn't going as well as he had hoped, that we weren't meshing right. I thought he was trying to be positive about the whole thing, and right away I started improving in terms of coming in and out with stories, being quicker and more concise with my analysis, eliminating a bit of the pizzazz and concentrating more on the technical side of the game.

It probably wasn't until last season, though, that I felt totally accepted. Keith started to laugh at some of my lines. He even began using some of my terms. The UNLV–Temple game was a watershed in that respect. Speaking of the Owls' Mark Macon, Keith said, "As Dick would say, Macon's a real diaper dandy." I nearly fell off my seat.

I returned the compliment; on a Vegas mistake I said, "Whoooa, it's a turnover. Whoooa, Nellie!"

In fairness to Keith, I have to mention that our teaming together was a feeling-out process for him probably more than for me. He was not only getting a brand-new partner but transferring to a different sport. He had been used to working with the Frank Broyleses and the Bud Wilkinsons, low-key professionals, and here came this zany, undisciplined wacko from cable with all kinds of sayings and quotes and lists. It was a shock to his system, I'm sure.

We really started to click last season before Keith went off to Calgary for the Winter Olympics. I thought we were really on a roll and was sorry we couldn't keep it up, but then Gary Bender was paired with me and he was equally terrific. I can't understand why Bender is maligned so much by the critics, because he's just about the nicest guy I've met in television. The man knows his hoops, he comes prepared and he's thoroughly professional in every way. I just think Gary's a victim of herd journalism: one guy jumps him and the rest climb aboard. He just laughs all the way from one network contract to another.

On the subject of ABC, let me issue a challenge to the other networks. On ABC, I've had the pleasure of working with Cheryl Miller, the former three-time Player of the Year for UCLA, who did some features in our basketball package, and David Robinson, the Admiral waiting in the wings to become the Trillionaire, who used to leave his Naval duties to come join us and work for ABC on the weekends. So right now I'm throwing down the gauntlet to the other networks: get your basketball teams up and send them on over. Cheryl, David, and I will take on all of you, three against five.

No chapter on my experiences in television would be complete without talking about Al McGuire and Billy Packer. I'm going to do a little bragging here because I think college basketball is one of the healthiest sports on TV primarily because Al, Billy and I sell the game at every opportunity. Critics say we're selling the game, yeah, but we're selling ourselves as well. If that's true, fine; it all goes hand in hand. The point is we've been ambassadors for this sport for a long time. And while we may not see each other often enough to be considered the Three Amigos, I have great respect for their work and the differences that make each of us unique.

Billy is the deep thinker of the cadre. He's the most analytical of the trio—the sharpest with the X's and O's and at breaking down the game. He really is a very serious issues man as well. He's the Socrates, the Plato, the Aristotle of hoopcasters.

Then there's Al. I don't know if you can describe Al McGuire with mere words. You have to see him in action, feel the charisma, the heat of his personality. He'll poor-mouth himself as a coach and announcer, giving credit to the players and his long-time assistant at Marquette, Hank Raymonds— "All I did was wear the flower in my lapel," Al says—but don't believe him for a minute. A more wily gamesman never existed. Al is one of the great con artists of our time. A promoter par excellence. He laughs at the rest of us "color" guys to the tune of about a million dollars a year, if all his outside interests and income are taken into account. Into his *bank* account—which leapfrogs by the second. Al has always had a special feel for people and situations; he coached that way, too, totally in control of the flow of things. If Billy's Plato, maybe Al's Walt Disney. And I'm Robin Williams. Vanilla. Strawberry–chocolate chip. And tutti-frutti.

The bottom line is we're all salesmen. We're guys who love the game. We like to battle and disagree with one another— mostly in the pages of *USA Today*. (If that paper and the Hedda Hopper of TV sports, Rudy Martzke, didn't exist, nobody would know whether we agreed or disgreed on anything.) Billy said Proposition 48 didn't affect many players. I said it did. Billy said he's come around to liking the three-point shot. I still maintain it's way too short. Al seems to stay above the fray; Al's so laid back, he may not know what "fray" means.

At breakfast at the ACC tournament once, Al was sitting with my wife while I had to leave the table and run around the hotel lobby looking for tidbits and quotes from coaches and players for a later telecast. McGuire had the ACC final to do that week, but do you think he was worried? "Lorraine, your husband is an absolute nut," he told my wife. "Look at him. He belongs in a rubber room."

Jim Simpson saw Al and me at the arena before one of the
ACC games and came up to us pretending to shovel away all
the bull we were heaping up on one another. Later, as I was
getting ready to do my opening for an ESPN telecast, Al ran
up behind me and made all kinds of faces in front of the
camera. In turn, when somebody was interviewing Packer at
the NCAA finals in New Orleans, I stuck my head in and got
in a couple of bits myself. It's all in fun. I hope nobody ever
takes us too seriously.

But Billy shouldn't, either. Mr. Packer had some things to
say about me during the '88 NCAAs that I thought were way
out of line. The big side-story of the tournament was the opening at UCLA after Walt Hazzard got the Ziggy, and the rumors were flying that Jim Valvano was going to take the job.
We reported on ESPN that Vee was in LA to meet with the
AD, and for some reason this got Billy all hot and bothered.
"In Valvano we have the number-one hyped guy in basketball
using the number-two hyped guy in basketball, Vitale, to upstage the tournament," Billy told Rudy Martzke.

Number two????

There was no call for that kind of cheap shot. First of all,
everything I said was true, and we said it in the context of a
news show. It *was* news. I was doing my job, reporting a fact.
Second, how did this upstage the tournament? The Final Four
is also the national coaches' convention, and when you get
that many coaches together you're going to have rumors, and
this was a hot one. But how does that detract from the games?
Valvano himself was puzzled, telling me, "Dick, I never realized we were so powerful that we could upstage the national
championship." Billy ought to be big enough to realize that
there are things that are important to our sport that don't
necessarily happen on his telecasts. I love the game, but it's
a game, and he shouldn't take it or himself so seriously.

Naturally, as he does so often, Valvano got the last word.
On our pregame show before the Kansas–Oklahoma final,
Vee said, "Now I'm gonna tell the real reason I turned down

the UCLA job: because the number-two hyped guy in college basketball wouldn't take the job as my assistant."

Billy doesn't talk about it much but he was one terrific player at Wake Forest. A tough little guard who played with Len Chappell on some great Demon Deacon teams, one of which went to the Final Four; he could really stroke it. I first met Billy when I started doing games for ESPN in ACC country. He would be announcing some of the same games for Raycom and we'd wind up sitting in adjoining booths. I was a little awed, thinking of what he had achieved. I consider him the true pioneer in this field, the guy who paved the way for McGuire and me. While Al didn't start in television until after he got out of coaching in 1977, Packer has been doing the NCAA championships for fourteen years.

Billy and I were at a practice before the McDonald's high school All-America game in Detroit a few years ago when we went out on the court and measured the three-point line. That's when the standard distance was considered 19 feet, 9 inches. Well, Packer went off. It's not 19-9, he said. That's from the line to the middle of the rim. But they measure the foul line, which has always been 15 feet, from the backboard. And from the backboard, the three-point line is 21 feet. This bothered Billy a lot. I'll admit I went along, trying to sound impressed, like I knew what the hell he was talking about and that it mattered; he was into this like a science. But that's Billy.

More recently, we got into a discussion about Proposition 48 again. This was expressly for *USA Today,* and Packer and I were together in a room. No, not a padded cell. Of course, Al was supposed to be with us too, but he couldn't make it in person, so they hooked him up to us via a phone line. McGuire probably had a speaking engagement making another ten G's somewhere; he sounded as if he was sitting by a swimming pool.

At the 1987 NCAA finals in New Orleans, Al invited me

to appear with him in front of this huge pep rally down by the river. Thousands of fans were there. The cheerleading squads representing Indiana, Syracuse, Vegas and Providence were there. Al and I were with our wives on the deck of this huge riverboat docked by the pier, and we discussed what we'd talk about in front of the crowd. I told Al that whatever he did, please not to ask me to pick a winner at the start of the conversation because we were supposed to do an hour and as soon as you name one school, you lose the supporters of the other three.

So what did this rascal do? Right out of the box: "Dickie!" he said. "Let's give it to 'em right now. Your pick to win the NCAA championship?" When I said Indiana, the kids from Vegas, Providence and 'Cuse were ready to hang me.

Another story captures the essence of the differences between McGuire, Packer and Vitale. A few years ago I was doing some studio work during the NCAA tournament for ESPN. A limo brought Billy and Al out from Providence to Bristol to research some teams and look at some taped games that we had saved. We were glad to oblige, and upon arrival Packer and McGuire went into Scotty Connal's office to monitor the games.

Two hours later there we were, the three semi-Amigos of college basketball, all together in a live, personalized set scene characteristic of our careers: Packer deep in study of the intricacies of the various games on the tapes; McGuire flat on his back, bored out of his mind, and at this point, in fact, asleep—he stretched out and told the limo driver to wake him when it was time to go; and me standing, awestruck, shaking my head in bewilderment, wondering how such three diverse guys ever made it to the ranks of the PTP's.

COACHES:
THE ROLLS-ROYCERS

Take off my ESPN blazer, remove my ABC headphones, strip away the glitz and glitter of the video waves and underneath it all will still be a Coach. Capital C, baby. C-O-A-C-H. An honest and honorable tag I have always been proud to bear. Hey, I've said it before, I'm proud to have been a coach, I'm proud of the guys who work the profession now. They're my friends and buddies—most of them; I hope they feel the same about me, and I'll continue to praise the individuals and cheerlead for the species as long as there's life and breath in me.

One of my cohorts at ESPN, Bob Ley, is always on my case about it. "You're the president of the coaches' society, the head of the coaches' union," he says. And he's right. That's why it distresses me when coaches get in battles among themselves. Norm Sloan of Florida and Jimmy Valvano of North Carolina State got in one—with me in the middle. Paul Evans of Pittsburgh and Rollie Massamino of Villanova—a real donnybrook, which Dave Gavitt, the commissioner of the Big East, had to step in and break up. Bobby Knight and Dale Brown down at LSU—a very ugly quarrel. Brown and Tennessee's Don DeVoe. Another bad scene. I wish they'd all kiss and make up. Well, at least make up.

It's tough enough in the coaching business today—with coaches being buried by the media, the fans and the alumni, not to mention the guys in the striped shirts every night—without having to watch your back because the guy on the other bench wants to rip you to shreds. Coaches should air these things out in private, at the National Association of Basketball Coaches meetings, or over the telephone, or over a beer in the summer. Get everything out on the table. Don't go sniping at your fellow coach.

I've always tried to be fair to my guys whether I've been on the sidelines or behind the mikes. My relationships with coaches have been the highlight of my professional career. They're such a disparate bunch, but as everyone who's ever heard me knows, there are a few basic categories; the Moaners, the Rising Stars, my Paisanos. We'll get to them all. But first, my tribute to the Super Seven, the crème de la crème, the Rolls-Roycers.

Between the lines, for one game, the man I'd want as my coach in the basketball battle of the century would have to be the General, Robert Montgomery Knight of Indiana. In between the language and the harrassment (most of it teasing), Knight has always treated me like royalty. He's taken me into his locker room, given me time and information. I've had lots of fun with him.

I'll never forget my first taste of the General, though. It

was when I was just about winding up my stint as a high school coach. Knight was the head coach at Army, and he was working at a summer basketball camp at the New York Military Academy near West Point. It was a warm summer day, and the gym door was open. I heard the balls bouncing. And then—I couldn't believe it—I heard this *voice*. "DEFENSE. This is about DEFENSE," the voice came blasting out the door and careened through the trees outside. "I'm going to teach you to TAKE the CHARGE. And you're going to learn some GUTS."

There were several bleeps in there. Bleep, bleep. You bleeping bleeps. Bobby is the captain and king of the All-Bleep team. But I'll leave those out. Just as I got inside, all of a sudden Knight blew the whistle and sent two kids to opposite ends of the gym. One of the kids was this little chubby guy who looked like he had never played the game in his life. His mother had written the check for two hundred dollars or whatever and said here, go have a good time. He had the black socks and the underwear hanging down below his basketball shorts. The guy at the other end looked quick and athletic, a player.

"I'm going to roll this ball to midcourt," Knight bellowed. "When I roll the ball, you guys are going to take off and see who can get the ball, UNDERSTAND? Whoever gets the ball is on offense. The other guy is on defense and has to protect the BASKET. GOT IT? It's not real DIFFICULT. Now, when the guy with the ball drives to the basket, the other guy gets in his way. He doesn't let him score. No. He takes the CHARGE. I want to see him TAKE THE CHARGE."

With that, Knight rolled the ball out there. Well, the chubby kid was about a half hour late getting to midcourt. The other kid blew by him and went in for the lay-up. Immediately Knight blew the whistle, sprinted out on the floor and was in the chubby kid's face. "I want you to do me a FAVOR, kid," he screamed. "I want you to apply to the NAVAL Academy and put me down as your number-one recommendation. Bobby Knight recommends ME. Because I want to play against you every day of the week!''

That was my first experience with Knight up close. I told that story, at the Naismith Award banquet where Knight got the award as Coach of the Year for 1987. After he spoke, Knight pulled me aside. "That wasn't even the worst," he said. "At John Havlicek's camp I had a drill where I'd tell everyone we were going to learn how hard they could hustle. I lined them up all around the court, and when I blew the whistle I wanted everyone to sprint into the center jump circle. There must have been 300 kids going full speed, crashing into each other, banging heads, piling on top of each other. John looked at me like I was crazy—like I wanted him to get sued or something. I got rid of that drill quick.''

I started watching Knight's teams at West Point; you talk about overachieving! He had kids like Billy Shutsky; Rollie Massimino had coached Shutsky at Hillside High School. He was tough, physical, a battler with great shot selection. Knight made him tougher. Shutsky would scratch your eyes out for a loose ball. Oh, how teams hated to play Knight's Army clubs. All the biggies would come into the NIT, play Army, and go home with the big L. They'd feel lucky enough to go back home with all their little L's intact—limbs, baby.

And the Army brass! They loved those wins but they must have hated the part of the Knight experience when he'd rage up and down the bench at Madison Square Garden shaking his fists at generals and getting in the faces of his own administration. If a guy was an officer and sat on Knight's bench at Army, that guy had better be up rooting and roaring like it was any other war or Knight would be after his butt.

They tell the story about the time Army lost a big game and one of the scrambled-egg officers at West Point came into the locker room afterward congratulating all the players for their "effort.''

"Effort?" Knight screamed. "EFFORT? What the #$%@# is that? These guys are going to be fighting a war! They're going to be second lieutenants with their $#@%ing lives at stake! If all they give is effort, you might as well get the body bags ready NOW! What the hell are you talking about, effort! We go for victory here. We got our asses kicked tonight. We LOST. You can take your effort and SHOVE IT!"

Knight hasn't changed much, of course. Last season I was the subject of a similar outburst one night after I told him I thought his junior forward, Ricky Calloway, who had helped win Indiana a national championship the year before, had played a good game.

"What do you know about it?" he started in. "You don't know anything about the game. Calloway didn't do #$%@. Just like [Steve] Eyl. Check out Eyl [a senior forward who had been starting]. Three big games. He plays sixty-eight minutes and gets zip. Zero for sixty-eight. You gonna tell me about Eyl, too? Calloway and Eyl, they'll sit their asses next to me on the bench because they can't play!"

"Bobby, you're too tough on these guys," I said.

Whoops.

"What do you know about tough, Vitale?" Knight said. "That's why I've won all my life. That's why I keep winning. Because I'm tough and these @#$%#'s need discipline."

Sure enough, the benching of Calloway and Eyl turned around Indiana's season. Knight went on and on that day about his treatment of players. I'll say this—and I've said it on the air: There's two guys who stand alone in the history of motivation in sports. Vince Lombardi was one. The General is the other. The people in Chicago talk about Mike Ditka of the Bears, but Ditka has miles and miles to go before he catches up to my guy Knight.

My guy. Hah. I didn't think he was my guy another time last year when he put on that intimidation act against me. Sometimes it's Knight's way of teasing, to get loud and nasty and in your face. Intimidation City. At a practice the day before his game with Northwestern in Evanston we were sitting there talking, having a regular human-being type of conversation—he had thanked me for sending flowers for his mother, who had passed away that week—when he walked to the other end of the floor where his team was in their shootaround.

My ESPN producer wanted to get some information on Northwestern, to find out what Knight thought of the Wildcats, so I walked down to ask him. He was sitting on a table talking to a Chicago TV guy at the time.

"Hey Bobby, what about Northwestern?" I said.

"What about #$#@ NORTHWESTERN?" he screamed. "I'm not telling you about Northwestern. Can't you see I'm busy with this guy? Can't you see I'm doing something? What do you have to interfere for?" He was getting louder and louder and cursing, naturally. I just turned away but then the Italian temper in me surfaced. I've got a little volcano in me too, you know. So I whirled around and let Knight have it.

"Let's get one thing straight right now, Bobby," I said. "I'm not one of your $%$#@ players. I've had enough of your act. I'm not one of your players. I'm just here trying to do a job." We were nose to nose. Then I went stalking off the court.

But here came Knight. "I'm not going to stand around and massage your $%$#@ ego like I have to do all these other guys," he said. "I was only playing with you. I was kidding. And then you take it like that."

"How am I supposed to know you were kidding?" I said.

Five minutes later we were laughing and shaking hands and hugging, having a blast. He also said he had just finished telling some other media people that he thought I was an okay guy and that he appreciated some of the things I had said about him.

"Hey, I never know when you're serious and when you're not," I told Knight. "I have my dignity too, in front of all these people."

The payoff is that the TV guy from Chicago was taping this whole episode and showed his audience the entire incident to its completion.

I think Knight and I have a relationship now where we can

either kid around or really get on one another and show mutual respect either way. Take the three-overtime game Indiana played up at Wisconsin in '87. For a long time the Big Ten had been complaining that the league wasn't on TV enough. That's why they contracted for our Big Mondays package as the late game after the Big East. So now we had Indiana with Steve Alford, Keith Smart and company against second-division Wisconsin. What should have been a blowout instead became a real knuckle-muncher and went three OT's before Indiana pulled it out on what I thought was a shaky call down the stretch.

I don't want to take anything away from the Hoosiers, but J. J. Webber of Wisconsin and the rest of his teammates played their hearts out and should have won the game. For the effort—uh-oh, there's that word again—and energy the Badgers gave, the folks in Madison should have put on a parade for the team, that's how great the intensity was for fifty-five minutes. To show you what the school thought of the game, Wisconsin presented the senior players with a tape of the marathon contest at their year-end banquet—even though it was a loss!

Anyway, after Indiana came away with the W, Knight devoted most of his press conference to going absolutely nuts about the lateness of the game and how TV was ruling basketball and how they shouldn't have to start games this late just so the Big Ten can get on TV. He ripped TV. He buried ESPN. "I don't need this [TV] for recruiting. I don't need this for attention," Knight said. "My team won't get back to Bloomington until the middle of the night. My kids have to get up for class tomorrow. Where's the priorities here?" On and on he went.

But I got the last word. Following the season Knight was being honored as Coach of the Year at the Naismith banquet in Atlanta. I was a speaker as well. Everybody there seemed to be worried about who would introduce Knight, so I volunteered.

After I told a few stories on him, I related Knight's harangue

against TV and against the late starting times that night following the Wisconsin game. "Now I know you're a genius,
Bobby," I said. "You've got the pride, the knowledge, the
discipline. You get the kids graduated. You stand for all the
good things in the game. You've won three national championships. Count 'em. 1976. 1981. 1987. You're brilliant. The
greatest . . . But did anybody tell you that if you had done
your job with the national champions that night in Madison,
Wisconsin, instead of getting your sweet ass outcoached, the
game would have ended an hour earlier?"

If I had to rate coaches in terms of all phases of the game—
X's and O's, motivation, recruiting, preparation, organization, public relations, media cooperation, kids graduating,
following up after they graduate, caring, keeping in contact
with their players, image, standing in the community, all the
rest—I'd put Dean Smith of North Carolina right at the top.
The Dean, the Michelangelo of coaches. I may be going overboard here, but I think the guy is a real artist at work. He
excels in all the areas. That's why he's already in the Hall of
Fame. His record, his consistency, the numbers just blow my
mind. I enjoy talking to him about basketball. I enjoy being
in his company.

Back when I was just starting in TV, the Raycom production
company linked up with the ACC. The first Raycom ACC
game was to be North Carolina versus Detroit and I was
assigned by ESPN to do the game. I didn't know this, but at
the time Smith was very upset. He called Raycom and pro-
tested my being the color man since I had been the coach at
U of D. He wasn't missing a trick. Dean didn't want any bias
shown on a telecast, anything that might detract from the
program at North Carolina. I can understand this even though
I could have told him I'd be objective. Raycom called Dean
back and said I was ESPN's announcer and I had to call the
game. We went on without incident. Anyway, several days
after the game Smith called Raycom and told them I'd done

a fine job. It was only recently that I found out he had actually tried to get me off the telecast.

Smith gets so much praise and favorable press—especially from me—that it wears on opponents. His standing in the ACC and North Carolina itself is such that it's driven not a few coaches right out of the league. Lefty Driesell's resentment of Smith has been well documented down through the years. Lefty didn't exactly pile up the W's against Deano, if you know what I mean; Maryland used to invent the most preposterous ways to lose to North Carolina when Lefty was around. But I believe Bill Foster left Duke partly out of frustration at having to play second fiddle to Dean and UNC. Norm Sloan left N.C. State for the same reason. (Mike Krzyzewski and Valvano have accepted Smith's standing and dealt with it more successfully.)

Sloan, for one, still waxes sarcastic about Smith's reputation for detail and for practicing all kinds of game situations. I came late to Sloan's practice at Florida one day. "Why are you late, Dick?" Stormin' Norman said. "You should have been here to watch us work on all our special situations. I had them practice our behind-by-27, ten-minutes-left drill. What to do, down 16 with eight seconds to go. How to point when a teammate gives you an assist. How to jump off the bench and cheer. All that good stuff." Norm had everybody in the gym rolling. "All I hear you talk about is Michelangelo. At least you could call me Leonardo da Vinci."

My favorite story about Dean's reputation concerns the time an N.C. State fan went into a barber shop in North Carolina the year after Norm Sloan's David Thompson–led Wolfpack (which was on probation and couldn't go to the NCAA tournament) finished with a perfect 27–0 record. "How about that State?" said the Wolfpack fan.

"Pretty good," said the barber. "But just think what Dean Smith would have done with that team."

Even Dean himself got on me last year for the hype. He told me he thought I got Indiana psyched sky-high when I picked the Tar Heels and Michael Jordan to beat the Hoosiers in the '84 NCAA game in Atlanta, and that I motivated Syracuse when I picked Carolina in their '87 NCAA matchup in the Meadowlands. "Don't pick us all the time," Dean said. "It's all bulletin board material."

He really does try to avoid the spotlight as much as he can. At the Final Four in Dallas in '86, Ley and I had Dean on ESPN for an evaluation of the teams. He was just great, smiling and looser than I've ever seen him. It was a treat to finally get an interview, because after games he'd always begged out and pushed his players for the publicity. Especially his older players.

Dean's devotion to his seniors and upperclassmen at the expense of his freshmen—no matter how great the freshman—is legendary. When *Sports Illustrated* wanted to put the Tar Heel starting lineup on its cover as the number-one team prior to Carolina's championship season of 1981–82, Smith would not permit a freshman by the name of Jordan to appear in the picture. The magazine ran a picture of Smith and *four* starters. Naturally, the guy who hit the winning basket to win the NCAA title was the freshman. During the '87 season when *SI* went ahead and put freshman J. R. Reid on the cover, labeling him Carolina's "Main Man," Smith exploded: number one, because he also had two NBA first-round draft choices on his team, Kenny Smith and Joe Wolf; and number two, because he was afraid J.R. would get big-headed and even more cocky than he already was.

I mentioned Dean's numbers. Think about the ACC over the last quarter-century. North Carolina's been number one or number two almost every season. Smith's won one NCAA, and taken the Tar Heels to seven Final Fours. Seven! Smith's teams have won the NIT, and he's coached an Olympic gold medal winner. He practically invented the foul-line team huddle, mass substitution (his famed "blue teams"), the run-and-jump defense, the motion passing game, the four corners. He's amplified a structured "team-play" psychology with the

way his players point at one another after good plays, the way
he keeps his bench involved, and how he lists individual statistics not in order of points scored but by a complicated set
of figures that takes in all aspects of the game. His mind is
always working: team, team, team. Even John Thompson said
he learned so much about the game when he worked under
Smith with the Olympic team in 1976.

Everybody kids Dean about his only vice, chain-smoking.
But last season I think he finally cut back some because of
his doctor's warning. Right after Temple, number one at the
time, beat the Tar Heels in that awesome 83–66 pounding in
Chapel Hill, Owl coach John Chaney smacked Dean in the
breast pocket where those cigarettes were and bellowed, "I
told you, coach, no smoking. None. No smoking." It was a
heartfelt warning, not a joke.

Dean only smiled and said, "After that game, I'll probably
have to take up drinking."

Smith told me he was down to only eight cigarettes a day
last season. That's okay, but for such a disciplinarian in every
other walk of life? I told Dean my dad used to puff three
packs a day, just light 'em up, until one day he had a heart
attack. "Why don't people stop smoking before, not after,
they have a heart attack?" I asked him.

No answer. Five minutes later I turned around and he was
puffing away walking down the hall.

His health willing, I'm sure Dean has his eye on Adolph
Rupp's record of 875 career victories. Going into the 1988–89
season he has 638—about nine or ten average Carolina-type seasons away from the Baron. Don't bet against him making it.

One day when I was at the University of Detroit, Smokey
Gaines, my assistant, and I were watching a practice session
for some high school all-star game when he introduced me to
a tall, bulky fellow from St. Anthony's High School in Washington, D.C., who had just been named the head coach at
Georgetown. After rapping for a while and jointly observing

all the talent, we left the gym. I remember it to this day. I turned to Smokey and I said, "Mark it down, Smoke. Put it in concrete. This guy is Hall of Fame, all the way."

It was simply John Thompson's aura, the stature he had about him, call it style or charisma or whatever. The way he presented himself, his knowledge of the players and the game— I just knew this guy would be a huge success.

Everything about John is huge, of course. It was only after he cut down on his eating and hopped the exercise bike to get in shape for Seoul, South Korea, in '88 that our Olympic coach kept within shouting distance of three hundred pounds.

John and I have our tiffs, semi-kidding though they may be. He accuses me of being a typical tennis father, worrying about national rankings rather than just letting my girls enjoy the game. I accuse him of intimidating the referees and opposing coaches, which he constantly attempts to do.

"Don't ask me about the Olympic team," he shouted at a press conference last season. "Ask Vitale back there, he's already picked it."

"Damn right, big fella," I called out. "We'll go with David Robinson, Danny Manning, and J. R. Reid up front, with Gary Grant and Rex Chapman in the backcourt."

"Who's gonna guard anybody on that team?" he said. (Well, I had the front court right, anyway.)

Thompson reminds me of no one so much as Joe Louis: the power, the strength, the aggression and intensity, the way his teams always keep coming at you. Danny Ferry, who's seen some pretty tough practices under Krzyzewski at Duke, said after working under Thompson at the Olympic tryouts that he now understands why Georgetown is so tough on defense: "This defensive intensity was just incredible."

Standing with that towel over his shoulder, doesn't Thompson look like he's after the heavyweight championship of the world? Mike Tyson, step aside; Georgetown is coming at you. John stands, he stalks, he bellows. It's Intimidation City and don't you not believe it. Just ask Paul Evans at Pitt. "Thompson intimidates everybody. He's bigger than the President."

Thompson shrugs off the charge. "When you're six-ten and black and have a big mouth," he says, "it's inevitable that you get accused of being an intimidator."

Even in the years when he didn't have the dominating center in Patrick Ewing or, now, Alonzo Mourning, Georgetown attacked teams with a hungry defensive pressure that was a scary sight to behold. Coaches always talk about getting their teams to play hard. They are usually happy, even in defeat, if their teams have played hard. Well, playing hard is where Georgetown starts, and that all stems from Thompson.

John recruits the kind of inner-city athletes who relate to fierce competitiveness. In a phrase, they're basketball street-fighters. Not for nothing is Georgetown known as the LA Raiders of college basketball; the Hoyas even wear uniforms suspiciously close to silver and black. If you can't run and jump and press, you won't play at Georgetown. If you don't like defense, go elsewhere.

John says that if you ask one hundred kids what position they play, all hundred will tell you their offensive position. "If they say 'forward' I ask them offense or defense?" Thompson says. "They don't have an answer. Fathers say they've got a son six-eight who can play guard. I ask them, can he check Isiah Thomas on the perimeter? We need somebody like that. That stops 'em."

Thompson says at Georgetown he looks for the people who "appreciate the music of defense." And that usually means drums. Because the Hoyas absolutely pound people into the court.

Other coaches have to envy the defensive intensity that Georgetown displays every season, but one of the raps John takes is a valid one. A few seasons ago when he had Ewing and Michael Graham, and again in '88 when the Hoyas engaged in a pair of widely publicized fights with Pittsburgh, I had to criticize Thompson because I felt he was letting his team's instincts for physical play get out of hand. Thompson says he doesn't condone fighting, that he's told his teams that the first guy who throws a punch won't play. But the fights keep happening, and I firmly believe that it's the coach who is ultimately responsible for the players' actions. He should keep a tighter rein on his kids.

Characteristically, Thompson would say after each incident that he hadn't seen the fight break out, so how could he comment? That's a cop-out. "I've seen worse fights in the streets," Thompson said after one skirmish with Pitt. "I've never seen anybody get hurt in a basketball fight."

C'mon, John. Somebody should have shown Thompson shots of Rudy Tomjanovich's crushed face after Kermit Washington decked him in a Rockets–Lakers game several years back.

But when you get right down to it, there were more fights in the college game last year than just those involving Georgetown. The Hoyas' aggressive, physical style can always be controlled by the whistle. But it's up to the referees. If the officials have the guts to come in and control the action, there's not going to be a problem.

On the other hand, Thompson takes most of his raps because of envy, jealousy, fear, and, I am certain, not a small amount of racism. Let's face it; this enormous, 6-10, three-hundred-pound black dude just out of high school coaching turns up at Georgetown, reverses a losing program, molds it into a giant and becomes a media heavyweight in the process within a few years—that made a lot of tongues wag. I'll say this, too: John is the single most important coach to his school. By that I mean, if Knight or Smith or Digger Phelps, say, were to leave Indiana or Carolina or Notre Dame, those programs would survive and remain among the elite of the sport because of their reputations and traditions. If Thompson ever left Georgetown, it would be el foldo for the Hoyas. Good night. Over and out. He's that much responsible for the success there.

And I'm tired of hearing the other knocks: that he controls the Big East, that he gets kids into Georgetown that don't belong, that he keeps his players under too tight security from the public and the press, that his operating style is steeped in Hoya Paranoia.

It's all image. There is no way Thompson bullies or pushes around Dave Gavitt, the Big East commissioner who in his subtle fashion is one of the most influential and powerful guys in the game. As for controlling the Georgetown players' dealings with the outside world, hey, at least the guy's consistent. As long as he's doing it for everybody, I have no qualms about the policy. If he let this or that kid speak to the networks and not to the local newspapers or vice versa, that would be one thing. But I've never gotten any kind of special attention nor have I seen other media people get any, so I can appreciate and respect the policy. Remember, John Wooden had the same kind of system at UCLA and he did fairly well with it.

Georgetown is one of our great academic institutions. The bottom line is that John gets his players into programs where a support staff works with them so that they keep up in their studies and eventually are graduated. His graduation rate is super. So if the guy can expose kids to that kind of learning environment and they adapt well enough to get through, who is to say they didn't belong there in the first place?

Jerry Tarkanian at UNLV has a different problem. Nobody thinks much of the academic reputation of his school. To compensate for this, Tark and his wife, Lois, have almost gone overboard in trying to sell what a great school Vegas is. It's almost become embarrassing. Now they're putting out graduation numbers and everything, just like the Knights, Smiths, and Thompsons. I kid Tark, "Jerry, we're going to have to start calling you 'the Harvard of the West.' "

At heart, though, Tarkanian still is the Father Flanagan of the game—taking chances on dropouts, transfers, marginal students, academic risks, attitude problems, even kids who've been in trouble with the law. If there's a kid with a checkered past who can play a little, Tarkanian's phone will ring and the kid will get a shot.

There was a time when the Tarkanians had great resentment about Jerry's reputation—Lois is still his greatest backer: she lambasted me, for example, when in a coaches' poll in my basketball magazine Dick (Hoops) Weiss, one of the premier basketball writers in the country, ranked her husband only twelfth. But now Tark tells the jokes himself:

About the time he brought in a transfer player to meet the UNLV president and assure him the kid could make the academic grade.

"Ask him anything, just anything," Tark called out to the president from the back of the room.

The prez held up three fingers on each hand. "How much is this, son?" he asked the player.

"Uh . . . uh . . . six?" said the player.

"Give him another chance!" shouted Tark.

Or about the time Jerry was coaching at Long Beach and he heard that a star player was not going to class. "You will show up in class," Tark told him.

The next day the coaches heard back that the player had popped into the classroom, refused to do any work and told the professor not to get on his case, he knew the basketball staff would get him a C anyway.

Tark confronted the player that afternoon. "Don't ever embarrass me again," he said. "Tomorrow you will go to your room, sleep all day and be at practice at three o'clock. You will not go to class ever again."

As obviously apocryphal as these stories are, I've told Tarkanian that continuing to recruit players like Lloyd Daniels, the wandering New Yorker who never belonged in college and busted out of Vegas after a drug arrest, is not worth it any more. Tarkanian has reached the point where he is too good a coach, too famous a name with too established a program, to have to resort to recruiting the social and academic dregs of society—no matter how great they are as players.

I've been all over the country watching different teams and I can tell from a practice session how organized and prepared a coach is. I'd put Tark in a class with the giants when it comes to having his players ready to play in the pressure cooker heat of the game. Last year before the Runnin' Rebels' important upset of Temple, Tark stayed up until four-thirty in the morning watching tapes.

One thing he has over all the big names, too, is his adaptability. He doesn't restrict his players to one style of play. He recruits athletes and gets the maximum out of them by allowing them to demonstrate their abilities in an open-court situation. Flexibility is the word, I guess. Vegas runs and guns up and down the floor, but it's a controlled, organized fast break and it all comes from that pressing defense. John Wooden told me that what makes Tark truly unique is that he's the only coach who's won playing the zone defense in a slowdown game like he did at Long Beach State, and then with the pressure defense and a fast-paced style like at UNLV.

He's also one of the few coaches who can get the superstar player to sit on the bench and understand he's still part of the team. That may be as difficult a task as there is in coaching. He's been to the Final Four twice—in 1977 and 1987. Some people felt he had the best team in the country both years. It won't be another decade before Tark's back again.

And surely he's done the job sellingwise in a place that's not exactly hard-pressed for entertainment. Tark's had it rolling in Vegas for years. Take your Duke zanies, your Palestra fanatics, your WAC conference wackos—nobody supports a team as boisterously as the coochy-Gucci crew at Vegas. And Tarkanian is the celeb among celebs. The pictures in his spectacular office tell the story: Jerry with Wayne Newton, Jerry with Don Rickles, Jerry with Frank Sinatra. What's the deal, Tark? No Jerry with Dick Vitale?

My wife and I were at a party that one of Tark's doctor friends in Vegas threw for him. It was an amazing bash—all his former players were there, as well as Bobby Vinton and a host of celebrities. The quandary for me was that Paul Anka was in town appearing at one of the hotels and Lorraine and I wanted to go see him. It was getting late and I kept bugging Tark about Paul Anka. Finally I said we had to leave the party.

"I'll get you a ride," Tark said.

And with that this beautiful blonde came up, took us outside, called for her Rolls-Royce and drove us to the Golden Nugget. When we pulled up, the hotel staff came pouring out to help us. She whispered into this guy's ear, that guy's ear. In a flash we were practically on the stage shaking hands with Paul Anka. It turns out the blonde was Elaine Wynn, the wife of Steve Wynn, who *owns* the Golden Nugget.

The next day, speaking at a coaches' clinic in Vegas, I told the audience about our experience: "This is the kind of thing that happens to a one-eyed, bald, Italian old man who can't play a lick. Imagine if I could play! Do you want your players to be recruited by Vegas or what?"

I wouldn't mind my players being recruited by Denny Crum at Louisville, either. When I think of Crum, I just think of this: he gets them there. In the 1980s: two national championships, two other appearances in the Final Four. One of the biggest stories of the 1987 tournament was that Louisville was *not* invited. That's a rep to be proud of.

One of the things to be admired about Crum at Louisville is that he plays the toughest schedule around; he doesn't load up with cupcakes. That got him into hot water in '87 when his team was shut out from the NCAAs because of its 18–14 record. Still, if the gutless Metro Conference had done the right thing and not let Memphis State play in its tournament—the Tigers were on probation—thereby allowing Memphis to win the tournament, Louisville might have received a bid. To this day, Crum is bitter. And he has a legit gripe. If I were Louisville, I might have pulled out of the Metro. The Cardinals would be in demand by conferences everywhere.

Crum is a much better bench coach than he's given credit for. People observe his Cool Hand Luke style on the bench and figure he's not into the game as much as the other guy. The general feeling is that he's got great athletes; all he does is turn them loose. But I've watched the Louisville practices. Crum is similar to the other men in this category. They don't

win just on reputation. They don't win just because they have
the best players. They get the best players, define their roles,
and put them into a team concept.

If there's one area where Denny has been deficient, it's in
adapting to the three-point shot. He hasn't recruited many
long-range shooters, hasn't put the trey into the Louisville
offense. I get the feeling he hasn't even bothered to work on
a defense for it, he despises the shot so much. Knight and
Tarkanian incorporated the trifecta into their offenses in '87
and both made the Final Four because of it. Denny was stub-
born. Similarly, our Pan Am team didn't do the job of guarding Brazil's three-point maniacs and that might have cost us
the victory in the final.

It's possible that Crum's laid-back style works much better
over a long season with players he has recruited and coached
for a few years rather than in a short-term, all-star situation.
Even some of Denny's players on the Pan Am team—David
Robinson in particular was quoted on this—were critical of
his lack of discipline for the squad. But the test of superstar-
dom in coaching is time. Denny's teams always seem to peak
at just the right time, storming into the tournament with a
full head of steam. And Denny has done the job with different
guys over a long period of time.

I also happen to think that Crum was the one guy who could
have continued the UCLA dynasty after John Wooden retired. Crum had been Wooden's assistant for a long time,
remember, before leaving for Louisville. I believe he would
have sustained the program in Westwood and prevented it
from becoming the Luke and Laura, General Hospital–type
soap opera that exists today.

Following his '86 championship I met Denny by chance in
the Atlanta airport. He was on his way to Florida to play some
golf. We were standing there shooting the breeze when a kid
came running up for an autograph. He said: "Can I have your
autograph, Mr. Vitale?" Then he looked at Crum and said:
"Can I have yours too, Mr. Smith?"

Which about epitomizes Denny Crum and his personality.

He's never been out front in terms of publicity, hype, recognition or the microphones and cameras. He's the Quiet Man among the superstar coaches.

Speaking of which, every season brings about various episodic dramas, not to mention loud noises, down the road from Louisville in Lexington, Kentucky. By merely coping with that and keeping the Wildcats in the thick of things nationally, Kentucky coach Eddie Sutton rates a place among my Rolls-Roycers.

I keep telling Eddie I'm betting he doesn't last five seasons at Lexington, so intense is the pressure of this job I consider the toughest in sports in America. The manager of the New York Yankees has only George Steinbrenner to please. The Notre Dame football coach can save a season with seven victories and a bowl appearance. At Kentucky the head man has an entire state of Steinbrenners breathing down his neck and if he doesn't win the NCAAs—forget about simply getting into the tournament—the season is a failure.

When Sutton was hired by Kentucky at the Final Four in Lexington in 1985, a broadcaster by the name of Vitale was left with egg on his face. I had found out that Lute Olsen of Arizona was already meeting with the Kentucky TV package people, that he had been offered the job and it was just a matter of his accepting. So I went on the air with it for ESPN. When Olsen backed out—and after Gene Bartow at Alabama-Birmingham refused to return for another interview out of pride—the Kentucky people turned to Sutton.

"I'd crawl from Arkansas to Kentucky for this job," Sutton said in a remark that burned a few bridges down in Razorback land. But people should remember how far Sutton had traveled. I used to do clinics with him when he was a little-known coach at little-known Creighton. And before that he was forced to recruit players at the College of Southern Idaho (a junior college) before the college had even built a gym!

What Sutton realized was that at Kentucky a coach always

has a chance—a chance at a national title. When Kentucky calls, a recruit answers. When Kentucky talks, a kid listens. At Kentucky a coach never has to worry about being a fundraiser, a ticket salesman, getting attention or recruiting. The Wildcats always get their share of the best players, the blue-chippers.

I was in Lexington last year doing a radio call-in show and discussing the advantages of changing the Hoosier Dome doubleheader featuring Indiana–Notre Dame and Kentucky–Louisville to a two-night tournament when the phone rang and a student started berating me for that idea. Only the caller wasn't a student; it was Eddie Sutton. I recognized him right away; it takes more than a name change to fool Dickie V. I think his opposition to the tournament stems from the pressure it would put on him to try to win it year after year. UK's alumni would accept nothing less.

The doubleheader has been the least of Eddie's problems at Kentucky, however. To hear him talk, the main detriment to success at Kentucky has been that very success.

"Because we are who we are, we get all these kids with great names and reputations and they're bigger than life in high school before they even get here," Sutton told me last season. "Then they can't live up to the billing, they have to share time, they get discouraged. It's a helluva way to put a team together."

Sutton was obviously proud of his record at Arkansas. "Look at [Sidney] Moncrief, at [Ron] Brewer, at [Alvin] Robertson. They weren't heavily recruited big-timers. You have to go after the marquee names here but, damn! I wonder if we need to sign them all."

Last year Sutton found out that Rex Chapman was a basketball god in the state. When he questioned Chapman's shot selection publicly, the state was not pleased. Sutton had words with point guard Ed Davender, who objected when the coach replaced him with his own son, Sean. (Coaching your son is usually a can of worms waiting to be pried open.) All season he was hesitant about how much playing time to give his famous freshmen, LeRon Ellis and Eric Manuel, who in turn were hot and cold and everywhere in between. Kentucky was the number-one team in the polls early in the season but struggled throughout.

After the Wildcats suffered an embarrassing loss to injury-depleted Auburn—the Tigers played without Jeff Moore or Mike Jones—in the middle of the season at Rupp Arena, Sutton was walking out the door when the overwhelming significance of Kentucky basketball socked him square in the jaw. It was a little eight-year-old boy sobbing his head off.

"What happened, coach?" the boy said.

Wow. You don't think that's pressure?

The next day, going to practice, Eddie felt so humiliated about the defeat he refused to walk by the crowd that was lined up at the ticket counter for the next game, and instead snuck in a side door. The Wildcats held a vicious three-hour practice session that afternoon as well as a team meeting. Sutton thought the Cats weren't concentrating. He gave his players a test of about ten questions, among which were:

1) What was the score of the Auburn game?

2) Who made the winning basket?

3) Who are our next three opponents?

Several of the Wildcats had no idea about who took the game-winner. A couple of the guys were no where near the right score. Concentration? Case closed.

Expectations? A few seasons ago I was walking out of Rupp following a close Kentucky victory over Ohio State, then a top-ten team with Kelvin Ransey and Herb Williams. It was a helluva game during the coaching era of Joe B. Hall, before Sutton came to Lexington. In 1978, Kentucky under Hall had won the national championship, albeit, as Joe said then, "joylessly" because everybody in the Bluegrass *expected* the Wildcats to win it. As I walked out of the Ohio State game the fans in front of me were complaining. "The Cats choked again," one said. "We should have blown them out by twenty-five."

It's no place for anything less than a Rolls-Roycer. They've got one there now, but for how long?

Speaking about not staying around, my last pick for the Super Seven is basketball's original Travelin' Man, Larry Brown. I always kid Larry that I really can't put him on my All–GQ team or in any other category of coaches because he's moved so much I never know where he is. But after the job he did taking his overachieving Kansas team to the national title, there's no longer any doubt—the man is a Rolls-Roycer all the way.

What Larry achieved in the 1988 tournament is one of the three best jobs of coaching I've ever seen, ahead of Rollie Massimino's perfect game for Villanova against Georgetown, and right behind Jim Valvano's N.C. State title against Houston. I only put Valvano ahead of Brown because of what he had to accomplish just to get into the tournament, first beating the Perkins-Jordan Carolina team, then getting by Sampson and Virginia for the ACC title. Without that automatic berth, the Wolfpack might well have been left on the outside looking in.

So Larry, my hat's off to you. You're the only non-Italian among my top three overachievers.

The recognition's been a long time coming for Larry. Part of the problem was that his reputation for moving on has obscured what a good job he did while he was around. He's coached Carolina and Denver in the ABA, then Denver and New Jersey in the NBA, with a term at UCLA along the way. And everybody was watching for him to leave Kansas almost from the moment he got there. Early in his career there he told me, "Dick, it's just not fair. You and everybody always say I never stay in one place very long. I've been in Lawrence four seasons already—summer, fall, winter, and spring."

My All–GQ team got a rise out of Larry, too. "Don't ever put me on the same list with those guys," Larry said. "They wear so much polyester, if they ever stand next to a radiator the whole building will go up in flames."

But on a serious note, here is a guy who is a great teacher and motivator, a class individual brimming with integrity, a person who gets so close to his players and assistants that his leave-taking has been more and more painful each time it's happened. And the coaching job he did last season with a team that was just wiped out by injuries and academic problems was an absolute masterpiece. Remember, this was a team that looked like a long shot to make it into the NIT, never mind the Final Four.

As I've told him, Larry Brown is just the kind of coach college basketball needs. *Come back to college, Larry.* I can understand the challenge of taking on the Spurs, the lure of the big bucks they offered, the chance to build with a franchise player like David Robinson, the knowledge that whatever you did at Kansas would never top that last act—but I truly hope that Brown will end up back where his teaching, motivating and molding skills can do so much good. I still stand by my prediction that he'll end up at North Carolina as the successor to Dean Smith someday. But wherever his travels takes him, I wish Larry all the best. Individuals like him bring a real touch of class to the college game.

PAISANOS AND WACKOS, MOANERS AND MR. CLEANS

PAISANOS

Is there any better word for them? Start with Jimmy Vee—yeah, Jim Valvano, at North Carolina State. I go way back with Vee, who played in the backcourt at Rutgers with Bobby Lloyd, the brother of Dick Lloyd, who gave me my first college job. Vee was a good shooter in his own right, a tough kid from Long Island, a street fighter from a basketball family. That Rutgers team went all the way to the NIT semifinal before running into the Salukis of Southern Illinois and the great Walt Frazier.

Valvano's late father, Rocco, was a coach. His brother, Bob, is coaching in Europe. I got to know Vee as a coach, sitting in diners talking hoops when he was at Bucknell and I was at Rutgers. He almost beat us one year; Dick Lloyd was very concerned because Vee was getting a lot of notoriety and some alumni figured he should be coaching Rutgers instead of Dick.

Later when Valvano was at Iona and I was coaching Detroit, he came out to play us and I was worried how to get my kids up for his team. As Vee used to joke, "Iona? I used to introduce myself from Iona University and people looked at me like I was crazy. They'd say, 'You're so young to own a whole college!' " Luckily, though, Iona had just beaten St. John's, so I could throw that name at my kids and they listened. That night, when it became apparent we would blow Iona away, I started working on a delay game, spreading the court, holding the ball, etc. But the fans wanted blood. As we walked off, they booed like crazy. "Vee, I saved you. Help me out," I said.

"Vitale, you're nuts," Valvano said. "First you blitz me, embarrass my butt. Now you want *me* to get the fans off your back!"

For all his comedic shtick, Valvano is a master on the bench. He develops spectacularly unorthodox teams—check out last year's Wolfpack of Charles Shackleford, Chuckie Brown and that gang—simply because he's so unorthodox. There is no rhyme or reason to his substitution pattern, but he gets away with it. He's a seat-of-the-pants coach. Game situations totally dictate what he does, but that way he keeps everybody on the team involved. And for controlling the tempo in a tournament atmosphere—well, look at the record. A couple of ACC tournament titles, another pair of NCAA Final Eights, one NCAA championship—all when his teams probably had no business being there. Everybody thought Vee was joking again when he said last year his goal was to go 7–7 in the ACC, knock off enough cupcakes to hit 20 wins and get into the NCAA tournament. But that really is State's MO.

Of course, when Vee's approach doesn't work, he leaves himself open to a lot of shots. I gave him some myself last year when he lost in the first round of the NCAAs to Murray State. I had just finished telling Bob Ley that the three coaches I would want on my side in the NCAA tournament were Vee, Bobby Knight, and Dale Brown, when the results started coming in. Boom! N.C. State falls to Murray State. Boom! Indiana loses to Richmond. Boom! LSU gets knocked out by Georgetown. My three sharp picks were down and out. But like I told Vee, I could understand losing to Georgetown or Richmond, but how does he explain being the only coach in history to get bounced from the NCAAs by a dance studio?

But what about that '83 run to the championship where Vee used the clock and the foul situations at the ends of games? Sure, Valvano fouled his way to the national title, but that was dictated by the game situations and his personnel. He was just using the rules of the game to his advantage, and isn't that part of being a great bench coach? They eventually had to change the intentional foul rule because of Vee. That's a legacy, baby! And he was awesome with the media in Albuquerque after State won. Who can ever forget his line when he said he was so happy, his wife, Pam, was going to get pregnant and he was going to name the kid "Al B. Kerky."

I kid Valvano that he only recruits players with names ending in vowels. Look at his '88 squad: Del Negro, Corchiani, D'Amico. Sounds like a construction business. But seriously, what coach ever capitalized more on a national championship than Valvano? He's athletic director, cookbook author, radio and TV star, marketing man, sales rep. For a year after the title he gave speeches during which he'd open a box and start selling his diary of the championship season. Larry Brown says that prior to his game against Vee in the '86 Midwest regional final, Valvano delayed the coaches' big joint press conference while trying to convince Brown to cooperate on some deal to sell laminated team pictures of the Final Four teams. And they hadn't even played yet to see who would get into the Final Four!

"Immediately after dinner Vee will be outside the hall," I tell banquet audiences, "selling autographed copies of the North Carolina State team jockstraps."

According to Rollie Massimino of Villanova, I never give him the proper respect. He may be right. The day before the Wildcats won the NCAA tournament in '85 we did an ESPN show from Claiborne Farms in Lexington, Kentucky, in which we broke down the final teams, position by position, player by player. At each spot, the winner came out Georgetown. At the coaching spot, advantage Georgetown: John Thompson had more experience at postseason tournament time.

Well, you know I heard about it after Rollie pitched that Don Larsen gem against Big John. A couple of years later—I'd just done my coaches' top-five list for ESPN—we had a game at 'Nova and I told my producers to just watch, Massimino would be in my face. Sure enough, we walked into the gym and basketballs came flying at me from every which way.

"Vitale, you Sonofa$%$#@!" Rollie read me the riot act.

"Hey, Rollie, quit yelling," I said. "You were number six on the list, baby, number six, it just never got on the air. We ran out of minutes."

(I told every coach that they were number six, that we just ran out of minutes. Works every time. Until they see my Super Seven, that is.)

Massimino is close enough to his players that he isn't afraid to play the clown for them. One night at Syracuse he put on a sheet and turban in the locker room, posing as a swami with a crystal ball, and predicted a W over the Orangemen. It didn't happen. Who ever heard of an Italian swami? But the guy is one terrific teacher and motivator who will not accept a kid who won't blend into the Villanova "family" or do things his way. Individualism is a no-no. Rollie lost Pearl Washington because of this philosophy—and the Pearl always had huge games against Villanova. Washington would dipsy-do down the lane for a basket and I'd say, "Hey Rollie, you like that little 'individual' move?" But the coach stuck to his guns.

Rollie was very hurt by the Gary McLain article in *Sports Illustrated* about his cocaine use—crushed, really, because of this very family-oriented system. Al McGuire used to have the philosophy that a coach shouldn't have to be a bartender, sob sister, or Ann Landers. He wasn't there to hear the players' problems or keep tabs on them or worry about where they were or who they were with; a coach wasn't a social worker. But in this day and age I don't know any coach who doesn't preach to his kids about going to class, about avoiding drugs, about not associating with gamblers, about staying away from trouble. And Massimino is one of the guys who goes way beyond that, who cares the most.

And yet when the guillotine comes down, the coach gets it. Rollie got blamed by McLain for his involvement with cocaine. It was a terribly cruel cheap shot. My feeling was that if McLain was sincere about rehabilitation and helping others with a "message," he should have taken the thousands of dollars he got from *Sports Illustrated* for telling his story and put it into a scholarship fund for kids to clean up their act. McLain showed no class. He hurt his coach, his teammates and the University as a whole by implicating everybody in the drug scene without mentioning names. That was a dark episode for Villanova—for all of college sport—and I was overjoyed to see Rollie and the Wildcats come back with a good season in '87–88, culminating in his dramatic run to the Southeast Regional Final.

Louie Carnesecca is the padre of the paisanos. What can I say? The gravel voice, the sweater, the face etched from the rocky crags of the Italian Alps. A St. John's practice can't start until I've kissed Louie's ring.

I call Carnesecca the Baryshnikov of basketball for his little sideline dances and swoops and slides. Once in the Garden he had no room to dance, so he actually climbed up on the players' bench chairs and ran up and down so he could see over their heads. The man is over sixty and he's still jumping up and down like a madman.

"What's the key to the game tonight?" I asked Louie once, since ESPN always likes to use a graphic about the technical elements the fans should watch out for.

"Key? What key?" Louie said. "Very simple. Put the ball in the hole. Cut the bull#$#@$. Key? Gimme a break. First, you try to score. Then, you guard them and try to stop them from scoring. If you score more than they do, you win. If you don't, you lose. How #$%$#ing simple can it get?"

And that's the Redmen in a nutshell. You don't have to scout St. John's. Carnesecca does the same things year in, year out, game in, game out. Classic half-court basketball stuff. Tough man defense. Walk the ball up. Solid offensive patterns. Get the ball to the key people. Louie gets criticized for putting audiences to sleep, but his team's movement without the ball and two-man games are beauties to behold.

It's fascinating to me that he gets the New York kids, who are used to the individual flash and dash of street ball, to stay in the area and compete for St. John's. But he harnesses them in a positive way. And his Italian point guards! Carmine Calzonetti. Frankie Alagia. Mark Jacksonalli. If a New York Italian can play, it's pretty tough to get him away from Carnesecca. Fortunately for the rest of the Big East, there aren't a lot of Italians who can play.

Louie was an assistant at St. John's under Joe Lapchick, the Big Chief; he played baseball at the school with a man who might someday be Commander in Chief, New York governor Mario Cuomo. When the Johnnies play at Syracuse, Mario's got to lose some of that upstate vote.

Carnesecca tried the pros for a few years. He coached the Nets in the ABA with Rick Barry. But he lives, eats and dies with St. John's too much to have stayed away long. Louie suffers on every basket, the same way Massimino does. Guys like that have to stick to college ball; if Massimino had gone to the Nets a couple of years ago, the suffering would have devoured him. I'm still not so sure Ricky Pitino, who left Providence for the Knicks, will want to stay in the pros. He may be built just like the others.

Which brings me to the lead singer of my Italian stallion barbershop quartet, Norman Sloanini. I changed Norm Sloan's name after he attacked me in '87 at the NCAA tournament. Here I was, a quiet guy minding my own business, and he buried me. Got a lot of ink, lots of pub. Said he was "sick and tired of Vitale talking about all the Italian coaches who run and sweat and hug people." He tried to soften it by saying "But I really like the paisanos; I even like garlic bread." Hey, I didn't mind Norman's stormin' so much. But the Italian Coaches Association was hot, let me tell you. Valvano and Carnesecca were really mad.

See, I think Norm used me to get at Jimmy. I think he's always been a little envious of Vee, resentful of the fact that he was never treated with the same love and admiration that Valvano gets in Raleigh. They both won national championships with the Wolfpack, but the media and Sloan's peers always pointed out his NCAA title was won by players who got State put on probation the year before. That's a sticky subject with Norm.

No stickier, however, than the fabulous Italian sauces Sloanini's wife, Joanne, fixed for me at a sumptuous feast in Gainesville last season when we buried the hatchet. The occasion was the Florida–Ohio State game, and Norm had Buckeye coach Gary Williams and me over for dinner. We taped it for ESPN with Italian music playing in the background, me announcing my Norm Sloan coaching five—all Italians, of course—and us feeding each other pasta.

But that same night, Dick Weiss and I were leafing through a Florida basketball yearbook, and we read that Sloan—in direct quotes—had accused me of using my position as a TV guy to recruit Vernon Maxwell for Valvano and N.C. State! I was livid.

The next day at practice I confronted Sloan. "Norman, what are all these quotes? I never even talked to Maxwell."

"You never talked to Maxwell?" Sloan said.

"Call him over and ask him," I said.

When Maxwell came over, he acknowledged that we had never spoken. He said that when he was visiting State, Valvano said he was good friends with Dick Vitale and if Vernon were to sign with State, I would announce it on ESPN.

I wondered why Norm hadn't checked this story out before going to the papers. I really believe he had such harsh feelings toward Valvano that he wanted to believe the worst. Then again, Norm forgets things. Five minutes later he gave me a story about his forward, Chris Capers, and how he never played much basketball in high school because he was in the band.

This was great stuff, so I was madly writing it down and asking what instrument Capers played. Again, Norm called the player over to talk.

"What instrument did you play in the band?" he said to Capers.

"I didn't play in the band, coach," said Capers. "I was too busy playing basketball all through high school."

These Italian coaches . . . Man!

WACKOS AND COMICS

One of my all-time favorite guys in the game is the Motivator, the Preacher Man, the coach at LSU, Dale Brown. If ever there was a guy who can rouse his troops against insurmountable odds and win when he has no business winning, it's Dale.

I'll just point out one instance a few years ago when I went into Baton Rouge to do an LSU–Kentucky game. The Tigers were plagued with the chicken pox. I mean, about six of them were down and out. Other guys were on academic probation. John Williams was out, several other key players were out.

Dale had barely eight guys on the roster and he was thinking about bringing in some football players just so he could practice and maybe use them in the game.

When I walked in Dale went into his routine right away. "Dick," he said. "I want to bring you to practice but I can't let you watch the players shooting and drilling because I've had that off-limits to the media all week. What I'm going to do is take you to a private team meeting."

Well, this meeting was like something out of the movies. He started whipping out videotapes and records and motivational stuff and the music was playing and it sounded like "Rocky." The players were ready to jump out of the building. He showed them tapes from back in 19-aught-6, whenever: "When we beat Kentucky here we had only six players and everybody fouled out of the game." Stuff like that. He had a list of motivational thoughts, one right after the other. You could see these kids were going to be ready to go out and battle.

Dale played one tape showing them hanging the banner at LSU when they won the Southeastern Conference championship a few years before. He played another from when the Kentucky national championship team of 1977–78 came in and LSU had several players foul out and still won in double overtime. He had the players listen to Bob Richards: "A genius is an average man." It was astounding.

I came out of there knowing this ball game was going to be a war. Everybody was looking for an NC'er, Blowout City, but after hearing all that, I opened our national telecast and flat-out said we were going to have a knee-knocker, a spine-tingler. In a one-game shot the magic word, emotion, means so much. And this night Mr. Dale Brown, the Preacher Man at his Billy Graham–best, was ready to roll. And sure enough, it was a wire game that LSU lost on a Roger Harden running jumper at the buzzer.

Another time I was doing an LSU–Georgia Tech game in Baton Rouge when Dale decided he'd let us in on his "freak" defense. Now you and I know the only freak defense is if you play five men and I play seven. Or if the guy making up the defense is some kind of freak. But . . .

"I'll tell you what I'm going to do for you guys," Dale said. "I'll let you in on the signals I'm going to throw from the bench. If I flash this, a zero, that means we're going to the man defense. If I throw this, a triangle, we're going diamond-and-one. If I go to a certain number code, we'll go half man-to-man, half zone, and then go to the freak."

Naturally, a coach wants the other team to be concerned when you're changing on every move they make. But this was going to be a riot, with the camera on Dale switching defenses as if he was a traffic cop.

Dale wanted to take us to dinner in his car because he wanted to play some more tapes for us. At least this time, they were all audio. We were driving along and when Dale switched on the tape, a guy came on singing about the LSU Tigers. "That's a great one," Dale said. "Let's go, Tigers," went the song, and Dale sang along full-blast. Then he grabbed another tape, which was another song about the Tigers, only the *latest* song. But it got stuck. So Dale panicked and pulled the car over to the side of the road.

Why were we sitting and waiting? Because some ESPN engineers would be coming along the road later and we knew they were mechanical enough to fix the tape. "We can't leave the road before we hear this tape," Dale insisted. And we didn't. We sat there by the side of the road until we'd heard him sing along with both songs.

And that night LSU won, too. Because of the freak. And I don't mean the defense.

One more Preacher Man story. Later in that same year that he had most of the Tigers down with chicken pox, Dale and LSU made their amazing run to the Final Four. I must have picked them to lose every game in the tournament because by the time they made the national semifinals in Dallas, Dale had headbands made up that said *Vitale 0–5*. Like I took the Ziggy. And now he was bragging to everybody that Vitale was a dummy and he was going to win the national championship.

When we got Dale on our pre–Final Four show—this was before LSU against Louisville in Dallas—he started running his mouth about how they were going to beat Denny Crum and the Cardinals. "There's no doubt in my mind," Dale crowed. "We're out to prove Vitale wrong." So I came on the show with Bob Ley and I said to Dale, "I have a challenge for you, Preacher Man. If you beat Louisville in the semis I will walk home immediately following the game. From Dallas all the way to Bradenton, Florida. I will walk all the way. Final gun, you win, I start walking. IF . . . IF . . . in the event *you* lose, my man, you, Dale Brown, walk all the way home to Baton Rouge. What about it? Is it a deal?" Alas, Dale hedged and let it hang. Not only did he not accept the challenge, I think he changed the subject. He said there was no way he would walk.

But man, did I have more shaky moments sitting in the stands during that game. I was writing a column for the *Dallas Times Herald* during the Final Four and I was watching the game with a pad in my lap, trying to figure out what to write, when LSU jumped out on Louisville at the half. I couldn't believe it. My wife was cracking up while I was sweating how I'd ever find directions to the Louisiana border.

An announcer isn't supposed to root. But you know who I was rooting for in that one.

A couple of other times I didn't root for Dale were on the occasions of those verbal shout-outs he's had with Don DeVoe and Bobby Knight. When he called Knight "a despicable human being" and said Knight flat-out cheats by putting his own players on the Olympic and Pan Am teams and getting his assistants good jobs so he can control the programs at their schools—that's a joke. It's ludicrous. Bobby came right back at Dale and said of Indiana's last-second victory over LSU in the '87 NCAA Midwest Regional final that he was worried until he looked at the other bench and saw Brown there. Hey, this was all Dick and Jane, Spot and Puff stuff. Na-na-na-na-nahh. Like two little kids sticking their tongues out.

Knight is an easy hit. You rip him and you get headlines all over. I was on a talk show with Brown in New Orleans; he buried Knight from head to toe.

The Brown-DeVoe thing also lacked taste. First Devoe called Brown "immoral" for hiring the high school coaches of outstanding players—Jim Childers from South Carolina along with his star, 6-10 center Stanley Roberts, is the latest—implying that the young coach wasn't qualified on his own and was just along as part of the package. Hey, I was in that situation myself once with a great player. But if a coach has credentials, why should his having nurtured a star be a disadvantage to his getting ahead rather than an advantage? I see nothing wrong with that.

Then Dale replied by questioning the morality of DeVoe's getting divorced! Whoa, now! That's a slap in the face to millions of people who may not have been able to live together as husband and wife but are good people nevertheless. They're not immoral!

Let's face it. Mr. Brown gets carried away with himself sometimes. I think he hurts his own cause. But to his credit, he recognizes that. I think the hiring of Joe Dean as athletic director has helped; Dean has great PR sense, and he's helped smooth out some of Dale's rough edges. Dale called a press conference just to say that he regretted saying what he'd said, and that sometimes his mouth runs away with him. I guess that's something we have in common.

Then there are the fellas who love having their names mentioned, positive or negative, doesn't matter. Any old way at all. What's the saying: "I don't care what they write about me. Just as long as they spell my name right." Way at the top of this category is Billy Tubbs of Oklahoma.

You talk about a fun guy. It's always great to nail Tubbsy because he'll always take it in good faith with a smile on his face and then ratatat you back with a hilarious line of his own.

What I like to get on Tubbs and Oklahoma about is the Sooners' defense. Or should I say lack of defense? I should. Now Tubbs can really coach. He recruits amazing athletes to light up the scoreboard in Norman. He admits he needs that kind of attack just to stay alive and withstand the football interest in the state. He needs a high-scoring offense to keep pace with the football Sooners' wishbone scoring machine.

As a result, more often than not Oklahoma basketball has come up short on the defensive end. It's no secret. Tubbs prides himself on his team's quickness and they will get out and press you, especially at home there in Norman. But in the NCAA tournament that defense of his used to keep falling apart.

One year I came on the air and said that for Christmas I was sending Tubbs a videocassette of Bobby Knight talking about ball-man defense. "Tubbs believes in giving up ninety points just so long as the Sooners get ninety-five," I said. "That's fine in the Big Eight, Billy baby, but you can't win the national championship that way."

Well, soon after that he established the Dick Vitale Defensive Award for his team. He gave the award to the Sooner player who was the most hard-nosed on D. He got a lot of pub for me because of that. So we help each other. Just spell our names right.

At the Final Four that season, as I drove up to the head-quarters hotel and got out of the car, here came Tubbs pushing away some coaches and jumping right out in front of me. "Hah, Dick Vitale," he shouted. "I'm ready to take the charge now, Dicky. Run me down. I'm standing my ground. It's a new day at Oklahoma. Now, the Sooners always take the charge." (And no less an authority than the General himself, Bobby Knight, told me that he thinks Oklahoma's pressing, running, shoot-fast-and-take-no-prisoners style will be the dominant style of the '90s. Take *that* charge, Billy!)

Just the other day I got word that something else had happened in Oklahoma. How's this for Iconsville? They got a league there now, I don't know where . . . they call it the Dick Vitale

League. A fan sent me the league standings and everything.

I have just one question. Do they take the charge in the Dick Vitale League?

Oh, and one more question for Tubbs. Why does he run up scores so? What goes around, comes around. There's nothing wrong with winning by a large margin if you're substituting. Beaten coaches don't expect the other guy to change his style, to go ball control or to a zone just to keep the losing team in the game. But a guy can tell when a game is a rout or a mismatch and it's time to go easy.

Tubbsy got cocky with that overwhelming bunch of Sooners last year; he had his team averaging about 115 points a game when Oklahoma came into New Orleans, where LSU and Brown nailed his hide. Then Oklahoma got upset at Kansas State as well. And finally, in the ultimate game for the national championship, the Sooner artillery broke down completely in the waning minutes and—man, oh Manning!—Kansas, which Tubbs and Oklahoma had beaten twice during the regular season, took the big enchilada.

I probably jinxed the guy. I called Tubbs an "offensive genius." Gracious pal that he is, Billy came back and said it's about time I got something right. I was like a hog rooting around in a field, he said; eventually, the hog had to find an acorn.

When I showed up in Norman last season Tubbs was waiting for me. His team had beaten the Big East's best, Pittsburgh, for the second year in a row and, of course, he equates me with the Big East. "Your Big East is okay, Vitale," he said. "Maybe right up there with the Trans America Conference. I can't really tell yet. But bring the rest of those 'Beast' teams down here, we'll kick their butts back home and then I can make a definitive judgment."

Typically, the Tubbsman explained away Oklahoma's propensity for head-bashing with his down-home humor. "I love to bury people," Billy said. "It only shows 'em where their deficiencies are and makes 'em want to get better so they can bury me." In his inimitable fashion Bad Billy also said, "If I call off the dogs to keep the score down, isn't that against the law? Hell, yes. It's called shaving points. I ain't goin' to no jail for calling off the dogs."

Tubbs is out of one Okie, Will Rogers, by way of another, Abe Lemons—still probably the funniest man in basketball. Talk about your wackos! Abe's the coach at Oklahoma City, which is an NAIA school now. But when he was there in his first go-round, the school was NCAA Division I and made it one year to the NIT. Lemons's team played so badly in the first half in New York that he made them scrimmage *at half-time!*

In March of '87 Abe had Ok-City coming to the NAIA championships as the only undefeated team in the country. I was so excited because ESPN was doing the tournament and I got all my Lemons material ready for the tournament banquet. Then my man Abe's team got upset by Georgetown—of Kentucky!

"The only difference between coaching in the NCAA and the NAIA is the NAIA is much harder," he says. "In the NCAA you just wait for Vitale and Packer to come do your game, set an assistant coach over next to him, and have him run relay back and forth between the TV table and your bench so's you know exactly what to do."

Lemons coached at Texas a few years before his outspokenness got him fired. He says the next car he buys will have a glass bottom so that when he runs over the men who fired him, he can see the expressions on their faces.

I love Abe Lemons. He's the guy who said you don't have to be experienced in coaching to be a coaching expert. "Take a look at Dr. Ruth, the sex expert," Abe said. "You mean to tell me she's had experience?" He was also never all that impressed with the sanctity of the college environment. "Some of the best people in the world never went to school. I know. I have some on my teams."

Behind all the lines is a wily hoops fanatic, let me tell you. The country-bumpkin stuff is all con.

Another one of Lemon's heirs carries out the same motif. Sonny Smith of Auburn. Sonny even likes country music! "I'm not gonna play dumb and be funny anymore, Dick," Smith told me last season. "Except if I can do it for money."

"Heck," said Sonny. "When the writers ask me all these questions and I'm funny, everybody thinks I'm actually dumb!"

Before he got to Auburn and stayed awhile, they used to call him "Suitcase Sonny" Smith for all the basketball jobs he was ready to wander around for. And who knows how long he'll stay there, since he knows basketball will always be second to football in Bo Jackson land. A bad second. A few years ago Smith was so fed up with the lack of fan interest and support from the administration that he up and announced he was retiring at the end of the season. Then the Tigers went on a roll, won the SEC tournament, swept into the NCAAs, and nearly made the Final Four.

Auburn sweetened the pot at home and Sonny stayed. He's developed some monster athletes there, too: Charles Barkley. Chuck Person, and last year, Chris Morris. Smith put on one of the more unbelievable coaching shows last year with that upset of Kentucky at Rupp without several of his best players. An Auburn kid named John Caylor hit the shot to beat the 'Cats, if you're still searching for the answer to the question that stumped the Kentucky players. Sonny was on cloud nine.

"The greatest win in the history of Auburn," Smith gushed to me in an interview afterwards. "I can't believe it. And John Caylor? The only reason I recruited him was I wanted somebody from East Tennessee who could understand the way I talk."

How about Jud Heathcote of Michigan State to wrap up the wackos? He's got the Caesar Augustus haircut to go along with the dry wit, and man, can he flash tempers with the best of them. I first met Jud when I was coaching at Detroit and he was the new man at Michigan State. He came in from Montana State where he had Micheal Ray Richardson, which was reason enough for him to be wacked-out before he got to me.

"Vitale, it's over," he said for openers.

"What, Jud? What's over?" I said.

"Our series. We're not playing you guys anymore," he said. "Don't give me any guff about a verbal contract, either. Michigan State won't be playing Detroit anymore."

If only he'd meant it. The year after I left he brought his Magic Johnson–Jay Vincent–Greg Kelser team in to play Smokey Gaines's 23–4 team and just blew us off the count at home. That loss may have kept U of D out of the NCAAs that year.

I rag Jud about all the publicity and attention he received for his matchup zone that season. That defense became the "in" topic at all the clinics after the season. Up to that time, everything was man pressure. Now the 2-3 matchup zones came into prominence. A few years later I was at a clinic with Jud. "The matchup looked great, big fella," I said. "Magic, Vincent, Kelser. Hmmm. How come you're playing the same matchup now and you're getting pulverized? Is somebody not matching up?"

"Get off my case, Vitale," Heathcote said. "You're a real genius now, right? You're unbeaten in TV. In the real world everybody wanted to schedule you when you were coaching except me. Because I had compassion."

But Heathcote was always cooperative with me in my role as a telecaster until two years ago before an Ohio State game, when I came out to an MSU practice and he wouldn't let me in. "I have to get these guys ready," he said. "They get too excited with you in here. All I hear is, 'Did Vitale see this? Vitale see that?' It's revolting." But last year he did let me come to practice—maybe because he knew his team wasn't anything anyone could get excited about.

If you could take the X and O and motivational ability of Jud Heathcote and combine it with the recruiting (and scheduling) ability of Bill Frieder, you'd have a perennial monster in the state of Michigan. But look out, Frieder—Jud had himself an awesome recruiting class last year, and the maize and blue are going to have a battle on their hands for state supremacy.

A few years ago Heathcote had a heart attack; I watch him in games now—the intensity he puts into it, the emotion— and I swear I don't know how his heart can take the abuse. Last year he rushed onto the court at Arizona, grabbed his seven-footer, George Papadakos, and *punched* him—whap, bap—two quick ones in the ribs. Two years ago he grabbed a loose ball and, furious at the refs, banged it down on the court. Of course, the ball bounced back up and smashed him in the face. Jud was also the victim in that strange clock foul-up at Kansas City in the '86 NCAA Midwest regional when Michigan State played Kansas. "Home-clockin' " he called it.

It's just as well Jud was already such a wacko. A loss like that can make a lunatic out of the sanest coach.

MOANERS AND GROANERS

If you watch Jim Boeheim long enough, you'll come to the conclusion that Syracuse has never committed a foul in the history of basketball. Jim is on the zebras from the jump ball to the gun. He's got a sarcastic sneer on the bench. Then he goes after them with his whiny voice. Together, the package makes him a Crybaby of the Year candidate practically every season.

Ultimately, though, reaching the Final Four in 1987 may have done more than lift the monkey from Jimmy's back at Syracuse. I think it loosened him up to the point where he is more at ease with the press, the public, and himself. As we all saw at those finals in New Orleans—where Syracuse played two outstanding games only to be denied the championship when Keith Smart hit the jackpot for Indiana—Boeheim was relaxed, friendly and outgoing, sometimes even smiling.

The Syracuse job is one of the toughest in the country. With the Carrier Dome and its thirty-thousand-plus mobs demanding the goods, Boeheim knows he's got to win and win big. Gone are the days when he wandered onto the Syracuse campus from nearby little Lyons, New York, as a walk-on guard. Actually, Boeheim has never really left Syracuse. He played for four years and ended up starting in the backcourt for the Orangemen, opposite Dave Bing. When he toured in the Eastern League, he was still doing graduate work at Syracuse. Then he was an assistant coach and finally head man. What other big-time mentor has been so closely affiliated with his school in so many capacities?

The paradox of Syracuse is that while Jimmy is plainspoken, conservative, common folks, his teams are multifaceted rainbows of running, jumping, no-holds-barred excitement. He is a terrific judge of talent, be it playing or coaching. Jim was the first guy to recognize the potential in Rick Pitino; he hired Pitino right off of Rick's honeymoon. "I have a guy on my staff who is destined for stardom," Boeheim told me about Pitino several years ago.

Moreover, he hasn't had the easiest guys to motivate and coach. Pearl Washington could be a downright difficult project in a practice situation. And he's had déjà vu with Derrick Coleman the past couple of years. Then, of course, there was his ongoing love-hate relationship with Rony Seikaly. These are all guys who consider themselves gamers who come to play in the big games, but they don't understand that they set the tone for the whole team's work ethic and practice behavior. When their attitude is "I don't like to practice," that's contagious.

Up in Alaska at the beginning of the 1987–88 season, Seikaly was already bad-mouthing his teammates for not getting him the ball. I was an observer when Boeheim had it out with

Seikaly, who claimed he didn't mean his statements the way they came out, that he wasn't "blaming" his teammates.

Jimmy jumped right in his face. "What do you mean, you 'don't *mean* it that way'?" Boeheim said. "You're saying you don't get the ball. If you say you're not getting it from them, you're blaming your teammates. You have to grow up, Rony. You're hurting people here. You're not getting the ball because you're not moving to get yourself free."

Boeheim may never be free of criticism at Syracuse. After that great season of '86–87 and before his preseason number-one-ranked team had even played a game in '87–88, a two-part diary of the road to New Orleans appeared in a Syracuse newspaper. It was written by former Orange co-captain Greg Monroe. It was pretty mild stuff, but the paper really played up the few quotes that were all critical:"A lot of games, we wondered what Coach was doing." "Sometimes Coach designs all the shots for just one or two players." Stuff like that. Almost as if the newspaper was looking for specks of dirt after a glistening season.

As if that wasn't enough harrassment, more came when Boeheim's prime recruit, Billy Owens out of Carlisle, Pennsylvania, finally made a qualifying score over 700 on his college boards, meaning he could play for the 'Cuse this season. It was thrilling news for Orange followers. But UNLV's Jerry Tarkanian, echoing many other suspicious coaches across the land, got up at a Vegas boosters luncheon and announced there was no way Owens had qualified, that Syracuse must have arranged for a "designated tester" to take Owens's test for him.

Rather than fly off the handle, which he might have done in past years, Boeheim treated that blast with equanimity. "Tark had to be joking," he told me. "He's probably just getting me back for last year when I spoke at the Vegas booster luncheon and presented him with a paper bag full of phony cash."

I know Boeheim is one of those guys who reads everything. He's very sensitive and criticism eats him alive. He doesn't

need raps anymore. He's paid his dues and established one
of the finest programs in the land. With recognition gone
aglimmering, sometimes maybe Jimmy has a reason to cry.

Ironically, with Syracuse having established a recent series
with Michigan, we have the perfect set-up for an annual Crybaby Bowl. Because if Boeheim doesn't lead America in tears,
Michigan's Bill Frieder surely must.

Frieder cries when he's got players, he cries when he hasn't
got 'em. He'll call me at all hours of the day and night. Two
years ago I didn't have Michigan in my Top Twenty. Late
one night, the phone rings. It was Frieder. "Vitale," he said.
(It must be an old Michigan tradition to call everybody by
their last name. Former Michigan athletic director Don Can-
ham did it, the new AD and football legend Bo Schembechler
does it, and so does Frieder.) "Vitale: You don't understand
what we got here. We got the horses. We can do it. We'll
show you before the year is over."

The Wolverines had Gary Grant and Antoine Joubert and
Glen Rice, among others. And they came through with a fine
season. Then they added Terry Mills and Rumeal Robinson
last season and I picked them number one. Another late night
phone call. "Vitale." It was Frieder. "Vitale: What are you,
crazy? Name me a team with freshmen coming in that has
ever been number one. Name me a team that lost such-and-
such three-point baskets that has ever been number one. Name
me a team . . ." He had all his stats ready, screaming that
they were too young, that they couldn't play, negative this
and negative that. With Frieder, I can't win.

Frieder has been a name in Michigan basketball for a long
time. He was the all-time gym rat of the Great Lakes. He
coached in Flint before going to Ann Arbor as an assistant
to Johnny Orr. He is a relentless recruiter, a workaholic, a
basketball junkie who cares for little else (except the new
Mercedes he treated himself to last year). They tell of the
time Frieder went scouting Doc Rivers, then in high school.

Somebody told him if Bo Derek was a ten, Rivers was a nine. Frieder ran to a phone and called his secretary. "Where does this Bo Derek play?" he screamed into the receiver. "Get out the file on Derek."

Frieder wears a towel on his shoulder like John Thompson; I call him the *lightweight* champion of the world. His crying is more or less a way of downgrading his teams. But I told him he can't recruit the Millses, Robinsons, and Sean Higginses of the world, all these high school All-Americans, and then say his teams can't play. Pretty soon a guy's team may start to believe they're not that good. After a loss, it could become a crutch: we're not good enough to win.

All coaches—like all people—have strengths and weaknesses. Like Boeheim, Frieder is dynamite on the recruiting trail. Also, like Boeheim, Frieder's taken knocks for his bench coaching. Rather than accept the criticism and build on his strength, Bill has gotten very defensive and paranoid about it.

Frieder remains the only coach to win back-to-back outright Big Ten championships in this decade and that's a major accomplishment. Still, I get on him about that balloon schedule he plays prior to the Big Ten season. Frieder tells me Michigan has exams in December. Hey, Bill, don't other schools have exams? He got mad at me last year because I kept referring to the Wolverines' record as 0–1 prior to the Big Ten. They had lost to Arizona but had beaten a bunch of no-names that I wouldn't count.

One night a caller phoned in to my radio show and said, "Do you know Frieder is 22–8 in Michigan's last thirty games decided by five points?" Holy cow. Really? You don't mean to say? I smelled a rat.

"That must be Frieder in the room feeding you those numbers," I told the caller. "Nobody could possibly care about numbers like that except Frieder. They mean nothing. Hey, Bill. Hey, Frieeeeeder. Where arrrrrrre you?"

Frieder's record shows that he's a terrific coach, even though he's had his disappointments in the postseason. He shouldn't be so defensive about his record. Can you hear me now Frieder?

Was I talking about criers? Hello to you, too, Wimp Sanderson. Alabama's Sanderson goes Boeheim and Frieder one better: He cries on *and* off the court. For all I know his name might even be short for Whimper.

From the moment I walk into his office at Tuscaloosa, it's always, "We don't have any players. We can't play at all." It's never, "Hi, Dick!" It's always, "Dick! We're never going to win another game in the SEC."

Sanderson has been crying so loudly and for so long that he found himself in a real boy-who-cried-wolf situation in the '87–88 season. Nobody believed him, and the Crimson Tide turned out to be pitiful. I had to feel for Wimp, who lost Derrick McKey, the scoring machine from his fine NCAA team of two seasons ago who decided to leave school early for the pros.

Sanderson has put some awesome numbers on the board for Alabama. But that season it all came crashing down. The only thing he could take much pride in was his office, one that once belonged to the legend, Paul (Bear) Bryant.

"Wow, Bear really sat here," I said. "Bear touched this. Bear walked around in here?"

Wimp wailed to the ceiling. "I wish Bear would listen to me," Sanderson nearly prayed. "Send me some players, Bear. Help me out. I need players."

One game I did for ESPN was Vanderbilt at Alabama not long after Sanderson had succeeded his popular boss, C. M. Newton, who had gone to Vandy. What a nervous wreck Wimp was that week! I'll never forget his wailing away. "They loved C.M. here," he said. "He was a hero, a god. Look at all the people gathering outside. You going to the Vandy shootaround? I guarantee you'll see all the 'Bama people in there rooting for C.M. Oh, I can't take it. You don't know the pressure I'm under."

"It can't be all that bad," I told Sanderson. I had never seen a coach carry on so. To this day my partner on that telecast, Jim Simpson, and I talk about that session in Sanderson's office. And to top off Wimp's good mood, they ended up losing that game to Vandy. He was a real basket case after the game—kind of like how I always was after a loss. Every time I see Wimp I sort of remind him, "It can't be all that bad." And it never has been.

One closing comment about coaches crying over officials' calls. The good referees don't pay attention one way or another. No ref will ever say that constant harrassment bothers him, but when you're talking about new guys, well, you're talking about human beings and the moaners and groaners just might get away with something. All coaches work the officials. But I still believe that the more a coach cries about the little calls, the less likely he is to get the one to go his way when he needs it.

MR. CLEANS

I guess the patron saint of the Mr. Cleans is the Wizard of Westwood himself, John Wooden of UCLA. One stat: The man won ten national championships in twelve years. This is only the greatest achievement in the history of sport, that's all. When you consider that in order to win one—just one—NBA championship, a team can slip up three times in three different series—in other words lose *nine* games and still win the title—and consider that in the NCAAs you can't even lose once or you're gone, and that in Wooden's day you didn't even get into the tournament unless you won your conference . . . well, that's how amazing the Wizard's ten championships are.

Let me tell you, he's awe-inspiring enough for me to totally blow my act every time I'm in his presence. Whenever I've interviewed Coach Wooden on TV, I've been practically gaga with pride and admiration. I haven't been myself; I've recognized that but I can't do anything about it. This is a guy I wrote to when I was just a young kid starting out coaching. I asked him to send me his "Pyramid of Success" and it came right back with a personal note.

The first time I met Coach Wooden I made sure somebody took a picture of me with him. He's always carried himself with such grace and class, I wanted some of it to rub off.

Then there was the time I followed him as a speaker at a coaches' clinic. I was nervous for a week; then I made the big mistake of sitting and listening to him speak in that dignified, professional, low-key manner. He talked of the simplicity of the game and the importance of fundamentals.

When it was my turn to come on and light a fire, I tried to get excited and motivated and fired up. But instead I wanted to be like John Wooden. I was subdued and de-energized, calm and collected. I was Bomb City.

People told me the speech was okay, but I knew it wasn't. It wasn't Dick Vitale. I wasn't myself because I tried to be somebody else. I learned my lesson. But that just demonstrates the awe and respect I have for the Wizard.

There has never been nor will there ever be anyone else like Wooden. But I guess C. M. Newton comes about as close as you could expect.

Everything about the Vanderbilt coach exudes class. His clothes, the way he carries himself, his image. He got down on us TV guys a couple of years ago at the Final Four for always second-guessing his profession, but C.M. did it in such a kindly way that I couldn't even get upset and explain to him that what I try to do is not second-guess but "first-guess."

Newton is bound for an administrative position, I'm certain. He's surefire athletic director material if he doesn't have his eyes set on one of the conference commissioners' jobs. When the SEC commissionership opened up last year, after Harvey Schiller resigned to become our head honcho at the U.S. Olympic committee I understand C.M. was ready to step in. But then Schiller returned after a few days.

Whether I go to Vanderbilt or Alabama or Kentucky where C.M. played for Adolph Rupp on a national championship team or anywhere else, he's Mr. Popularity. He's revered everywhere. A lot of people in Lexington were surprised and disappointed he didn't get the Kentucky coaching job when Joe B. Hall stepped down, but I don't think C.M. would operate as well in a pressurized situation like that.

On the other hand, if anybody can adapt to any kind of situation it's got to be C.M., a guy who worked with Wimp Sanderson for years and turned around to be an assistant to Bobby Knight on the 1984 Olympic team. If there was ever a more bizarre odd couple than Newton and Sanderson, it might have been Knight and Newton. But isn't dealing with all kinds of personalities the mark of a solid administrator?

I owe C.M. and the Vandy athletic department thanks for rolling out the red carpet in Nashville and getting me into the Grand Ole Opry where I went up on stage and was taken on a tour of the place by Minnie Pearl herself. How-DEE! And where I met the singer Skeeter Davis, who turned out to be a St. John's fan. (Speaking of bizarre.)

Of course, Newton can't compete in the SEC with the players he gets at Vanderbilt. No, not much. Those usually happen to be players Kentucky and Tennessee don't want. Like Scott Draud and Will Perdue. Of course last season Draud, a deadly three-point artist, lit up Kentucky with 22 points. And all Perdue did under the delicate handling of Newton was improve from a no-chance project as a freshman to an NBA first-round draft pick as a senior. This while Vanderbilt came on to be a major factor in the SEC race and knock Pitt out of the NCAAs en route to the Sweet Sixteen. Maybe C.M. should continue coaching for a little while after all.

You know who I really hate to interview? Lute Olsen of Arizona, that's who. Talk about class and style, mention handsome and appealing, this guy always looks like he's just stepped out of a tuxedo commercial. I've told my TV producers: Don't

put the same camera on Olsen and me. I feel I'm PeeWee
Herman and Lute's Cary Grant.

Refined. Stately. Dignified. Name any adjective that has to
do with grace and elegance and you've got Olsen. And he
was a junior college guy, if you can believe that. Denny Crum,
Jerry Tarkanian and Lute all came out of the California JuCo
coaching ranks to strike it rich in the big time. Olsen, in fact,
took over for Tark at Long Beach State and kept the winning
alive there before moving on to Iowa and creating a religion
of the game out among the cornfields. He brought a whole
new feeling for basketball into that state and took the Hawkeyes and Ronnie Lester to the Final Four in 1980.

Then warm weather called and—the pressure in Iowa City
having reached the point where the people demanded more
winning than was possible—sanity prevailed. Olsen moved
back to the sun in Tucson where he took the horrendous
Arizona program and made it immediately respectable.

Olsen's just about ready to move up into the class of the
Rolls-Roycers. A few more banner years and he'll be right
up there with the Knights, the Crums and all the rest.

One thing I like about Olsen is his straightforwardness.
About the time he arrived at Arizona, I was knocking the
Pac Ten for being a mediocre league. It didn't rate anywhere
near the top five or six conferences even though the league
was attracting terrific coaches. Lute went after me: "The people out here listening to Dick Vitale should check his record
and investigate what he did as a coach." Hey, I won over 70
percent of my games at Detroit. When it was checked, they
found I was ahead of Lute at the time!

Later, though, when Walt Hazzard at UCLA was ripping
me and claiming the Pac Ten's goal should be "to shut up
Dick Vitale," Olsen went at it in a different manner. He said,
basically, let's not talk about it. Let's just go out and do our
job. If we deserve it, we'll get the praise.

Well, last year, boy did they get that from me! I saw Sean
Elliott early in Alaska and praised him to the hilt. Again, I

should have listened to Olsen. He's not one of these shrinking
violets who hesitates to admit his team is good when it obviously is.

"Dick, I'm not just mentioning this lightly," he said the
summer before the '87–88 season. "We are going to be good,
very good, *really* good. And forget about Jerome Lane and
Fennis Dembo and all those other kids you've got at All-
American small forward. Sean is the best in the nation."

In Alaska, after Elliott and Arizona took Michigan and
Syracuse and simply whipped them wire to wire—the teams
yours truly and *Sports Illustrated,* respectively, picked number
one—Olsen had his players give me the business.

"Hey Dick, where's Gary Grant? Where's Sherman Douglas?" The Wildcats blitzed me one night at a restaurant in
Anchorage. "Michigan couldn't finish third in the Pac Ten.
Syracuse? Who's she?" One of the Arizona assistant coaches
thought the players might have gone too far ragging me. He
thought I might have been annoyed at the attention.

Annoyed at attention? Are you kidding me?

Olsen's teams have always reflected his personality: Cool.
Alert. Imperturbable. Unwrinkled. Olsen knows his players
so well and trusts their judgment so much he lets them choose
their future teammates. Lute says he does the recruiting, but
the players make the final decision on whether a recruit fits.
A story is told about when Olsen was at Iowa and Joe Barry
Carroll made a recruiting visit. Supposedly JBC spent most
of the day with his stereo earphones plugged in and his head
down. Lute was worried the Iowa players would approve him
anyway, but the rejection vote wasn't even close.

All along I've talked about building programs. Gene Bartow is the greatest architect in the history of basketball. He's
the Frank Lloyd Wright of the game. When a guy steps into
a place that doesn't have a *basketball,* much less any players
or program, and then takes that team to the NCAA tournament in seven straight seasons, well, if I owned a hat, it would
be off to Mr. Bartow.

Gene's reputation as a builder and sustainer is renowned; his name pops up for nearly every good college coaching job that comes open. Kentucky. UCLA. More recently, Arizona State and SMU. The reason is simple: Bartow provides instant stability, organization and contacts. He's a class act. No tricks, shortcuts, or fancy frills. The man has taken two teams to the Final Four—Memphis State and UCLA—and he would have been the first coach to take three if his Alabama-Birmingham team, which had already upset Virginia and Ralph Sampson, hadn't stumbled on its home floor against Louisville in the NCAA Mideast Regional in 1982.

Bartow has had a fascinating career; he went from the losing depths at Illinois, withstood the oppressive spotlight of succeeding Wooden at UCLA, then started from scratch at Birmingham, where he's now AD, coach, and virtually king. The word is Bartow wants to start a football program at the University now, as if there isn't enough pigskin power floating around the state at Auburn and Alabama. Another word is always that, having accomplished the impossible at UAB, Bartow is ready to move on again.

Through it all he's been Clean Gene.

But don't mention that phrase in the vicinity of Wimp Sanderson at Tuscaloosa. Bartow and Sonny Smith are kissin' cousins, but Gene and Wimp are enmity personified. I'm talking serious dislike here. It stems from the bitter recruiting battles the two schools have had over Birmingham natives like Bobby Lee Hurt, Ennis Whatley and Buck Johnson, all of whom ended up in Crimson Tide uniforms. Name-calling, accusations of cheating and nasty rumors continue to foul the atmosphere surrounding what could and should be a fine rivalry. But it's a war with no truce in sight. When these men are in the same room—which is rare—there's tension, big-time style.

The ball of forgiveness is obviously in Clean Gene's court. Isn't godliness next to cleanliness?

THE NEXT BIG STARS
AND ALL THE REST

Of all the bright new marquee names appearing on the horizon, probably the easiest bet for pure stardom is the most difficult one to pronounce. Of course I'm talking about the K-man himself, Coach K, Mike Krzyzewski of Duke.

Krzyzewski comes from the world of another K, the Bob Knight Preparatory Institute for Budding Geniuses. It's no secret that the Mentor virtually got the job for Mike at Duke; after all, Krzyzewski came to Durham after a *losing* season at Army. How many guys are going to get hired anywhere with that little gem in the portfolio? But what I like best about

K is that he seems to have taken all the good qualities of Knight and left the bad ones behind. No verbal explosions, yanking teams off the court, throwing chairs, none of that has been evident amid the gorgeous Gothic atmosphere at Duke.

Krzyzewski played for Knight at Army, then coached under him at Indiana on that amazing staff that also included Bob Weltlich and Bob Donewald, who both went on to major head coaching positions. Kn and K grew so close that, after he had been at Duke for a few years, Krzyzewski had a major part in convincing Knight to cooperate with John Feinstein, a Duke grad, on his idea for a book on Indiana that turned out to be *A Season on the Brink.*

When the project didn't turn out exactly the way Knight had imagined it would, he was furious with Krzyzewski, and for a time the two had a serious falling-out. But by the time they played each other in the NCAA tournament in 1987, all that had been patched up.

Krzyzewski's Duke team that took the Hoosiers to the wire in the Midwest Regional that year was as good an example as any of his coaching philosophy. There were no outstanding stars—Danny Ferry was yet to bloom into the terrific all-round force he's become—and yet the Blue Devils, practically ten men, two full teams strong, came at you in waves with pressure defense; unselfish passing; a tough, hard-nosed intensity usually missing in ACC teams; and a family-type camaraderie that most other coaches can only dream of.

The first time Mike and his wife, Mickie, walked onto the Duke campus, he turned to her and said, "This is what college is all about." And I think we're looking at a long run here, a run (do I dare mention it) similar to that of the Master's over at Chapel Hill. Every chance he gets Krzyzewski goes out of his way to praise the student crazies that support the Duke team, both for their cheering on the court and for that fanatical tent city they set up outside Cameron Indoor Stadium to wait for tickets three and four days before big games. They've named the tents "Krzyzewskiville"; last March, after the Blue

Devils lost three straight on the road, the team returned by bus from Clemson to find that K-ville had not been ripped down at all but had doubled in size! That's support.

A couple of days later, before Duke's big home victory over North Carolina, Coach K invited all the citizens of Krzyzewskiville into Cameron to eat pizzas and watch a large-screen videotape of the previous Duke–UNC game.

"At most other schools, coaches have to worry about all the nearby alumni calling and getting involved and taking up valuable time. It's all called pressure," K says. "Here I don't have to worry about that because most of the Duke alums are scattered all over the country. Most of my constituency is these kids. And what they contribute is undying love and affection."

Mike took the X and O foundation from Knight, but I think he must have gotten his student relations from TV's Dr. Cliff Huxtable. The Duke situation really is a family; K is a friend and confidante as much as he is a coach. I'll never forget the tears in K's eyes after he watched Tommy Amaker play his last game for Duke in the '87 tournament, and again last year as he took his senior cocaptains Billy King and Kevin Strickland out of the game at the end of the team's regular-season finale, the rout of Carolina. He even lets his players take a part in coaching strategy and preparation. Krzyzewski has the final decision, of course, but he takes player suggestions to heart.

Most everybody who's gone head-to-head with Dean Smith and the Tar Heels in the ACC has spent too much time worrying about the Carolina style and tradition and image and press clippings. When K first came to Duke, the Blue Devils' old coach, Vic Bubas, told him, "Concentrate on *you*. Don't be concerned with anybody else." I think K has used UNC as a barometer and a role model without getting involved in any of the petty shenanigans that shadow a lot of rivalries.

"It's not like Dean and I go out and have a few smokes together," Krzyzewski once said, but there is a lot of respect on both sides now. Krzyzewski is winning some recruiting battles against Dean, and for the first time Michelangelo has a younger artist with staying power who can compete down the road at the same high level.

Gene Keady at Purdue is Mr. Intensity. He's from the old school—his players are going to work and work until they drop. All his life he had to gut things out, from the time he was a track star at Kansas State to when he got a taste of the big time as a football player in the Pittsburgh Steelers' camp. What a fighter this guy is! He acts more like a football coach than any basketball coach I've been around.

The Boilermaker boss let me sit in on a staff meeting one time and I have to tell you this guy is the chief honcho—right down to details, goals, the scouting, the charting of plays, the practices . . . he's out there getting down in it with his players. You can tell by the way Purdue competes. Hard. Spirited. Blood and guts. Opponents pay the price.

I love Keady because he's honest, candid, up-front. His players have got to love and respect that. When he lost Jerome Harmon to Louisville in the recruiting wars, he went after Denny Crum in the newspapers. He doesn't take one iota of guff from the General over in Bloomington. He nails Digger Phelps at Notre Dame for not ever playing Purdue. Phelps always says there aren't any roads from West Lafayette to South Bend. Funny, the football teams seem to find a way to get back and forth every year . . .

A lot of people in Indiana look at him as number three in the *state,* and that's awfully tough when you've built a program that's consistently in the top twenty in the nation. And if you check the records against each other since Keady came to West Lafayette—now don't get mad at me, Mr. Knight— Purdue isn't number three, it's number one.

Keady is Vince Lombardi–tough—there it is, the football again—and I don't believe he's entirely satisfied at Purdue. Remember, he was Eddie Sutton's assistant at Arkansas. He left and did a great job at Western Kentucky. The same for many years at Purdue. But still he's always been on the periphery of the big time. Keady's name is mentioned for just about every big-name coaching job that becomes available—Kentucky, New Mexico, Texas (his former college classmate at Kansas State, DeLoss Dodds, is the AD in Austin)—and I think there may be one more glamour stop awaiting him.

Not that he'd ever listen to me. I got into it a couple of years ago with Keady about fouling at the end of a game when his team had the lead. This was before the intentional-foul rule where a team retains possession of the ball. But the argument still applies if a coach can get his guys to disguise their intentions. "Less than five seconds left, you're up three points, the other team has the ball," I said. "Gene, you've got to foul before letting them shoot that trey and tie it up."

"Too risky," he said. "What if they make both free throws and then steal the inbounds? Now they've got the ball with a chance to win."

"Wait a minute," I said. "Too many things have to happen. They've got to make both foul shots, steal the inbounds, convert, score. If you can't inbound, you don't deserve to win anyway. Give them that chance for the trifecta? That's too easy an opportunity."

We went round and round on this one. Keady was laughing. Finally he said okay. "Look. Tonight if we get in that situation I'm going to foul. But if I end up losing that sucker, I'm coming after you. I'm taking the Vitale theory and sticking it where the sun don't shine. I'll be on your butt so fast, you won't know what hit you. You understand that?"

Sure enough, that night against Illinois the situation came up. But Keady turned gutless. He didn't foul. The Illini hit a three-pointer toward the end of of the game to tie. Luckily, Purdue won in overtime. Whew. I'm glad Keady didn't have to remember whose strategy did or didn't work. I didn't need an enraged former Pittsburgh Steeler on my case.

Of all the guys I've plugged on the air for better jobs, I've gotten the most flak for promoting Gary Williams of Ohio State. I'll never back down from that. This guy can flat-out do the job—anywhere, any time, any conference, any material. The Big Ten has already felt his sting in the two short years he's been in Columbus. Just wait until he gets some players; it'll be bye-bye to everybody else. The Buckeyes will be a top ten and national championship contender on an annual basis. Mark it down.

I first met Gary when we were both coaching high school ball in New Jersey. He had played at Maryland and I think that's where he would have loved to end up coaching. He's a protégé of Dr. Tom Davis, initially starting with Davis at Lafayette and then going with him to Boston College. Williams was head coach at American University in Washington before succeeding Davis at BC, orchestrating the same uptempo, full-court pressure, skit-skat game most kids love to play. He recruited two of the more amazing little guards in Big East history in Michael Adams and Dana Barros and then he got practically a carbon copy of them in Jay Burson at Ohio State.

One of the reasons Williams is close to my heart is because he's a pacer. I was a pacer. Up and down, up and down; the guy is never still. Gary is so wound up it looks like a crew of teamsters would need a straitjacket to keep him down. He's a yeller, a screamer. I was a yeller and a screamer. Williams's biggest plus is his preparation; he really knows how to get a team ready. Unlike a lot of intense, extremely hyper coaches, Gary also has the ability to rationalize away a defeat. That's another tremendous plus, because a lot of guys can't take a loss and come back to the gym ready for the next game or get their players thinking positive right away. Gary can.

He's another guy who refuses to back down from the Knights, the Frieders, the Lou Hensons, the guys who've established winning programs in the league. There's a terrific high school guard named James Jackson coming out of Toledo, and in the old days he'd have probably been headed toward a Michigan or Indiana. But when he announced his final five choices, U of M and IU were nowhere, while Ohio State was right there with national powers UNLV, North Carolina, Syracuse and Georgetown. With Williams on the scene, Ohio State will be in the hunt all the way.

Can I call a guy who didn't get a chance at a Division I school until he was fifty a rising star? How about a shooting star? Because John Chaney of Temple took off like a rocket once he finally got out of Cheney State, just outside Philadelphia, where he had built a Division II power and won a national championship. If Miami of Ohio is the football world's "cradle of coaches," maybe Cheney State is the basketball cradle; Vivian Stringer was the women's coach at tiny Cheney at the same time Chaney was directing the men's teams. Vivian went on to produce a top-five program at Iowa, and everybody knows what Chaney produced at Temple last season, practically everybody's number-one team for the better part of two months.

The dawn practices. The discipline. The lack of turnovers. No dunking, no high-fiving, no flash. Cardigan sweaters. The foghorn voice. Those laser eyes—has any coach ever looked more like his school's mascot than Chaney, that ancient, avuncular Owl?

When he finally got his chance at the big time Chaney took it by the throat and squeezed. He started recruiting from the Philly city leagues in which he had been a big star, and he got other big stars, usually guards like Nate Blackwell and Howard Evans; then from out of the city he got the pièce de résistance, Mark Macon from Saginaw, Michigan.

Chaney didn't play in the city's Big Five of Temple, LaSalle, Villanova, St. Joseph's and Pennsylvania, mostly because in those days hardly any black guys played in the Big Five. But after growing up with Wilt Chamberlain, going away to school at Bethune Cookman in Florida, toughening himself up over a decade in the Eastern League, and coaching at Cheney State, Honest John was ready for Temple.

Here's how good Chaney was as a player: The year Tom Gola won the city's Catholic League MVP, Chaney won the public league MVP. As a ballhandler he was the equal of

Temple's great Guy Rodgers; anyone who watched his ple team last year will hardly be surprised to learn that John was always in control of the ball.

Chaney's Temple teams play rough and tough; like him, always under control. They stress the simple skills of passing and catching the ball. Easy entry passes. No cross-court skip stuff. No bounce-pass gambles. Execution. Deliberation. He knows precisely what the other teams on the schedule can do as well. "Don't be beaten by the unknown; let us be prepared for everything," he says.

The simple warmth and humanity of the man draws people to him. Oh, he may rant on the sideline—how about his famous Evil Eye stare at a ref after a bad call? I've seen Chaney spend entire timeouts giving an official the Evil Eye without ever talking to his team. But he is not consumed by basketball. Chaney regularly treats his office staff to culinary treats he brings in from the city markets each week. And he is a closet gourmet cook who can concoct a Cajun or Creole special at the drop of a spice.

To understand the affection the little Owls have for their lead Hooter just watch him at the beginning or conclusion of a practice. He gathers his team around him in a circle on the floor for a kind of fireside chat. It might be about basketball, or it might not. That doesn't matter. What matters is his concern for the players.

I agree with him on his stand against branding kids "Proposition 48's" as well. "With Prop 48, we're heading back to the Stone Age," he says. "I blame the educational system, not the kid. Opportunity is what this country is about. Let the kid succeed or fail on his own merit, not because some NCAA body is limiting his athletic participation. What does Prop 48 do to aspiration levels? What about dreams?"

Following the tough one-point loss out at Las Vegas last season, I was in the Temple locker room. It would be the Owls' only regular-season loss. Most guys would be punching the walls, trashing the benches. What did Chaney do? He went around to all his players, gave them a strong hug and told them to forget about it. They would go on. Later, out in the hall, Chaney spotted Vegas's Jerry Tarkanian. More hugs for Tark. "I love you, Jerry," he said. "You're a great guy. We're going to do this again. We're going to keep playing. Just remember that because there's a lot of love here."

That's pure Chaney. Talk of love after a big defeat. But if I were Tark, I wouldn't be looking for much mercy next time.

To describe what a ferocious competitor yet fragile human being Bobby Cremins of Georgia Tech is and always has been, think about when he was a senior at South Carolina in 1970, and the unbeaten and second-ranked Gamecocks were upset in the ACC tournament by North Carolina State. Cremins was so ashamed over the season-ending defeat that he and a teammate scampered off to the mountains to hide out in a cabin for a full week.

Cremins's wife, Carolyn, calls him "Gloom and Doom" because while somehow expecting the best will happen, Bobby always fears the worst. He was a street-gang punk out of the Bronx when Frank McGuire rescued him and brought him south, and sometimes he acts as if he's more surprised than anybody he's in the forefront of college coaches.

Cremins is a strange breed and yet a terrific "people" guy at the same time. When he first crossed the Mason-Dixon line he already had the prematurely white hair and the garbled dialect—he got the nickname "Cakes" because he always sounded as if had a Hostess Twinkie stuffed in his mouth. But if he hadn't had the white hair, the prospect of the Tech job would have given it to him. It was one nobody in their right mind wanted because they knew there was no way they could win. Tough academics. Engineering students. The ACC. Recruiting against Carolina, Duke, and Maryland. The team was so bad the year before Cremins got there, winning 4 of 27, that the coach left to become a caddie on the pro golf tour.

Quickly, however, Cremins began stockpiling recruits who would become ACC Rookies of the Year: Mark Price, Bruce Dalrymple, Duane Ferrell, Tommy Hammonds, Dennis Scott last year. Five in six years. And he developed sleepers like John Salley into solid NBA contributors.

Like his mentor, McGuire, Cremins is not necessarily an X and O guy. He's a motivator, another seat-of-the-pants coach, who depends on the feeling and situation in a game to determine his actions. Also like McGuire, he's conservative. Doesn't run much. Doesn't sub much. Wants to keep everything simple. He must be superstitious, too, because he's been wearing that same pale yellow tie almost continuously since he left the Bronx.

When he got Tech to number one in a city notorious for losers, Cremins became the prince of Peachtree Street, probably more popular in Atlanta than the Braves' own bashful slugger, Dale Murphy.

Again, though, like the dead-ender he had always been, Cremins didn't relish the top. Some coaches are great on the lead; others prefer to come from behind and not be the ones everybody's shooting at. The Ramblin' Wreck played like a nervous wreck much of that Price-Salley '85–86 season, to the point that when they came face-on with their destiny in the NCAA tournament in the Omni, Cremins not only blinked but virtually pressed his eyes shut. "I hope it doesn't have a negative effect," he said of his own near-home court.

"I just wanted us to be a good basketball program," a desolate Cremins said. "I don't know how the hell all this happened. It's terrible." Bobby rode his team mercilessly that year, feeling the pressure of that early number-one ranking.

I think Bobby learned from that experience not to take it so seriously but to enjoy the roll while it lasts. I think he'd love to be in that position again. He'd know how to handle it this time. With his recruiting prowess and his street style in full bloom, Cakes should have another shot at the whole pie very soon.

THE BEST OF THE REST

Digger Phelps has never been the warmest guy in the world to Dickie V. I always thought it stemmed back to my recruitment of Phil Sellers at Rutgers, a guy Digger wanted very badly at South Bend.

Hey, as a Catholic kid growing up, Notre Dame was always the epitome of the big time to me. I've always praised the school, commended the basketball program and complimented Digger on his graduation rate, his game preparation and the like. Then last year I got such a cold reception from him that I finally asked him what the trouble was. It wasn't Sellers.

"No, that's not it at all," Phelps said. "I'm ticked off because you're always talking about Notre Dame joining a conference, how the Independents are dead and how Notre Dame should become affiliated with this or that league. Hey, why should the Irish join anybody else?" And then Digger gave his topper: "America is our conference."

Which is precisely why Phelps has problems with other schools and coaches. Most in the fraternity find Digger sometimes pompous, and condescending in the extreme. Knight and Krzyzewski joke that they're Digger's only friends in coaching, but it's not such an exaggeration. When he came to the Final Four a few years ago and charged that players were up for sale to certain schools without naming names or schools, it just left a terrible taste for everybody. Given the time and circumstances, everyone considered it an arrogant grandstand play by Digger.

But as a person, I can't say enough good about him. Here I thought all along that he wasn't very friendly, but after my automobile accident he made several calls to track down my wife and to get in touch with me in the hospital. He gave me a medal of St. Joseph for luck—the luck to stay away from any more of these accidents. I carry it in my pocket everywhere I go.

The excitement Phelps brought to Madison Square Garden

when he had that terrific Fordham team before going to Notre Dame was unequalled until the Big East Tournament started its annual show there. And it was so obvious even back then. The guy is a showman. He has charisma. He works a crowd like a Las Vegas emcee. And look at his record of knocking off number-one teams—UCLA in '74 (halting the all-time record 88-game winning streak), San Francisco in '77, Marquette in '78, DePaul in '80, North Carolina in '87—and you have to admit he is one terrific bench coach.

I think Digger prepares a team for that one big game as well as anyone; it's always difficult to wrest control of a game from Notre Dame, and the Irish seldom get blown out. In terms of changing defenses, mandating the rhythm and tempo of a game, he deserves all the plaudits. Maybe one of these years the Irish will sustain their abilities and play consistently over a couple of weeks in the postseason and Digger will get to strut as a participant again in the Final Four rather than as an observer.

Walt Hazzard helped John Wooden win his first national championship and I've got Walt on my all-time UCLA team (along with Kareem Abdul-Jabbar, Sidney Wicks, Marcus Johnson, and Gail Goodrich). But I've got to say that the UCLA program did not emerge from chaos when Walt took over in Westwood. If anything, it got worse.

I incurred a bit of Hazzard wrath a few years ago after Walt crowed loudly about the Bruins winning the NIT. The NIT? I said, great, now the chant at UCLA will be "We're number sixty-five! We're number sixty-five!" He remembered that a year later after UCLA won the Pac Ten conference tournament.

"Hey Dick, we're not number sixty-five now," he said. "And we want Vegas in the NCAA tournament."

I said, "Forget Vegas, Walt. Wyoming's in your bracket. Watch out for the Cowboys." Sure enough, in the NCAA tournament Fennis Dembo had a monster game. Wyoming won and UCLA was bingo, gone again.

Hazzard always has been a fighter and a scrapper and I know he was Wooden's choice to try and turn the UCLA program around from the sorry soap opera it's become. But I just don't think Walt's style went over well in Westwood. Hazzard got into tiffs with Lute Olsen at Arizona and Lou Campanelli at California among others. When Reggie Miller played there, opponents said UCLA was Cheap Shot City. There were some harsh words exchanged between the coaches during the UCLA–North Carolina series over the past couple of years. Good players have either abandoned UCLA or refused to come aboard, as if Pauley Pavilion was the Titanic and Wilshire Boulevard was an iceberg.

With all of that, I wish Hazzard the best of luck. And the same to Jim Harrick, the former UCLA assistant and Pepperdine head man who's just stepped into the Bruins' lair. Thirteen years post-Wizard, the UCLA job might still be the most difficult in all the land.

There are difficult places and there are difficult players. Paul Evans found a passel of the latter when he left the sanctity of Navy and the dream student, David Robinson, for Pittsburgh, where the atmosphere between coach and players was like grenade practice in downtown Beirut. Jerome (I Wanna Play Where I Wanna Play) Lane, Demetrius (Me) Gore, Charles (The Return of Ralph Sampson) Smith! What Pitt needed wasn't so much Mr. E as Mr. T to come in and crack some skulls.

Well, when Evans got through with them, the Panthers wished they'd been gang-beaten by the entire A-Team; the bruises might have healed more quickly. First Evans jumped into the faces of his players, and Lane responded by leading the nation in rebounding as a 6-6 sophomore. Then Evans jumped into the jockstraps of the entire Big East, taking on Villanova's Massamino, Georgetown's Thompson, and Commissioner Dave Gavitt himself. In the ensuing melee, Pitt also won the '87–88 league race due in large part to what may have been the best freshman class in the land.

Evans is Knight East, disciplinewise, and I'm not sure even the General can outcuss Evans at forty paces. Paul is brutally critical of his players—just like he had to be with such an unstructured bunch—and the results spoke volumes: Pitt is now on a par with Georgetown and Syracuse as an annual contender from the Big Beast.

I wonder if Evans used as many bunches of four letters while he was molding Robinson from a nonplayer into a spec-tacular number-one draft choice at Annapolis. I wonder if his fierce tongue and hard-guy persona would go over at a big state-supported institution that might not be prepared for the gritty urban renewal Evans brought to Pitt.

And wasn't it outrageous how, after that heart-breaking loss to Vanderbilt in the '88 NCAAs, his players—Charles Smith in particular—couldn't wait to bad-mouth him to the press? It was the exact situation I argued with Keady about—up by three with seconds to go, you can't let the other team come down and hit the trey—and Evans should have made it crystal clear to his players to give the foul, but coaches are human, and for the players to turn on him like they did when things got rough showed no character, no class at all. And then, at the Dapper Dan high school all-star game in Pitts-burgh a couple of weeks later, Evans actually got booed when he was introduced to the crowd! How can the team and the fans turn on him like that after the season he had? It all just shows that the task of turning some individuals into a team might be too much even for Evans.

Whatever he does, if Evans stays around and doesn't chuck it all for either his beloved sailboats or the NBA, college ball will have an annual controversy and explosion waiting to hap-pen in the Steel City.

I would be remiss if I didn't mention a couple of guys from a league I've never had the pleasure of doing a game from, but which is one of my favorites nevertheless, the Western Athletic Conference. Yeah, baby, the wackiest of the wacky, the WAC. LaDell Anderson at Brigham Young is one of the

real veterans in the profession having gone from Utah State
to the pro Utah Stars and back to Brigham Young. Sort of
what Louie Carnesecca did at St. John's, only LaDell switched
schools.

LaDell has all those Mormon missionaries helping him to
win games out in the mountains—those twenty-five-year-old
veterans—but hey, it takes some coaching to get guys who
have been away for two-year tour reindoctrinated into the
system. And what a system it is at BYU! Run, run, and run
some more. But let me tell you, that Cougar team I saw last
year passed the ball about as well as any group I've ever seen.
And in Michael Smith and Jeff Chatman, whom LaDell somehow stole out of Alabama, Brigham Young had two of the
best forwards in America. I think the Y's feat of beating
Wyoming, Colorado State, UTEP, and New Mexico on the
road over a period of eight days early in the season was the
team highlight of the year.

If it weren't for Don Haskins, the big ol' Bear down in El
Paso, I might never have gotten to be a college head coach.
As all those who remember ancient history might recall, a
few years after his national championship at UTEP, then called
Texas Western—one of the great upsets in NCAA history,
the Miners over Pat Riley and the Kentucky Wildcats, by the
way—Haskins flew to Detroit and accepted the coaching job
at U of D.

I think he kept the job approximately seven hours or something before deciding the big city life was not for him. Which
meant Detroit got Jim Harding. Which meant inevitably a few
years later Detroit got me.

Not that Haskins would have stayed there long. But the
Bear has been at UTEP for nearly twenty-five years now. An
institution. A legend. The last of a dying breed, I imagine—
those coaches who go to one school and stay there forever.

Haskins is one of the great disciplinarians in the game, a
defensive stickler out of the Henry Iba school. Careful shot
selection, a deliberate offense. At least, that was the sixties
Haskins. The great thing about the Bear is he never went into

hibernation. He's adjusted and the Miners can go up-tempo with you whenever you want.

Don has won and won and won some more. Last season he passed the five-hundred mark in victories. But I know he's getting soft because of what one of his players said the next day about the achievements: "All that means is the man must be getting real old." Haskins just laughed at that. C'mon, Bear. A few campaigns ago, Haskins would have shipped that trooper's butt out of town.

Know what's unique about Dr. Tom Davis of Iowa? He never demands any credit; it's always the players, the players, the players. When I was coaching, I never had any players. It was always the coach, the coach, the coach.

But Davis isn't fooling anybody. And don't let the kind-faced, chubby, rumpled image divert attention away from the viciously oppressive manner in which Davis's teams get after people. What a competitor!

Long ago Davis decided that the bounce pass was the best way to advance the ball; now he's made it almost a science. At Lafayette, at Boston College, at Stanford he always coached the same way: platoons, presses, aggression, frantic pace. It wasn't until he reached Iowa, however, that Davis was finally able to recruit enough athletes to really make his system work. Two years ago only a miracle rally by UNLV in the finals of the NCAA Western Regional to wipe out Iowa's 17-point lead denied Davis a shining hour in the Final Four. And he got even last year, bumping the Rebs from the tourney by a comfy 18-point cushion.

I always missed Dr. Tom's humor until two seasons ago, following my first national game for ABC. It was Louisville at Purdue, and Iowa was in West Lafayette for a game the next day. I was on the balcony of the hotel trying to wind down from my nerve-wracking opener when all of a sudden I heard voices shouting out: "A . . . B . . . A-minus . . . C . . . Aw, give him a D."

It was Davis and his Iowa coaching staff ragging me about

the telecast. "We're giving you an A-minus but keep hanging tough," Davis called out.

"You better be an A-minus tomorrow when that crowd starts rockin' and rollin'," I said.

Sure enough, Iowa got on the A train and came away with the W. I once compared Dr. Davis with Paisano Valvano in an Iowa–North Carolina State game. "Watching these two is like reading William Shakespeare and Mickey Spillane simultaneously," I said. "I'll let the viewers decide who is Shakespeare."

I've mentioned the next guy before, but one of my biggest influences in the business was Bill Foster of Northwestern. When I took the assistant's job at Rutgers I was amazed at all the organizational tools at my disposal, and much of that came from Foster. He brought a sense of pride to the state university of New Jersey. He did the same for Utah, Duke, and South Carolina. He had at least one 20-victory season in each place. And now at Northwestern he's trying to resurrect another moribund program.

The amazing thing is, Foster has practically come back from the dead for this restoration. A few years ago he had a heart attack while coaching a game for South Carolina against Purdue. He was at the age where it seemed about time for him to get out anyway. I've always believed he'd make a terrific league commissioner: he's so well-organized, just a great administrator. The Atlantic Ten Conference would have been an ideal place for Bill, with all his ties back in Jersey. But he's stuck it out, coming back to the bench again and again, and there he was last year, still jumping up on every play, pounding the backs of his players and letting them pound him back. I worried: How can his heart take all that?

Before Northwestern's January '88 game with Indiana— the defending national champions, remember—Foster told me he just wanted to make it respectable and not get blown out. He had lost three of his top seven players that week, two by injury and one an academic casualty, and yet the Wildcats

played their hearts out and won the game in overtime. It must
have been one of the two or three biggest upsets of the season,
truly astounding.

"Do we have to play anymore, Dick?" he asked me. "I
just wish the season ended tonight."

Foster's got Mike Adamle, the former NU football player
turned sports announcer, working hard on recruits for him.
And the rest of the alumni are solidly behind him as well.
Academically, Northwestern is the Duke of the Big Ten, however, and it will be a long road back.

Why does Foster still coach? Same reason Bo Schembechler
still stalks the yard markers at Michigan or Jud Heathcote
keeps on going at Michigan State. You get addicted. You get
crazy. It gets under your skin: the spotlight, the events, the
game. If I wasn't so set in TV, I think I'd want to be out there
on the lines again myself. Did I hear massive groaning?

George Raveling, with whom I go back even further than
with Foster, epitomizes what our country is about. George
was an orphan, a guy who came from nothing, took basketball
and made it a career, first as a player for Jack Kraft at Villanova, then as an assistant coach under Kraft and under Lefty
Driesell at Maryland. George got his first head position at
Washington State in Pullman, which is not the end of the
world, but the rumor is you can see the end from there. Then,
after recruiting a dream team as head coach at Iowa, he returned to the West Coast to direct the program at Southern
Cal.

One of the most literate guys in the game, George has an
extensive library that might even make another George, Will,
salivate. His recent critics are now saying maybe Rave has
been spending too much time reading those books and not
enough time recruiting. But USC is a hard sell—both to players, who if they are lured by LA at all are more often than
not UCLA-bound, and to fans who have their choice locally
of every recreation known to man. And some unknown.

If anybody can get the job finished at USC, though, it is

Raveling—a grand marketer in the old hard-driving tradition. Once I attended a team banquet at Iowa after a season in which the Hawkeyes finished barely over .500. The Iowa fans had gobbled the dinner tickets up instantly. The lights went out. Each player came walking in. Gifts. Speeches. Awards. Tons of tears. Big-screen video highlights. Barbra Streisand singing "The Way We Were." The place went nuts, drowning in emotion. And this for a team that won half its games! Imagine the show Raveling might put on if he ever won the national championship.

I don't know why Rave has struggled so mightily at Southern Cal, unless it is due to his one weakness as a coach. And that is that he sells his players and teams with the same energy he expends on everything else, leading to tremendous overkill and outrageous expectations.

Of course, getting rid of USC's three best players—Tommy Lewis, Bo Kimball, and Hank Gathers—didn't help matters. The three allegedly wanted a voice in naming the successor to Stan Morrison in Trojanland; when they didn't get consulted and Raveling was hired, there were some brickbats hurled and the players transferred. I think cooler heads might have ironed out the situation, but Rave was enraged that the kids were being influenced by outside agitators and he let them go.

In two seasons the Trojans have yet to recover. Last year Lewis (who went to Pepperdine), Kimball and Gathers (who wound up at Loyola Marymount and led that team to a 110-point scoring average, an unbeaten record in the WCAC, and a berth in the NCAA tournament) combined to average more points than the entire USC team put together.

Raveling wrote the single best book on rebounding, *War on the Boards,* and I still predict he'll come back to make a war of it against UCLA and the rest of the Pac Ten. But when Rave asked me last season to evaluate his team, I told him I thought he was doing too much coaching rather then letting his guys play. The Trojans would work on pressing and trapping and opening up the court, but they had far too little talent to try all the things George wanted to do.

Of course, this past fall he had oodles of talent to work with as John Thompson's assistant on the Olympic team. That was his second Olympic assignment, having worked under Bobby Knight in 1984 at LA—another experience he might want to forget in that he and Knight had it out a couple of times over the handling of Patrick Ewing.

At any rate, everybody in the game who knows Rave is rooting for him. Remember, the man is an expert at rebounding, and that is exactly what I expect him to do. Soon.

Which brings us to Petey Carril, without whom no list of coaches in any classification would be complete. Carril is the Princeton guy who takes on all the biggies and is never embarrassed. Carril is the cigar-chomping, jacket-flying midget who looks like he should be making book on the game, not coaching it. Carril is the Bowery Boys character who stomps the length and breadth of the Ivy League making basketball a riotous funhouse even in those storied halls of academe.

Bottom line, my man Petey—the protégé of Butch van Breda Kolff, under whom he served and with whom he put away a few brews at Old Nassau—annually gets more out of less than any coach in America. Virtually an unknown nationally, Carril has taken the backdoor cut and made it into an art form at Princeton. Once, his underdog Tigers won the NIT. Another year his exquisite backcourt of Brian Taylor and Teddy Manakas thoroughly embarrassed a North Carolina team that boasted Bob McAdoo, Bobby Jones and a host of other Tar Heel celebrities.

My friends have laughed at this, but I firmly believe that, given an NBA shot, my stogie-puffing dwarf buddy Carril would be an instant legend in the pros. His personality, knowledge, ability to communicate and, most of all, to hang loose under trying circumstances would serve him well at the highest level. Sure he's a slow-down, walk-it-up devotee at Princeton.

But he has to be. Petey could adapt anywhere; it's a shame he has never had the talent to make any headway to the limelight.

Last summer at the Nike camp right there at his home stomping grounds in Princeton, Carril's predicament became clear. I was sitting with Petey watching all the great high school players run and jump and dunk over each other. Out there on the court were Alonzo Mourning, headed for Georgetown; Billy Owens (Syracuse); LaPhonso Ellis (Notre Dame); and Shawn Kemp (Kentucky). Carril was just shaking his head and his cigar from side to side with a bewildered look on his face. "There's no way I'll ever get to coach these guys," Carill said. "I can't stand it anymore."

That's the coach's life, baby.

MAT PTP&T NTM WAPTLB OAL TBUHW

(My All-Time Prime-Time Players And Teams Not To Mention Words And Phrases To Live By Or At Least To Better Understand Hoops With)

In my nine years of broadcasting games on television I've seen enough dunks and dribbles to force most basketball junkies to switch to roller derby. But you think I've ever had enough? Nah. Lemme see them. Show me what you got. I still might have some openings left on my all-time teams (all-time defined as the period from when I started on television in the 1979–1980 season through 1987–88). If you think you've got somebody better, let's hear about them. Remember, Larry Bird and Magic Johnson had left the college ranks before I began riding the video waves, so you won't see them mentioned here. But just about everybody else is. Call them the VETEs. Vitale's Elite Teams of the Eighties.

CHAMPAGNE AND CAVIAR *(THE BEST TEAMS)*

1. North Carolina, 1982
2. Georgetown, 1984
3. North Carolina, 1984
4. Georgetown, 1985
5. Houston, 1983

The Tar Heels of Worthy, Jordan and Perkins who finally grabbed the brass ring for Dean Smith were the best team I saw during the decade, but the Ewing-Graham-Williams Hoyas that won it all two years later weren't far behind. Ironically, that year's Jordanesque Carolina squad might have contested Georgetown, whose '85 team was stopped from repeating only by a perfect game from Villanova, but got derailed by a defensive gem by the General. (Surprised neither of his Indiana champs of the period make the list?) And if the Phi Slamma Jammas were only fifth in greatness, they were easily first in electricity—though second in the nation thanks to a coach called Vee.

THE PTP'ERS *(THE BEST PLAYERS)*

PG—Isiah Thomas, Indiana
2G—Michael Jordan, North Carolina
C—Patrick Ewing, Georgetown
PF—James Worthy, North Carolina
SF—Danny Manning, Kansas

These are the mostest, the crème de la crème, the finest college players of the decade at their position. I want to make a distinction right way, though, for my man Isiah at the point. Thomas was more of a lead guard than a point guard when you consider that most guys who make their reputation at the point are distributors, creators, players who break defenses down rather than shoot the rock. The thing that set Isiah apart was his ability to score as well as pass. His leadership carried the Hoosiers all the way to the Final Four in '80–81, where he simply tore apart North Carolina in the championship game. Isiah had terrific pride and a certain cockiness about him that all leaders have to have. The runners-up at the position are Darnell Valentine of Kansas, a more traditional point guard who thought pass first (probably because he was a suspect shooter), and three New York City–area kids who came out of high school in the same year: Pearl Washington of Syracuse, Kenny Smith of North Carolina, and Mark Jackson of St. John's.

At the two-guard or shooting guard spot, who can forget Dr. Dunkenstein at Louisville, Darrell Griffith, who flew the Cardinals to the national title in '80; Danny Ainge of Brigham Young, with his unforgettable coast-to-coast lay-up to beat Notre Dame in the '81 NCAA tournament; Alvin Robertson of Arkansas, who locked people up defensively and threw away the key; or Chris Mullin at St. John's, a national player of the year? Nobody can—but nobody's close to the winner at this position either, the all-universe Jordan. Last season I was talking about a few of the new high school players on the horizon possessing Jordan-type qualities and Bob Knight, who coached Michael in the '84 Olympic Games, said forget it. "There will never be another Jordan in our lifetime," Knight said. Case closed.

Hey, what about big Ralph Sampson at center? Hey, what about Akeem the Dream—he's gone on to become the best center in the NBA. The Admiral, David Robinson, always seemed a bit soft for my taste. And David did big things for only two years. Remember now, I'm only considering these players' college careers, which leaves Ewing far and away supreme. Three Final Fours in four years. One national championship and an opposition steal and opposition perfecto away from two others. The prime gladiator in the game.

And who made that steal? Why, Worthy, of course. Jammin' James was the root and core of the '82 champion Tar Heels; his spectacular junior season gave him the nod over an unbelievable field of candidates including Wayman Tisdale of Oklahoma, Kevin McHale of Minnesota, and Maryland's twin tornadoes, Buck Williams and Len Bias.

Then at the small forward I have to go with Manning, who may be the most versatile player I have seen in this era. He could play any position effectively. And the ability he developed late in his career to take over and close out games gives him the edge over a supporting field of Dominique Wilkins of Georgia, Mark Aguirre of DePaul, and the X-Man, Xavier McDaniel of Wichita State. The job he did taking Kansas to the top of the mountain settled it. My fabulous five won four different NCAA titles among them.

ALL–FRANK LLOYD WRIGHT
(THE BASKETBALL ARCHITECTS)

> Dave Gavitt—Commissioner, the Big East
> Vic Bubas—Commissioner, the Sunbelt
> Gene Bartow—Coach: Memphis State, Illinois, UCLA, Alabama-Birmingham
> Bill Foster—Coach: Rutgers, Utah, Duke, South Carolina, Northwestern
> Lute Olsen—Coach: Cal State Long Beach, Iowa, Arizona
> Bobby Cremins—Coach, Georgia Tech

For Gavitt to coax the various and sundry basketball eagles into the same nest and lift the Big East onto the same level as the ACC, the Big Ten and the SEC in such a short time has to be the building job of the decade. Marketing, selling, putting the TV contracts together—it was all due to the organizational abilities of the former Providence coach and athletic director. Bubas has done a similar job but on another level in the Sunbelt; I always thought the former Duke boss got out of coaching much too early. As for the coaches, Bartow took both Memphis State and UCLA to the Final Four (he was the first successor to John Wooden, of course—at the time the no-contest toughest coaching job in the history of sports) and then built a program at Birmingham completely from scratch, getting the Blazers into the NCAAs seven years in a row. Who else but Foster has won twenty games at four different schools? Northwestern will be the most difficult mountain to climb to that level. As for Olsen and Cremins, maybe it takes prematurely silver hair to raise the dead back to annual Top Twenty prominence.

ALL–VELCRO VARMINTS *(THE DEFENDERS)*

> PG—Tommy Amaker, Duke
> 2G—Alvin Robertson, Arkansas
> C—Patrick Ewing, Georgetown
> PF—Kevin McHale, Minnesota
> SF—Paul Pressey, Tulsa

Guys who stuck to their men like Velcro; guys who sacrificed their bodies at both ends of the floor; guys who played the capital D. Nobody ever placed more or better pressure on the basketball coming up the floor than Amaker, who barely edged out the phenomenal little muscleman, Gene Smith of Georgetown. A lot of people thought Smith could play in the NFL. That was a pair of defensive demons—as were a couple of my favorite defensive point guards last season, Michigan's Gary Grant and Purdue's Everette Stephens. Robertson should have worn a mask on the court, he stole so many balls. Ewing was the ultimate Terminator in the lane; he again beat out Olajuwon and Robinson for this spot. McHale's long arms afforded him the opportunity to block a ton of Big Ten shots. I almost chose Utah's Danny Vranes for this position until I remembered McHale's arms. And at small forward, a surprise: Pressey played on the point of Tulsa's devastating press but he certainly could guard any and everybody. For some latter-day Pressey oppression, you need look no further than Duke's Billy King.

ALL–WINDEX WIPERS *(THE REBOUNDERS)*

Buck Williams, Maryland
Kevin McHale, Minnesota
Charles Barkley, Auburn
Clark Kellogg, Ohio State
Jerome Lane, Pittsburgh

These are the Clear the Glass, Sweep the Board fellows, the guys who went after a rebound as if it was their last meal. (As if Barkley could possibly imagine that any meal would be his last.) And I'm not talking about centers. Centers are tall, strong, always under the rim anyway. I don't count centers as Windex men. My Windex men love their bounds, their rebs. They grab that stat sheet every night and their eyes go directly to the "R" line. Barkley was a combination of power and agility. He chewed up the glass along with his occasional four pizzas. Lane, who in his sophomore year at Pitt became the smallest player (6-6) in thirty years to lead the nation in boards, once told me he fantasized about getting 30 rebounds in a single night. Don't bet against any Windex Wiper.

ALL–THOMAS EDISONS *(THE CREATORS)*

Isiah Thomas, Indiana
Darnell Valentine, Kansas
Pearl Washington, Syracuse
Kenny Smith, North Carolina
Mark Jackson, St. John's

Sound familiar? Innovative geniuses with the ball, this crew all jostled each other for the premier point guard spot. I used to sit there putting myself in an opposing coach's shoes and watch guys like this operate. I couldn't believe it. There was absolutely nothing a coach could design that took away from the skills players like this possessed.

ALL–RAMBOS *(THE INTIMIDATING TOUGH GUYS)*

PG—Scott Skiles, Michigan State
2G—Bruce Dalrymple, Georgia Tech
C—Patrick Ewing, Georgetown
PF—Michael Graham, Georgetown
SF—Xavier McDaniel, Wichita State

Dalrymple, one of my all-time overachieving hustlers, may have spent more time diving to the floor than dribbling on it. Ewing and Graham were especially effective in that Hoya reign of terror of the early eighties when Patrick would control the lane while Crack 'Em Graham pounded anybody who got in their way into the floorboards. Graham's fearsome shaved noggin was matched only by X's similarly bald pate. Skiles might have been lost out there were it not for an inherent toughness that rose to the occasion, most memorably against Georgetown in the '86 NCAAs. I gave the forward spots to Graham and McDaniel only because Buck Williams made my rebounding squad. But look at the guys I've had to leave off: Jeff Ruland of Iona; Karl Malone, the Mailman, from Louisiana Tech; Sam Clancy of Pittsburgh. Was Clancy tough enough for this team? Yeah, he's the same guy who now plays some mean football for the Cleveland Browns.

ALL–SECOND LIEUTENANTS *(THE ASSISTANT COACHES)*

Jim Maloney, Temple
Wade Houston, Louisville
Bernie Fine, Syracuse
Tim Grgurich, UNLV
Pete Gaudet, Duke

These guys might as well be second head coaches, as much as they aid and abet their bosses in developing players and grabbing those W's. Maloney, a Philly guy from birth, was a head coach at Niagara before he was thirty years old; he coached the great Calvin Murphy and is a terrific x and o guy as well as being John Chaney's details man. Houston has been with Denny Crum a long time and is obviously looking to make the next step up. His son will be one of the oustanding high school senior players in the nation this year and will probably want to play under his dad. The question is, will that be at Louisville?

Fine has been looking to move for several years now. A low-key, quiet type, he's a typical New York City work-aholic who is as responsible as anybody for Syracuse's re-cruiting successes. Grgurich, another former head man (at Pitt) doesn't really want to do it again. He could have had the San Diego State job a couple of seasons back but elected to stay with Tarkanian at UNLV, where he is a tremendous organizer, both of practices and of the recruiting system. Then there is Gaudet, who used to be the head coach at Army but now is the perfect complement to Mike Krzyzewski in Durham.

ALL–ROLAIDS RELIEVERS *(THE SIXTH MAN)*

Jeff Moe, Iowa
Gary Graham, UNLV
Garde Thompson, Michigan
Terry Gannon, North Carolina State
Benny Anders, Houston

It takes a special kind of personality to be able to first swallow some pride and sit the bench while the starters are announced, and then come off the bench cold and light up the night. For a couple of years Moe came out smoking for the Hawkeyes, especially shooting the trey. Thompson was another Big Ten Bombs Away guy who had a great attitude coming out of the bullpen. On the other hand, there's the bench sparkplug whose forte is defense, and that was Graham. I think Tark should have used Graham more in the '87 NCAA semifinal game, taking Indiana's Steve Alford head-on. A guy who did wind up playing for a national champion was Gannon, who filled in admirably all of that wondrous '83 season for the Wolfpack. When Derek Whittenberg went down, Ernie Myers came in to replace him while Gannon remained sixth man, so valuable was he as a motivational force off the bench. Then there was Anders, who played for the twice runner-up Phi Slamma Jammas but who never felt he got enough PT. One year at the Final Four Anders came duded out in tuxedo and pink tie and cummerbund. Still, he was all dressed up with nowhere to dance.

ALL–FREQUENT FLYERS *(THE LEAPERS)*

    Michael Jordan, North Carolina
    Dominique Wilkins, Georgia
    Darrell Griffith, Louisville
    Clyde Drexler, Houston
    Len Bias, Maryland

Who can forget the all-time Dunkathon in the '83 NCAA semifinals when Louisville, the former Docs of Dunk (now without Griffith) went sky-on with the Phi Slamma Jammas? On an afternoon of the spectacular, Drexler was the most spectacular. But when you speak of throw-downs and facials and hang-on-the-rims, you must remember the powerful Bias and, of course, the Human Highlight Reel, Wilkins, who among his stuffs has the monster mash, the windmill spin and the backwards somersault, not to mention the look-out below, dive bombing, sound-barrier-be-damned special. Don't tell me Dominique wouldn't have won the NBA Slam Dunk Contest over Jordan if the thing were held anywhere but Chicago.

ALL–MUHAMMAD ALIS *(THE COCKY ARROGANTS)*

Scott Skiles, Michigan State
Kevin Williams, St. John's
Len Bias, Maryland
Fennis Dembo, Wyoming
Derrick Chievous, Missouri

I don't care what the odds were; when Skiles walked into an arena, it was, "I'm badddd and what're you going to do about it?" Bias had the same kind of persona while Williams will be remembered as the sinewy guard who jumped in Patrick Ewing's face whenever one of those Georgetown–St. John's brawls threatened to break out. Dembo and Chievous battled each other from afar the last four seasons over who could lead America in talking trash.

ALL–AVISES *(THE UNACKNOWLEDGED, WE-TRY-HARDER GANG)*

Danny Callandrillo, Seton Hall
Brooke Steppe, Georgia Tech
Ricky Pierce, Rice
John Bagley, Boston College
Brian Shaw, UC-Santa Barbara

These guys never got the national attention or media respect they deserved for outstanding careers for one reason or another. In Callandrillo's case, it was because he played on bad teams, but night in, night out, this kid gave forty minutes of the toughest effort and most effective ball you could imagine. Similarly, Steppe played on horrid clubs that went everywhere but into the win column. Pierce's drawback was that he played in the Southwest Conference, Bagley's that he just looked too small and too wide to be anything but a hockey goalie. Now both of these guys have had long and happy NBA shelf-lives.

Shaw, meanwhile, just concluded a dazzling career in another league that goes unnoticed, and will get his shot as the Boston Celtic's number-one draft pick.

ALL–BOMB SQUADERS (*THE LONG-RANGE SHOOTERS*)

> Steve Alford, Indiana
> Mark Price, Georgia Tech
> Kiki Vandeweghe, UCLA
> Danny Ainge, Brigham Young
> Trent Tucker, Minnesota

Alford should cut his NCAA championship ring in half and give a piece to Dr. Ed Steitz. Price also lived on the perimeter with the trey. If those other three guys had had the trifecta to play with in their careers, their numbers would have been astronomical. Tucker came out of Flint, Michigan—maybe no city has produced per capita as many blue-chippers as this one, guys like Jeff Grayer of Iowa State, Roy Marble of Iowa, Glen Rice of Michigan, Andre Rison of Michigan State, Terence Greene of DePaul—and maybe no Big Ten player has ever shot better from as far away as he did. Jeff Malone of Mississippi State and Del Curry of Virginia Tech are still playing HORSE to get onto this squad.

ALL–DOW JONESERS (*THE UP-AND-DOWN STAIRCASE*)

> Chris Washburn, North Carolina State
> Dallas Comegys, DePaul
> Antoine Joubert, Michigan
> Rob Williams, Houston
> Billy Thompson, Louisville

Washburn deposited coaches in Fantasy Land dreaming of what he could do with that vast wealth of talent. Only in his last year did Comegys achieve any consistency after a career of semi-CYO play. Joubert was going to be the next Oscar, the next Magic, but it was unfair to ever believe this chubby, limited athlete could achieve much more than he did. Williams polished off a bizarre career by not scratching, going 0 for 8 from the floor in the Final Four while Thompson, perhaps the most enigmatic of all, went in one season from being a loafabout bench-warmer to a major star on a national championship team. *You* figure these people out.

THE RANDY NEWMAN ALL-STARS *(SHORT PEOPLE)*

Spud Webb, North Carolina State
Muggsy Bogues, Wake Forest
Michael Adams, Boston College
Billy Donovan, Providence
Darren Fitzgerald, Butler

I'm talking about guys under six feet tall who have been major factors in college basketball. Adams, 5-9, was told by his high school basketball coach to try wrestling. Bogues—what? 5-3? Maybe?—would have forgiven people if they suggested he try the circus. These little guys are inspiration indeed to all the youngsters who might think that basketball is not for them just because of their size. When N.C. State coach Jim Valvano first saw this new point guard, "Spud," whom his trusty assistant Tom Abatemarco had spent so much time recruiting, he nearly fainted. Wizened pros in the NBA still need smelling salts after trying to keep up with Webb.

ALL—AIRPORT

Martin Nessley, Duke
Steve Stoyko, Michigan

Geoff Crompton, North Carolina
Mark Eaton, UCLA
Manute Bol, Bridgeport

These guys look great on the traveling squad but usually don't earn much PT. I say usually. Eaton and Bol, neither of whom worked up a sweat in college, are now usually ranked one and two in blocks in the NBA. Crompton once weighed in at a cool three hundred pounds. When Michigan coach Bill Frieder wants to inject some life into his squad, before a big game he sends Stoyko sprinting to the top of the bleachers in Crisler Arena. Then Stoyko sprints down again onto the court where somebody feeds him a pass and he roars in for the dunk. Practice ends. The Wolves are psyched. Bus to the airport at 6:00 A.M.

ALL-ZEBRA *(THE REFEREES)*

Henry Nichols
Joe Forte
Lenny Wirtz
Paul Galvin
Dick Paparo

And anybody else who ever put on a striped shirt and blew a whistle. I got enough T's in my time not to want to make anybody mad.

ALL-RIP VAN WINKLES *(THE SLEEPERS)*

David Robinson, Navy
Chuck Person, Auburn
Karl Malone, Louisiana Tech
Armon Gilliam, UNLV
Vinny Del Negro, North Carolina State

This is a bunch who were unknowns out of high school, who never got five thousand letters from colleges and invitations to visit, who were not wined and dined by politicians and young debutantes. Valvano took Del Negro practically as a walk-on and probably because his name ended in O and Jimmy needed another recipe for manicotti. All the kid turned out to be his junior season was the MVP of the Atlantic Coast Conference tournament.

ALL–JOHN MCENROES *(THE CRYBABIES)*

> Mark Aguirre, DePaul
> Kelly Tripucka, Notre Dame
> Jeff Ruland, Iona
> Reggie Miller, UCLA
> Derrick Coleman, Syracuse

I'd say a lot about this bunch of moaners and groaners— terrific players even with their snarled-up faces—but I don't want to hear any more complaining than we're already subjected to. You want to really see them cry? Let's flip a coin and give them a coach. Heads, Jim Boeheim; tails, Bill Frieder.

ALL–TOM CRUISES *(THE NO-CONSCIENCE, NEVER-MET-A-SHOT-THEY-DIDN'T-LIKE TOP GUNS)*

> Tim McAllister, Oklahoma
> Alfredrick Hughes, Loyola of Chicago
> Reggie Miller, UCLA
> Freddie Banks, UNLV
> Rafael Addison, Syracuse

We're talking pathological shooters here. Ricky Grace, last year's star point guard at Oklahoma, told me that whenever he so much as thought about shooting, McAllister looked at him as if he was nuts. As if he was saying, "Don't you know who *always* shoots the rock around here?" McAllister did; he is easily the most selfish player I ever saw, with Hughes a close runner-up, although Alfredrick had an excuse—he was the only scorer Loyola really had. Miller has proven he's not as one-dimensional as he sometimes looked, while Banks and Addison usually appeared to be heaving their mortars *without* so much as looking.

ALL–DIAPER DANDIES *(THE FIRST-YEAR PLAYERS)*

 PG—Pearl Washington, Syracuse '84
 2G—Mark Macon, Temple '88
 C—Pervis Ellison, Louisville '86
 PF—Wayman Tisdale, Oklahoma '83
 SF—Reggie Williams, Georgetown '84

The freshmen, the new kids on the block, the rookies. And I'm only rating them here on their first season, not their overall careers. Hey, yeah, Michael Jordan became a great player. But just because he drained the national championship points as a freshman doesn't mean he had as spectacular a first year as Macon at the same position—and he didn't. Macon also beat out Darrell Griffith here; the infant Owl is simply the best first-year man I have had the pleasure to watch in any year. Similarly, Ellison and Williams get the call at their positions over the more obvious Patrick Ewing and Mark Aguirre. The former pair helped win national championships for their teams; the latter two only got to the Final Four. Tisdale was a lock at power forward; I chose the Pearl over Isiah Thomas basically on his thrilling rookie finishes in the Big East tournament.

ALL–GQ *(COACHES AS BEAU BRUMMELS)*

> Larry Brown, Kansas
> Lute Olsen, Arizona
> Digger Phelps, Notre Dame
> Lafayette Stribling, Mississippi Valley State

I needed some help here, being a K-Mart haberdasher myself. Brown had been left off my past collections in this category, a mistake which if repeated, I am told, would have forced Ralph Lauren to sell both his ranch and his townhouse. Stribling's still my man, though. Lafayette, he shall return. George Raveling used to be on the list, but he's gone to some awful sweaters on the sidelines lately. By the way, a worst-in-show here to Bob Knight of Indiana. Even I know red is out. And to Nolan Richardson of Arkansas. Polka dots haven't been in since Pinky Lee.

ALL–JUDGE CRATERS *(THE WHERE-DID-THEY-GO DISAPPEARING ACTS)*

> Kevin Walls, Louisville
> Ricky Ross, Wichita State and Tulsa (not to mention
>   JuCo stints at Santa Ana and College of Marin)
> Efrem Winters, Illinois
> Bruce Douglass, Illinois (Tandem MIA)
> Raymond McCoy, San Francisco and DePaul

Some heavy competition here, ironically much of it from overpublicized Chicago-area youngsters. Besides Winters and Douglass, who played as many sharps and flats as Ferrante and Teicher, and McCoy, who was considered the equal of Isiah Thomas as a high school senior and wound up his sorry career as the Blue Demons' designated foul shooter, Teddy Grubbs (DePaul), Walter Downing (DePaul and Marquette) and Lowell Hamilton (Illinois) have been additional major

busts from Chi-town. Tony Bruin at Syracuse and Dave Pop-
son at North Carolina were bumped off this team by Walls
and Ross, whose underachieving was truly monumental.

THE GLINDER TORRAIN ALL–NAME REVIEW *(FOR THE DAYTON CENTER WHO EXPLODED UPON THE FINAL FOUR IN 1967)*

> Fitzgerald Bobo—Duquesne
> Endy Basquiat—Northeastern
> Calodeis Cannon—South Alabama
> Aparicio Curry—Detroit
> Kral Ferch—Montana State
> Anicet Lavodrama—Houston Baptist
> Napoleon Lightning—St. Francis (Pa.)
> Tamas Peredy—Vermont
> Lamont Sleets—Murray State
> Goliath Yeggins—West Texas State

NAME OF THE DECADE *(WHO ELSE?)*

> Fennis Dembo—Wyoming

And now, for those of you who have stuck it out this far,
what you've needed from the start: the comprehensive dic-
tionary of Vitalespeak.

THE DICKY DO'S AND DON'T'S GLOSSARY

Area code J—The jump shot from three-point range, or any
shot taken from another area code.

AT—Air Time.

AWOL—Absent without leave. A mystery player who has again
disappeared from the game.

Blender—Mixes perfectly. A good role-player.

Brick City—Throwing rocks. Shooting poorly.

Carl Lewis—A speedster.

Creampuff Delight—Automatic victory. Weak team a stronger one has no business playing.

Crunch Time—The stretch. The last four minutes of the game.

Cupcake—See Creampuff Delight.

Dipsy-Doo Dunkaroo—A flashy, spectacular, acrobatic dunk, usually from close in.

Doughnut Offense—Hole in the middle. A team without a center.

Dow Joneser—An up and down player, like the stock market. Hot one night, cold the next. A yo-yo man.

Drilling Reggies When You Need Pete Roses—Going for the long bombs instead of moving in and getting higher-percentage shots.

Fan or Funnel—the defense forcing the ball either to the sideline or to the middle of the lane, respectively.

Finalize—to finish the transition; steals and fast breaks don't mean much if you don't get the points at the end.

Flash to the Gap—Move to the open areas of the defense.

Glass Eater—strong rebounder.

High-Riser—One who plays on another level, à la Michael Jordan.

Human Spaceship—A guy with a wide body ready to explode.

Ice the Shooter—To call time-out before a foul shot, usually a crucial one, to make the shooter think about the situation.

Indianapolis Raceway—Playing at the fast pace up and down the floor, à la Indy 500.

Isolation Man—A one-on-one player.

J—The jump shot.

Johnny One-Note—A one-dimensional player.

M & M'er—Mismatch.

Matador Defense—Waving as the dribbler drives by.

Maestro Man—The conductor, the orchestra leader. The point guard making it all happen.

Marconi Special—Telegraphing the pass. You can see from thirty feet away where the man will throw the ball.

Maalox Time—Last minute of a close game. The stomach is churning.

Monster Mash—A vicious dunk, ramming it down onto somebody, usually with two hands.

NBN—Nothing But Net. Also Nothing But Nylon.

NC'er—No Contest.

Pac Man—A guy chewing up the other side on defense.

PT—Playing Time.

PTP or PTP'er—Prime-Time Performer.

Penetrate the Seams—Find the openings in a zone defense and drive.

Pine Time—Sitting on the bench.

Pink Slip—The rejection special, a blocked shot.

QT—Quality Time.

R & R—Rip and Run in fast-break style.

The Rack—As in "take it to . . . "—the basket.

Rock and Roll Time—Crowd outburst at a big momentum play.

Shake and Bake—Fancy one-on-one moves.

Slam Bam Jam—An exciting dunk, usually on a fast break.

Slasher—A driver, penetrator.

Space Eater—A guy with a wide body.

Strawberry Shortcake—After a good season, the NCAA tournament.

Surf and Turf—A great player. Eating big time. Club 21.

TO—Time-out.

Three-D Man—Drive, draw and dish. Someone who can penetrate to the basket, draw the defense to him, and dish the ball off to an open man.

Tickle the Twine—Shot hits NBN.

Times Square—A lot of congestion. Playing a slow-paced, deliberate offense.

Transition—Running up and down the floor changing from offense to defense or vice versa.

Uncle Mo—Momentum has arrived in the form of a slam dunk or big block or an eight-point run.

Velvet Touch—Sweet shooter, silky and smooth.

W or L—Win or Loss.

Wilson Sandwich—A huge blocked shot inside, forcing the shooter to practically eat the ball. Sometimes called a Spalding facial.

ZZZ Time—Sleeptime. The game is terrible.

The Ziggy—If you don't know by now. . . .

IF I WERE KING

Enough beating around the bush. Let's get down to brass tacks here. There are several trends going on in basketball that I don't like and that I think should be changed. Crown me king of the game for a few days and here's what would happen.

PROPOSITION 48

I commended the NCAA for ruling that a student-athlete has to qualify out of high school with a core curriculum. This meant that the kids had to have taken English and a foreign language, the basic sciences, math, history or government and the like and pass those courses. In the past, too many young-sters were being admitted with a 2.0 average in phys ed courses and electives. But now it must be a core, a solid foundation. I think that's healthy. I believe the NCAA's goals of bringing sanity to the term "student-athlete" and of making them re-alize there's more to life than a jump shot are admirable ones.

But here's where I differ with the boys from Shawnee Mis-sion, Kansas. I would like to see the NCAA use the SAT scores as a diagnostic means of placement rather than a strict requirement of eligibility. Everyone admits the SAT is prej-udicial to minorities and kids from rural areas and the lower economic groups; let's not increase that bias. A lot of innocent kids can get hurt along the way.

Why not, for example, increase the grade-point average by which a student becomes eligible? Then there wouldn't be such a dependence on the SAT. The rule states now that students must have a 2.0 and a 700 on the SAT or they are ineligible to play their freshman year in college. In addition to losing a year of eligibility, they can't practice with the team. That's a heavy penalty for a kid who has done the job in the local classroom, achieved say a 2.4 or 2.5, but can't score that 700 on the SAT. I say, allow kids to qualify with lower test scores if they've got the grades.

Okay, if they're going to keep the rule about the 700, then at least allow the kids to practice. Every single one of the Prop. 48 youngsters I've talked to tell me they go ahead and play some sort of basketball in college. But where? In intra-murals, maybe. But also out on the college playgrounds. Down the street. Since they can't play in organized city leagues, all they can do is go hang out and play. That's dangerous. First of all, they're not feeling too good about this anyway. Sec-ondly, we're exposing them to some questionable elements. There are some real characters out there just waiting to get

their hands on these kids: agents, gamblers, the drug creatures.

This is the first time in the kids' lives, remember, that the
one thing they've been able to excel at—basketball—has been
taken away from them. We act as if by denying them basketball, they're going to go marching straight to the classroom
to study. Who are we kidding? Why not let them at least
practice in the gym with the varsity, then have a mandatory
period of study hall after practice. And don't take the year
of eligibility away, either. Let the players begin their five-
year-to-play-four the year they enter school: the first year then
automatically becomes their no-play season. I think that's
penalty enough.

Furthermore, stigmatizing the Prop. 48 victim is wrong. It
just aggravates me when I hear on TV, "He's a Prop. Forty-
eighter." I do it myself, we all do it. But for the Marcus
Libertys at Illinois and the Terry Millses at Michigan and the
Brian Shorters at Pittsburgh, that label stays with them. It
has to be difficult to walk around campus or into class and
everybody knows they got less than 700 on the boards and
they're probably being stared at and ostracized. If a kid is
ineligible without the stigma of a low SAT score, he just
doesn't play for a year and it's forgotten.

I say throw the term out the window. I know we need
rules and regulations, but I almost agree with Temple coach
John Chaney who says that if his college admits a youngster,
if that school feels he or she meets the criteria, that youngster should be able to partake of any and all facets of college
life, including athletics. That means they're eligible to play,
period.

I think it was the tennis legend Arthur Ashe who said he
would make the kids get their butts into the library as well as
onto the courts. There's nothing wrong with that. But with
some of these students who are such gifted athletes, I think
you can motivate them to learn about education even more
through the positives of college sports.

SUBSIDIZE A SEMI-PRO LEAGUE

We have too many kids going to college who flat-out don't want to be there, but see college ball as the only route to the pros. That's where this idea comes in. I think there should be a league organized and operated by the NBA solely for those kids who are not qualified and who have no desire to be in college. This would be similar to baseball's rookie leagues. There are a lot of people who don't go to college, there are all kinds of vocations out there. But the system we have now forces a kid like Lloyd Daniels or Chris Washburn to make his mark on a college campus, where he doesn't belong.

Daniels bounced around four high schools in four years before winding up at UNLV. Washburn tried to pretend he was a student at North Carolina State. Neither of them belonged in college, let's face it. Some kids just don't have the capacity or desire to sit in a classroom and learn. But the system says a coach must win, so the coach has to recruit the best players available. The system says if a kid wants to go on to play pro basketball, he needs that experience at the collegiate level. This is a user mentality.

Why not have a league subsidized by the NBA with the dual purpose of training the kids for life in the big league as well as for a separate vocation? The colleges meanwhile would be recruiting only those students who want to be students as well as athletes. The majority of kids want to go to college anyway, no question about that. But these others would be in a sort of minor pro league.

The Continental Basketball Association is already set up as a feeding mechanism for the NBA, but I don't mean that. The CBA is for guys who are still chasing the dream after college and a lot of others hanging on for a paycheck. It's more like baseball's Triple-A leagues. The league I'm talking about would be a full-fledged rookie operation where the players would learn what the pro life is all about—everything from the travel to how to deal with the media. It would be the perfect place for a Tito Horford, a Charles Shackleford;

it would have given a Moses Malone or a Darryl Dawkins a year's experience before getting thrown to the major-league lions. Players who chose to bypass college would be drafted by the pros, but wouldn't be allowed into the NBA until they'd played one full season in this league, no exceptions. It would be a great outlet for the kids, and a good proving ground for the pros.

SALARIES AND AGENTS

Agents are dead wrong when they entice undergraduates with cars, clothes, girls, money, and all the other perks. But it has to be a two-way street. College youngsters are old enough to know right from wrong. They know from the moment they become a big-time prospect, be that at fourteen or eighteen or twenty-two, that they can put their hand out and sell themselves and become a prostitute for big bucks. But the question is, are they going to avoid the sleazy way and direct their lives in a laudatory fashion?

There are a lot of fine, upstanding agents in the sports world; there are also a number of slime rats waiting to make a quick rich hit on unsuspecting kids.

I think we could alleviate some of the problem by changing a few of the rules and by coming up with enough compensation for these young athletes who make thousands and thousands of dollars for their schools and for the NCAA. First, let's give them $150 a month in addition to their scholarships. Moreover, as part of that scholarship, how about one round-trip paid back and forth to home? That's in addition to room, board, and books.

Hey, my feeling is that above all, the kids have earned the money. Think of the pressure they're under to play and produce, the hours they put in, the results at the box office that their work and play provides. I don't want to hear about how they should only get what's available for the normal student; the big-time student-athlete is not a normal student. The latter doesn't go through the practices, the workouts, the weight programs, the conditioning sessions, the pressure of new kids coming in to take their jobs. It's a year-round thing these days. My point is, if these youngsters got this extra money, it wouldn't eliminate the agents or all the cheating, it wouldn't make the handouts disappear, but certainly it would lessen some of the temptation to start with nickel-and-dime stuff. That's where so much of the cheating begins.

Where would the money come from? This idea came out of a radio show Digger Phelps and I did together. It's very simple. In its most recent contract with CBS, the NCAA received $165 million in exchange for that network's right to televise the NCAA championships. One hundred sixty-five mil over three years. That's $55 million per year. Why doesn't the NCAA take $25 mil of that right off the top and distribute it to the schools—there are something like 280 playing at the Division I level—and the schools in turn lay that on the kids?

What about the tennis player or the wrestler, what about the other kids in the other non-revenue-producing sports? Hey, I respect the work ethic of all these athletes. My daughters work their tails off in tennis. But they're not under the same kind of gun. Nor is there the exposure and visibility that football players and basketball players bring to a school. I think these kids deserve it, that's all.

Years ago scholarship kids used to get $15 per month but they wiped that out. Now it's just room, board and tuition. But how do you recruit nationally when you have to walk into a living room and tell a kid who's been wined and dined by every school in America that you'd love him to attend your place, but he's got to pay $500 to fly to your campus? Coaches have ways around everything, it's no secret. They get an alumnus in the summer to get kids jobs that pay well, but many times these jobs are phony. The coaches are now putting it in the minds of their players that this security is going to be there for them whenever they need it. Don't worry about a thing.

Once a player has his coach in a situation like that, it's an awkward deal. Scare City. What's wrong with one paid trip? The school flies the kid to the campus in September and flies him home in June. If he wants to visit Mom and Pop in between, it's got to be through family cash. This is one area in which I think Dick Schultz, who took over the directorship of the NCAA last year, will make inroads in terms of bringing some logic and sanity to the process.

The argument says that if we pay $150, the kid is going to want $500, that schools will just out-bid each other under the table. I don't buy it. That's just searching. There certainly will be people who still cheat, just as there are in the legal profession and the medical profession. There's scum everywhere. We just want to reduce the chances of that happening. The positives outweigh the negatives here by so much.

And while we're talking money, let me get this off my chest: I think the payoff for a school that makes the Final Four is way out of line. Schools that reach the promised land, the national semis and finals, now get more than *one million dollars* each. I think, and I know my buddy Packer agrees, that that's a very unhealthy situation. It's just too much money.

When there's a payoff that big you get all kinds of pressure on a school to do whatever it takes to get there. Today schools get something like a quarter of a million dollars just for losing in the first round, and there are athletic departments that put that money in their budgets right from the start. This puts incredible pressure on the coach to make the tournament and meet that budget goal. It's like a salesman who's got to meet a quota or lose his job. You can get into a situation where the coach feels he's got to cheat to survive.

I would take all the money generated by the NCAA tournament and divide it among all the Division I schools, whether they made the tournament or not. Let the schools use the money to give their players a little something, like that $150 a month and round-trip home. There's enough pressure on a coach to win already without adding to it.

RECRUITING REGULATIONS

The first thing that really frustrates me about recruiting is that the evaluation period in which a coach can look at a player has been shortened to the point of being ridiculous. It's broken down now to certain weeks where the coach can watch the kid play and certain weeks he can't. I think a coach should be able to see a kid over his entire basketball career.

I'm thinking here of the borderline player who gets hurt, the kid a coach needs to see more than the permitted four times. Reduce the observations at practice, that's fine. Keep all the assistant coaches and recruiters away from practice. But I think it should be okay to watch a kid in as many games as a coach wants or needs to in order to get a valid opinion of him. It's very important to watch a player in games, especially the "sleeper" types who may not be able to play at the super big-time level.

The early signing period—now mid-November for a high school senior entering college the following fall—really has to be rethought as well. I have a lot of trouble with that and here's why.

In almost all cases a kid who signs that early national letter of intent has not been admitted academically to the college he supposedly is going to represent on the basketball court! What kind of priority is that? That's a joke, an absolute farce, that's what that is.

Any student-athlete who signs with a school—*whenever* it may be—must already have been approved by the admissions department of that school. That should be a flat-out prerequisite. Period. Finished. Case closed. Or as my old friend Howard Garfinkel always ends his arguments, Next?

I'm serious about this. The player's resume and transcripts should have been submitted; the school should have gone over his courses and test scores and proven to themselves positively that he or she should be accepted to the school. I'm not talking about eligibility now, Proposition 48 and all. That comes later.

Let's get that admissions department approval before anything is signed on the dotted line.

The last couple of years we've had examples—Larry Johnson at SMU, John Pittman at Kentucky—of players who signed with a school early only to find out later that they would not be admitted. In the meantime, other coaches had to stay away from recruiting them to places where they might have been accepted. The kid is obligated, committed to that signing. If he breaks it and wants to go somewhere else, he's ineligible for a year.

This loophole in the process also makes it possible for coaches to stockpile recruits and then ship them out if they find better players. In other words, to fish and cut bait at the same time. A coach can always find reasons not to admit players. They'll never confess to running off kids but it happens all the time, in this case running them off before they even come on.

Under my system, once a kid is admitted and signed, a coach must honor the player's scholarship. No hanging him out to dry.

Speaking of leaving things hanging, a real pet peeve of mine is coaches who recruit players, sign them early and then decide to leave their school for a head coaching job elsewhere. Where does this leave the recruit?

Let's be clear on something. I don't care how beautiful Duke University is, or what a wonderful academic reputation Stanford has, or how great it is to play in the Carrier Dome at Syracuse, or what terrific contacts a kid can make at your Kentuckys or UCLAs or DePauls—the overwhelming reason a young man goes to play basketball at a college is the coach. When the coach leaves a school before the kid even has a chance to play for him, why should the kid be penalized if he no longer wants that school?

More often than not recruits stay at their original school, even if their coach has left. But that's because if they don't, if they transfer, they lose a season of eligibility. And that's wrong. I give you the case of Brian D'Amico a few years ago.

After Bill Foster of South Carolina signed D'Amico out of New York, Foster switched jobs and went to Northwestern. D'Amico no longer wanted to go to South Carolina, but because he transferred to North Carolina State he had to sit out a year. And what if he had followed Foster to Northwestern—Foster, the coach who signed him in the first place? D'Amico still would have been ineligible. In other words, the coach can coach but the player can't play. Or take Derek Martin, who had committed to go to UCLA before Walt Hazzard got fired. Now, if he wants to transfer, he'll have to sit out a year, and if he goes somewhere else in the conference, it's *two years*.

Get serious.

Here's what should happen: Following the early signing period, if there's a coaching change for whatever reason—a coach is fired, or he leaves on his own, or even in the event that he dies—in the month of April there should be another two weeks or so that a player can be rerecruited by all schools. Then let the kid make a new decision about where and with whom he wants to go. A coach is with a player for four years; he's in his face constantly and is part of his life far more than any other faculty member the player might see for one or two class periods. A player shouldn't have to expect the unknown: some coach with whom he had no relationship and for whom he might be unwilling to face the guillotine.

One of the things that really encourages me about Dick Schultz becoming the executive director of the NCAA is that we finally have someone in that job who's been a coach. Schultz coached at Iowa, and he can bring that perspective to the task of making the recruiting rules bear some relation to reality.

GRADUATION RATES

We always hear about the great coaches' graduation rates: the Dean Smiths, the Bobby Knights, the John Thompsons.

But what does that really mean? It means a lot and it could
mean more. Here's how.

The Vitale Plan is a refinement of a program that's been
knocking around in conversation for several years. I mentioned it once on the air and Dick Young, the late columnist
in New York, flew with it. That really flattered me.

Right now the NCAA has a fifteen-scholarship limitation
in Division I. My proposal is that if every athlete graduates
in the basic five-year plan, that school maintains its fifteen
scholarships for basketball. Since it's so tough for athletes to
graduate in the normal four years, for everyone who does the
coach gets a bonus scholarship with a top of twenty in the
program. For every kid on his team who doesn't graduate in
that five-year period, you can reduce the scholarships. One
miss, one less scholarship, down to ten in your program. When
a school lowers itself to ten, it's ineligible to participate in the
NCAA tournament.

What this would force coaches to do is recruit student-
athletes who are students as well as athletes, to go after the
kids who have a chance rather than just those who can make
their twelve hours and stay eligible. A coach keeps collecting
outlaws, he pays the price. Taken in tandem with the subsidized rookie pro league, this would help make college ball
what it was supposed to be: athletics for college students.

Do the majority of great players graduate? I don't know.
I do know that players of all abilities are graduating at a higher
rate than ever. Would this measure pull down the caliber of
big-time competition by eliminating many of the great players? Again, I don't know. What is the caliber now? How do
you determine that? I do know the game still would be exciting
and competitive. There are always enough good, intelligent
players for that.

The devil's advocate would say, what about a Michael Jordan and a James Worthy? What about North Carolina, which
runs as clean a house as anybody? What about Dean Smith
advising his players to go pro before they reach their senior

years, before they graduate? Maybe a coach wouldn't send his kids off if he knew he'd be penalized when that kid doesn't get his degree in the required time.

We could refine the rules somewhat. We might have to come up with an asterisk for kids who leave early. I think this program could be solidified. What this is is a start, a foundation. Of course, remember that Dean Smith also makes sure his guys come back to school and get their degrees. I've heard that was in Jordan's Chicago Bulls contract: that Michael must return to Chapel Hill in the off-season and get his degree or lose a certain amount of money. Jordan and Worthy, by the way, both have been graduated from Chapel Hill.

THE NCAA TOURNAMENT

Now I'm rolling, gang. As for the tournament, I think the size of it is fine as is. Sixty-four teams. Nobody gets a bye. Six rounds, two each weekend. Simple.

And don't you start in, Billy Packer, with that wacko idea about opening up the tournament to every team. Sure, it would mean just one more week of play. But I think it would be a total farce, destroying, absolutely destroying, the regular season. It would make the whole season totally worthless. How is it fair for a 2–25 team to play a 25–2 team in a one-shot-to-advance matchup?

And besides, *that system already exists.* It's called the conference tournament, baby, and through it just about every team in the nation gets a sudden-death chance at the NCAAs. Is that fair? Was it fair for little Siena College, after a 23–4 season, to have to beat 3–24 New Hampshire in a win-or-else game in '88? What's the point of playing the regular season when you can get knocked out of the tournament in a game like that? I say don't water down the season even further—*strengthen it.* Restrict the conference tournament to the top four teams in the conference. You'll still get those extra dollars from the tourney, losing only one payday in the case of an eight-team conference, but you'll be adding some real importance to those regular-season games that decide who's going to qualify.

The best that Packer and his crew can say for the open-door tournament idea is that it would eliminate all the politics involved in the selection process. But does it? We lose the excitement of seeing who's going to slip by into those last five or six spots, who's on the bubble, and there's still the question of who gets sent where and how far, who has to play whom and in which round. Do you really think there's no politics in seeding a tournament with 250-plus teams?

You're never going to have perfection with human beings involved in the process, but I think the selection committee usually does a terrific job breaking down criteria and choosing deserving teams. I might have had a quarrel with their not inviting Louisville in '87—the Cardinals were the defending champs, they had won 18 games and beaten several teams that were invited; they had played probably the toughest schedule in the country. Unfortunately, I think they based that decision more on Louisville getting blown out by Memphis State by 75–52 at the exact moment that they were sifting the figures in that Kansas City hotel suite.

Scoring margins are misleading. If they're going to go by point spreads, coaches will be trying to bury everybody as badly as possible. You think my man at Oklahoma, Billy Tubbs, might like that criteria?

If I were on the selection committee—remember now, I'd be the *king* of the committee—I'd give primary importance to a team's road schedule, the strength of its conference, and its intersectional record. Is a team loading up with cupcakes at home or playing a number of Division II schools? I know those don't count any more and the committee does use Jeff Sagarin's computer ratings as a basis of analysis. But in '87 when the committee sent Purdue out of the Midwest to the

East and lowered its seeding to third, committee chairman
Schultz said that the 104–68 beating Michigan gave Purdue
the day before the pairings were announced had a large bearing. Again, are they using margins or what? If that's going to
be an item in the process, they should specify it.

Moreover, I wouldn't keep giving automatic berths to those
smaller conferences whose teams aren't under the same pressures as the big boys. Does the Southland Conference champion really deserve a bid instead of the Big Ten's sixth-place
team? Some years, maybe, but not necessarily every year,
particularly if the goal is to put the best sixty-four teams into
the tournament.

If you want to give an automatic berth to a small conference,
fine, but then reevaluate it a couple of years down the line.
Take a look at how the teams from that conference have been
doing in the tournament. If they're getting blown away in the
first round year after year, then take away the automatic berth.
To take one example, the Colonial Athletic Conference has
certainly earned its spot based on the performances of Navy
and Richmond in recent years. And Cleveland State and
Southwest Missouri have done a lot to put the AMCU-8 on
the map. But is the Ivy League champion really one of the
top sixty-four teams? Not by their showing in the tourney,
they're not.

Taking away the automatic bid doesn't necessarily mean
that no one will ever get to the tournament, remember. There
are still at-large bids available, and if a few schools do well,
they can always get that automatic spot back. What I mean
is that the committee should be flexible. Don't treat all the
decisions about conferences like they're set in stone.

As for the sites, the committee must keep to what they
started in 1988 and at no time in the tournament let a team
play on its home court. Don't give me that song and dance
about how hard it is to get a school to host games if they
know their team isn't going to be playing. There'll always be
enough sites to play. Don't cry croc tears about the diminished
revenues if a North Carolina doesn't play in the Dean Dome

or a Kentucky in Rupp Arena. I don't want to hear it. With all that money the NCAA collects from CBS for the tournament, gate receipts should be the last of the considerations. Especially when it comes to fairness.

Ask Auburn's Sonny Smith if he felt the Indianapolis crowd and General Knight had any effect on the officials in the Indiana–Auburn NCAA game in the Hoosier Dome in '87. Ask Virginia's Terry Holland about losing to Alabama-Birmingham in Birmingham in '82. Talk to Purdue's Gene Keady about the Boilermakers' first games on the home floors of Memphis State and LSU in consecutive years in the NCAAs. Then wash your ears out with soap. The watershed game in this regard was Illinois at Kentucky in the Midwest Regional final at Rupp in 1984. A questionable call at the end of the game cost the Illini the upset and a berth in the Final Four at Seattle. Illinois coach Lou Henson had a right to scream. It's like Caesar's wife; it's all in appearances. If that call had occurred on a neutral court, a lot less would have been made of it. As it was, its effect was good because the NCAA changed the tournament rules: no more Regionals on a team's home court, which simply meant that in the pairings process a school hosting a Regional would be sent away from its Region. But now the committee should declare as policy that this holds in the Subregionals as well. It worked out that way in '88, but it should always be the case. No home games in the NCAAs. None. *Nada.* Next?

With all that money floating around, the NCAA needn't worry about a few empty seats anyway. If the games and rounds are promoted correctly, they'd get good crowds no matter what teams are involved. There are certainly enough solid arenas around the country that would consider it an honor and privilege to host the NCAA tournament. The Omni. The New Orleans Superdome (I've got nothing against those big domed monsters, either). Freedom Hall in Louisville. The Hoosierdome or Minneapolis's Metrodome. Kemper Arena in Kansas City. McNichols in Denver. The Kingdome in Seattle. There are enough, believe me.

THE THREE-POINT BASKET

Uh-oh. Got an hour? A day? The Steitz Supernova. The Trey. The Trifecta. The one rule that has changed the face of the college game more than any other. First of all, I think the game has been hurt by the way Dr. Ed Steitz and the rules-makers pushed the thing down the throats of the coaches, the vast majority of whom didn't want it. The coaches should have more of a say in something that governs their very livelihood.

But now let me admit that I'm not against the concept of the three-point shot. I liked it from day one. I just don't accept the distance, and I never will. It's just too close. I think it does many things that don't even get reflected in a boxscore. It rewards and favors the more dominant team. Who has the best players, the most talent, the inside power guys who make their names on the glass? The traditional schools, that's who. So now the new rule comes in and a coach has to extend his defense to protect against the three-pointer, and the North Carolinas and Kentuckys and Indianas with their great inside games just have more room to dominate.

Check some of the blowout competition early each year. This rule is really just another one favoring the rich getting richer.

What I would like to see is the three-point line moved back at least a foot. It's at 19 feet, 9 inches now from the middle of the ring. Of course, like Mr. Packer says, that right there is a ridiculous measurement when you consider that the free-throw line has always been 15 feet and that was measured from the back of the rim. But even if it's a 21-foot shot, I say it should be at 22-feet somewhere between the international line and the NBA line (23-9). Put the three-pointer in the range of the legit shooter, but not where every Tom, Harry, and Dick Vitale can hit it.

I believe it's really unhealthy for the game when teams start using the trifecta twenty-five, thirty times every night. That's not what the game is all about. UNLV's Jerry Tarkanian, for one, jumps in my face about this. He loves the rule and thinks it's great, because it destroys the zone defense and makes a team come and play man-to-man. But hey, I'd love it too if I had all Tark's athletes and could outpersonnel the other guy and take people apart man-to-man.

But the zone helps to negate terrific talent: it adds some balance to the proceedings. A coach can take away the superior athletes' driving ability with a zone and maybe steal a few games here and there simply by sage coaching. Against the three-pointer, you've got to spread out your admittedly inferior personnel so much, you kill yourself elsewhere.

THE SHOT CLOCK

Let's face it: Before the forty-five second clock we had a multitude of stalls and delays and slowdowns and outright sleepwalks, especially that ACC final in '82 between North Carolina and Virginia. TV is vital to selling the game, and there was nothing worse than sitting there watching Ralph Sampson and Worthy and Jordan stand around in a ball-control atmosphere.

So I have no qualms about the clock and the time. It's still enough time to use patience on offense, but at the same time it eliminates the farcical meltdowns.

Back to the NBA again. I know the pros get labels: run and shoot, no defense, very little coaching. But I want to tell you it just isn't true. The coaches in the league do a terrific job teaching patterns and breaking down the game. There are a lot of two-man and three-man plays. But what happens in the short twenty-four-second span of that clock is that it's such a fast-paced game that the average fan can't see the play developing. I think the pros would be wise to go to thirty seconds because even six more ticks would enable the people watching at home to observe the creativity of the triangle stuff, the split-post series, the backboard play.

Six seconds is an eternity. And the full forty-five enables

exciting things to happen; for instance, I've already pointed out Auburn's whipping of Kentucky at Rupp last season even while the Tigers lacked two of their big three inside power players. But what about Kansas's national championship victory over Oklahoma? If the second half of that second half wasn't the prime example of a team cutting the tempo, spreading the floor, dragging out each possession so that the quicker, stronger, more athletic and favored opponent would get frustrated, I don't know what was.

Remember, the Jayhawks ran with the Sooners in the first half even though Larry Brown tried to get them to slow up. But he just couldn't do it; the old adrenaline had come into play and the halftime count was 50–50. Everybody in Kemper Arena knew Kansas couldn't keep sprinting with Oklahoma for a full forty minutes even if Brown was using his bench like a maestro, keeping his munchkins fresh while the Sooner starting five wore down. But late in the game I thought Larry's strategy of having his big men, Danny Manning and Chris Piper, handle the ball most of the time in backcourt so that the quick, theft-minded Oklahoma guards couldn't get at it was a gem of a move. Kansas simply ran out each possession in the last ten minutes, a couple right down to the final ticks of the forty-five-second clock. The Sooners never got rocking and rolling again the way they like. Result? Kansas's slow, droll M (momentum, not to mention Manning) meant a spectacular W in the biggest game of all.

People don't realize that forty-five seconds is forever. The two biggest upsets in recent NCAA championship games before the clock were N.C. State over Houston in 1983 and Villanova over Georgetown in '85. People have said that with the clock, that never would have happened. Wrong. Research has shown that in neither game did the winning team hold the ball longer than forty-five seconds on a possession. Both Jimmy Valvano and Rollie Massimino executed their game plans perfectly, slowed the tempo, took only the high-percentage shot, kept the ball away from the more heavily favored op-

ponent and ended up with the W. And without actually stall-
ing.

INTERNATIONAL RULES

When it comes right down to it, I'm basically an international
basketball rules man. One of the reasons they put the three-
point basket in the college game was to decrease the congestion and slashing and banging that went on in the lower box
area of the court. Right along with that, I say widen the lane.

Go to the trapezoid-shaped lane, which is the one used in
international play. It's 12 feet wide at the foul line, expanding
to 18 feet at the baseline—wider even than the NBA, which
is 16 feet at the base. We could eliminate guys beating each
other up in the lane. Eliminate the big man just loitering near
the lane and then dunking on everyone. This new dimension
would force him wider. It would also open up the lane for the
little guy to penetrate and drive. Anything that puts more
speed and cutting into the game is a positive step, I say.

In addition—just like in international ball—let's eliminate
the referee's handling the ball after backcourt violations. The
nonpenalized team just grabs the ball, brings it inbounds and
takes off. Know what this would make obsolete? The bitching
and moaning that goes on all the time after a player has been
slapped with a violation—traveling or throwing the ball away
and the like. This would again speed up the tempo. Force the
violating team to shut up and get back in defensive transition.
It would be like soccer. Go-go-go.

There are a couple of international rules that I could do
without. The defensive team is allowed to knock shots away
even after the ball is in the cylinder. This is totally illogical
when matched with another rule forbidding offensive dunks
off the alley-oop pass. That second one was put in, I feel sure,
as a ploy against our American teams' great athletic leaping
ability. Maybe the first one was passed for the same reason.

There are a lot of egos involved in the rules-making at all levels. But for the most part—especially when it comes to sending our representative teams to the Olympics and to the Pan Am Games—I think we would do well to adjust our college game to the international rules.

FOUL-OUTS

I think we put too much power into the hands of the officials. A couple of years ago I did an ABC game involving Navy at Kentucky. The Admiral, David Robinson, put on a show. He was on his way to a 40-plus afternoon, maybe 50-plus. The Wildcats were going to win, okay, but they weren't going to stop David. All of a sudden it's coming to the stretch and Navy knocks Kentucky's 15-point lead down to just a few and is about to make it close. Just then came two of the worst phantom offensive fouls called on Robinson I've ever seen. They were fouls number four and five and now he was gone, whistled and legislated right out of the game. Know what I did? I got up from my chair at courtside in Lexington and gave David a standing O. Had to, I was so emotional about this. Keith Jackson didn't know what was happening.

That's the first time I'd done that in my life as an analyst.

My point is, we shouldn't lay the star's sitting down on the shoulders of the zebras. The kinds of violations in other sports that lead to ejections are more like technical fouls in basketball. Personal fouls are more like misdemeanors than felonies. John Elway gets to stay in the game no matter how many times he's called for intentional grounding or even unnecessary roughness. Wayne Gretzky won't get thrown out of a game unless he commits several major penalties, and he doesn't do that in a year, never mind one game. If a player is really getting out of hand, there's always the flagrant foul rule to punish him with. Why should we let the refs put a player out of the game for a number of, let's face it, often very subjective foul calls?

The Vitale Solution? When a college player is whistled for foul number five, give his coach the option: If he leaves the player in, the team is charged with a technical foul. Which is severe enough, meaning the opposition gets two free throws and possession of the ball. Or the coach could take the player out of the game himself. But anytime he's back in and commits a foul, it's a T (two shots and ball possession for the other side). The point being, let it be in the coach's power to play his star or not. Don't let the referees decide who gets to play the games.

VIOLENCE

A new bench-decorum rule came out last year prohibiting a coach from talking to a referee—and vice versa—unless the official calls both coaches together for a conference. Hey, that's bull.

That's just a protection for lousy referees. A good ref can handle a dialogue anytime, anywhere. It only becomes a problem if there's a lot of pushing and shoving going on underneath and the ref can't go to a coach, and he has to go to a captain or another third party, and then that guy goes over to the bench to relay the message to the coach. It's a party-line deal, a Third-Man Theme. It's a joke.

The ref should be allowed to talk to the coach. He shouldn't need to have a scoring or a timing situation, a dead-ball time-out, to relay the news that a problem is developing on court. It might be too late, anyway.

Let's say that J. R. Reid of North Carolina is really banging with Danny Ferry of Duke down low. Why shouldn't Lenny Wirtz be able to talk to Dean Smith as he's running up the court, "Hey, Dean, I'm going to tell you now that J.R. is doing too much pushing inside. We have to stop the incidental contact. Once more, and I'm nailing him." Why shouldn't he tell Mike Krzyzewski the same thing?

The good officials can handle these things. That rocking

and rolling down low, by the way, got seriously out of hand last year, resulting in several bench-clearing brawls. Georgetown–Pitt. Indiana State–Drake. Syracuse–Cornell. An Ivy League team? Hey what about this? The most serious might have been Towson State–Rider.

The college game has become so emotional, the fans so fanatical. Everybody is close to the action, every little movement is visible enough so that raw nerves can be jangled at the slightest hint of trouble.

In football you have a situation on the sidelines where the coaches are hidden among all those guys with the parkas. In baseball a lot of managers hide in the dugout or clubhouse. But in basketball the coaches are right out front doing their ranting and raving and screaming. Basketball players, too, are without protective armor. Fights have become too commonplace.

The NCAA responded to the increased violence by putting in the following rules after the end of the '88 season: Any player involved in a fight is ejected from the game and put on probation. If he's in a second fight he's out of that game and the next game. A third fight and he's gone for the season.

That's much too lenient, particularly at the start. I'm not worried about punishing the third fight; I want to prevent the first one. My solution? Anytime a player throws a punch, he's out of the game, and not just off the court, either; I mean off the bench and into the locker room. He doesn't get to sit there and simmer and stew and maybe provoke some more nasty stuff. He's gone. Not only that, *he's suspended for two games*. Again, automatic. No questions asked. The seriousness of a fight has to be at the discretion of the referee, but mostly a guy can see if a punch is thrown. And whenever one is, that's it. Goodbye.

THE CALL-MAKEUP CALL

One last harangue about referees. I'm probably thinking too much as a coach here, but I'm so sick of what I refer to as the "gentleman's call" where Sherman Douglas of Syracuse, let's say, drives down the lane and crashes into B. J. Armstrong of Iowa. On any offensive charge in the NBA there is no score and that's the way it should be. But in college we have the score and the non-player-control foul when the ref rules that the player released the ball before the contact. So here comes Douglas and here comes Armstrong stepping in. Bango! Up jumps coach Jim Boeheim of Syracuse, and up jumps Dr. Tom Davis of Iowa. The official waves in the goal for the Orangemen (thank you, Mr. Boeheim) and now we're going the other way, foul on Douglas and B.J. will shoot the one-and-one (thank you, Dr. Tom). It's a balancing act: deuce here, deuce there, and everybody's happy (thank you, gentlemen, and we'll see you next time).

It's a call and a makeup call at the same time. Get it outta here, Eddie Steitz!

COACHING RESPONSIBILITIES

Everybody in the coaching fraternity will probably slap their thighs over this one from a guy who began the seasons at Detroit scheduling Hiram and Hillsdale, but I think a reasonable effort should be made by our major traditional powers to beef up their December schedules. When I was at U of D, an independent without a league schedule to get us to the NCAA tournament, I was constantly in a win-or-else situation and I desperately needed W's. We didn't dictate who we played anyway. But Bill Frieder at Michigan, Boeheim at Syracuse, Cliff Ellis at Clemson, John Thompson at Georgetown—you others know who you are—gimme a break!

Frieder and Boeheim play so many cupcakes early on it's a wonder they haven't come down with glucose attacks. Frieder plays every small school in the state; he'd make up a "Southwestern Central Michigan" to get a W. Boeheim plays fewer road games than the San Quentin prison team. Ellis's Clemson squads have definitely been hurt by the patsies he finds for them when they finally enter ACC play. And big JT? Sometimes I think Don Ho is the Georgetown athletic director. The Hoyas' schedule usually looks something like: St. Leo, Hawaii Loa, Mama Poa and Papa Papaya. Appetizers are fine for the beginning of the season, guys, the first two games maybe, but in the future let's get to the main course a little earlier.

Games against Division II schools no longer count against a coach's record and that's why some of the big names schedule the little fellas, as practice sessions. Those games in Hawaii don't do anything for the sport. I don't think they develop anybody, bodies or minds. There are too many good tournaments around in early December for a team to consistently take that easy road.

What about getting back to some good old-fashioned area rivalries? One of the happiest developments in recent years was the resumption of the long-dead Kentucky and Louisville competition. Then last year those two schools hooked up with Indiana and Notre Dame for the start of an annual series of Hoosierdome doubleheaders. That's the kind of thing that I think should be the responsibility of coaches everywhere, to build interest in the game.

I want to see Georgetown and Maryland start playing again; maybe those old buddies, Thompson and Bob Wade, will get it together, although I heard that when the idea was proposed last season Big John put the kibosh on it. Let's see Wimp Sanderson and Gene Bartow kiss and make up and get it on for Alabama against Alabama-Birmingham. Tennessee–Memphis State would be another great matchup. It's time for Frank Broyles, the AD at Arkansas, to recognize that Nelson Catalina at Arkansas State has a legitimate program and a beautiful new facility. and what about Notre Dame and Purdue? Digger and Gene Keady would be dynamite on the same floor.

I say let the fans enjoy these matchups. More important, let the players enjoy them. Don't tell me that anybody prefers seeing these dog-pounders and fill-ins for the automatic W's instead of a competitive game against a nearby state rival.

Most of the schools I've mentioned are virtual locks for the NCAA tournament every year anyway; the coach can afford an L. These games aren't going to hurt them. Let the tournament committee announce—and demonstrate—that it's paying close attention to the strength of schedule in the selection process, and not just looking at the supposedly magic 20-win mark, and maybe we'll see some more of these games. There are so many positives to gain. Most important, it's a matter of what is logically right and best for the game and the players and the fans.

I remember seeing the Clemson team in the Dallas airport one year when they were busily loading up on creampuffs. "Hey, Dick Vitale," Ellis said. "You got to get off our backs about the schedule."

So I asked his players, Horace Grant and the rest, "Would you guys really rather play these pushovers where you see about fourteen minutes of PT and get a forty-point win and it doesn't mean anything, or play some legit clubs who will make you better?"

The Tigers didn't say anything in front of their coach, but I could see the looks on their faces: *He's right, baby.*

Lastly, I think every school should take it upon themselves to educate their players regarding all the elements they will face as big-time student-athletes. I'm talking about how to deal with agents, with alcohol and drugs, with the media and self-communication, with the fans and public relations. I long for the day when our colleges' priorities are concentrated in turning out upstanding human beings who also just happen to be fine basketball players.

It would be nice to be king, but then it's great just being Dick Vitale, too. I can't overemphasize how flattered, how utterly flabbergasted I am at what's gone on in my life since I started doing television. Sure I'm a ham. Naturally I'm a hot dog. I'm full of mustard and sauerkraut and catsup besides. Whatever you want on a wiener, I've got it. But I've now developed a relationship with college basketball that transcends anything I could have imagined.

I go to the games and dance with the cheerleaders. I go up in the crowd and sign autographs for the fans. I've led bands, doing "Hail to the Victors" at Michigan. I went to Notre Dame, and Tim Brown, the Irish Heisman Trophy winner, rubbed my head for luck. At almost every arena where I go now, the word is out that Vitale is coming. At Oklahoma last year they had a group holding a sign: *Dick Vitale Is Our PT PEER*. These guys were all dressed up in blazers and skull caps trying to look like me. Some of them had glasses on; I had to knock them off. That's history, baby. That's bye-bye. The Zoo Crew at Northwestern. The Bleacher Creatures at Wisconsin. I'm an honorary member of all these gangs now.

It's almost like a Pied Piper deal. Banners, signs, buttons. You think it's easy being a cult figure? But seriously, I really do try to have time for everybody. I just love people. And remember, this didn't just start with me on TV. Who was the first pro coach to throw basketballs out to the crowd? Last March at the NCAA Tournament in Kansas City, Nike brought out a tee shirt with my caricature on it. I was really disappointed I had to knock Spuds McKenzie off the best-seller list.

But this celebrity thing is amazing. And to think I'm the guy who's still in awe of celebs! When I go to Los Angeles, I always hang out in Hollywood, cruising the streets looking for the stars. Last year I got one of those maps of the celebrities homes and, man, was I in paradise. I saw Burt Young, the guy who played Sylvester Stallone's brother in all the Rocky movies. Burt was out walking his dog. Got him to pose for pictures. I went right up to Lucille Ball's door. "Hey, Lucy," I called in my best Ricky Ricardo accent. "Lucy, I'm hooooome."

Later at a little restaurant on Rodeo Drive, Goldie Hawn came inside for a few minutes. Unfortunately, I was in the men's room at the time. But when the people told me she had popped in, I popped out. I searched all up and down the street for Goldie, poking my head into shops asking if anybody had seen her. Alas, no luck. Missed Lucy and Goldie in the same afternoon.

The last time I was in LA was for the NBA finals between the Lakers and Pistons. I was doing the games for ABC Radio, and when I got to the airport and climbed into a cab, the cab driver recognized me right away. "What are you doing here?" he asked. "I knew you did college games, but I didn't know you covered the pros too, Mr. McGuire."

I knew I wasn't McGui-ah; McGui-ah wasn't the one there to cover the team that had given him the Ziggy.

The whole period of those NBA finals was like old home week to me. Ten years earlier I'd dreamed of taking the Pistons to the top of the mountain, and now, after more twists and turns than anyone could have imagined, there we both were. I was there the night they—we—played the first game at the Silverdome, and thanks to the new arena the Pistons are moving into for the '88–'89 season, I was there the night they played the last one.

And I had to laugh when I walked in and saw Greg Kelser, who was at courtside doing the games on the Pistons radio hookup, and Roy Hamilton, my jump-shooting kid with the flying elbow, who was there as an associate producer for the CBS telecasts. Hey, I said when I drafted those two that we'd get to the championship round together, didn't I?

I really got chills seeing the Silverdome rocking and rolling with 41,000 screaming fans. It was everything I'd dreamed of when I took the coaching job there, and I've got to admit that I felt some twinges of envy seeing it happen. It was the first time in a long, long time that I wished I was back in coaching. Then I thought about the long nights, the ulcers, the pressures, and the pain of the Ziggy, and I realized that the safest and best way to be in the middle of it all is to be right where I am now.

You know, I'll never understand why people get so carried away with a guy like myself talking about a game. All I am really is the guy who got the axe, the coach who got the Ziggy.

The limousine rolled up. The boss fired me. A little while later a guy gave me a microphone. I wasn't made from broadcasting school. But I happened to survive. Big deal.

I actually still think of myself as the fired coach trying to make a living. That's why I have the work ethic that I do. I know that attitude will never change. I treat every telecast like the NCAA championship, every performance as if it's my most important event. It's all going to end someday, I know that. One day some blond, blue-eyed Adonis will come in and tap me on the shoulder and say it's over. The party will end.

But I'm going to have a nice run while it lasts. I savor every minute of my life. Especially now, since the accident that nearly cost me and my family virtually everything—that is, each other.

It was July of 1987 and we had just returned home to Florida from all the national junior girls' tennis tournaments in California. We came home and all this mail was everywhere. It was unbelievable, the paraphernalia that had piled up. Speaking engagements. A book contract. Radio deals with WFAN in New York. Talk shows. Everything seemed to be going such great guns that Lorraine and I and the girls decided to go out to a restaurant to celebrate.

It was July 10. We were driving home around nine o'clock, coming up Seventy-fifth Street in Bradenton, a couple of minutes from our house, when a Ford Bronco came whipping out of control over the double line and headed straight for us, head-on. It had the high bumper and the big lights on top. But right then it looked like the front was coming right through our windshield.

Fortunately Lorraine, who was driving, slowed down, so that when the other car hit us we didn't have any momentum of impact. But I can still see that car coming at us plain as day, the kids inside it and everything.

My seatbelts were on but I jerked to my left just in time to see Lorraine's head hit the windshield and start gushing blood. She ended up needing twenty-one stitches to patch up the hole through her chin and face. I turned to the left to shove my girls down in the back of the car and I hit the windshield myself.

The collision completely shattered the socket under my right eye—my one good eye. And it was a mess! I had just undergone an eye operation a few months earlier; they operated on my right eye to give me more muscle control over my blind left eye. There was some risk involved, but I wanted to get enough control to keep my bad eye from wandering on camera. But this was a hundred times more scary. I knew something bad was happening to my right eye—my one fragile link to the world. If I lost that, it was going to be the end of this color man's career.

In addition, I broke my nose and my ribs. I broke my foot, which had jammed on the floor board. A nerve was later diagnosed as being completely damaged in my face from my eyelid down to my mouth. I had no feeling in it, only complete numbness, and later the doctors said I may experience that for the rest of my life.

Nowadays I can touch my cheek and shave, but the feeling in it comes and goes. They say that's a good sign, that it means that the nerve isn't totally severed. Of course, when I was in the emergency room I was practically hysterical because everything was blurry and I was afraid I would never be able to see again.

My daughters miraculously were unhurt, didn't have a scratch on them. But Lorraine was bleeding horribly and they were working on her face. I was in a brace in the emergency room because they were worried about my back and neck. The blood was pouring out, so finally they got the contact lens out of my eye and the doctor came in for a look.

"The one good thing is you have complete mobility of your eye," he said.

For a week I was in the hospital, and then as I'd go for rehabilitation I met folks who made my accident seem like nothing. Every athlete should do rehab at a hospital and then see if they complain about their place in life and their salaries ever again.

The doctors decided against surgery because they felt the risks were too great, but they were worried about me getting a sinking eye because I'm involved in TV, where looks are a consideration. The wall was shattered. They wanted to repair it by taking cartilage from my nose and operating around my eye. But then an eye specialist from Michigan, Conrad Giles, got involved and said definitely not. "Let nature take its course, Dick," he said. "It's too sensitive an area. But you have to be checked periodically."

I missed all kinds of games and engagements, not to mention the US Olympic Festival and a vacation trip to Hawaii. But the bottom line was how close . . . one moment I'm on top of the ladder . . . and the next I'm not sure if I'm ever going to see again.

Cards and letters and flowers rolled in. Knight and Thompson and Phelps and all the coaches sent messages. I cried in my bed one day; it was incredible I could receive all this caring.

But I'll never forget what happened and the fleeting nature of life. I carry a picture of my eye from right after the accident; it hemorrhaged so badly that from the top of the eye down my face was a mass of black. I have that picture with me everywhere I go. It reminds me whenever I think things are going so smoothly that it all could change very quickly.

Having gotten the Ziggy, having been axed from coaching, having lost my eye, been involved in a major accident, been divorced, suffered some major internal bleeds with my stomach . . . I've had a lot of adversity. But I've proved I'm a survivor and a battler and that I can fight back when things go wrong.

Fear drives me. I'm just as insecure as the next guy, probably more so because I've been a coach and now I'm in TV. But as long as I have my health and my family and basketball, and the Man upstairs who gave me love and enthusiasm and the capability to express myself a certain way keeps me around, I guess Dicky V will be okay.